# Miami, Florida:

## A Sunshine State's Unauthorized and Unredacted Journey

**A Memoir**

**By Lyonel Gerdes**

**Tome I**

# Dedication

This Tome I of "Miami, Florida: A Sunshine State's Unauthorized and Unredacted Journey..." is dedicated to all the remarkable "femme fatal" ladies who had graced the beginning chapters of my journey here in Miami. It is, of course, dedicated to that mid-70s Miami/Haitian group of remarkable friends named "Les Pépés" from Little Haiti's dawning days. It's undoubtedly dedicated to the unforgettable FIU International Studies' Graduate Class of 1984, and this memoir is finally dedicated to all the Roots Uprisings' Reggae band members of the late 70s and early 80s for their transformational Reggae music vibe at the Coconut Grove's Village Inn Bar and Restaurant.

# Acknowledgment

I shall acknowledge the names of the people who had provided me with many invaluable informations in the course of writing this book memoir of mine. This project could not have been this smooth without their indefatigable help and assistance. Here are the names of the persons who had made themselves available through hour-long interviews, research sharing, books referrals and stories' recollection. For their support and contribution, I will forever be grateful to Roger Biambi, Marcus Garcia, Elsie Etheart, Pierre Andre Clitandre, Castro Desroches, and the late Bernard Etheart.

# Contents

Dedication .................................................................... iii

Acknowledgment ........................................................ iv

Prologue ..................................................................... vii

PART I ..........................................................................1

Miami's Little Haiti's Nascent Years ...............................2

Living With the Gelin's Brothers ..................................25

Gasner Raymond Was No Longer With Us....................38

The Start of My Bachelor Pad Days ..............................43

Fast Forward To 2024 Miami and an America in Decline ...........54

My Rental Apartment At Isidor's Family Home .............64

Coconut Grove's Village Inn: A Bar/Restaurant for The Ages .....93

PART II........................................................................157

Could Africa's Decolonization Be Haiti and America's Last Hope? ..........................................................158

The 1980s: A Transformational Decade for Everyone ...............197

Brutal Government Crackdown of Haiti's Independent Press.....207

The Lady Who Thought Me There Was
More to Love Than Sex ................................................235

The Day Reggae Music Died at The Grove ................................247

PART III ................................................................286

On The Black American Experience ...........................................287

A Cozy Evening Recital with The Legendary Michel Legrand ..299

FIU's International Studies' Graduate Class Of 1984 with Dr. Mark Rosemberg .................................................................318

The Inspiring Parties at Mike and Peter's Chicken Coop Pad.....341

Francis Fukuyama Ought to Rewrite His End of History Book ..347

Epilogue ...............................................................362

About the Author .......................................................375

# Prologue

The last time we departed was when I sat guilt-ridden on that Pan Am flight, taking off from Port-au-Prince's International Airport en route to Miami, Florida. It was on that early Wednesday afternoon of July 30th, 1975, that I was thrusted to a land completely unknown to me. My hasty departure was nothing short of miraculous, as it occurred a day before my birthday. Had I missed my flight that day and not made it to the US before my 21st birthday, I would have been disqualified from receiving my green card upon entering Miami's Immigration office on any day past that deadline. During the almost two-hour long flight, I could not help traveling back and forth, revisiting various parts of the lows and highs of my life journey. Images from my adopted provincial city of Les Cayes, where I spent my early childhood, ran through my head, and so were the visual imageries of Port-au-Prince, where I was born and returned later to live there at age 12. It was one of the pivotal moments in my life, flying on that one-way ticket, to begin with my Sunshine State's unauthorized, unredacted journey.

Sure, my life till then, for those who read my last two book memoirs, had not been what one would have viewed as a joyous walk on the paths of both my childhood and adolescent life for I was an unloved, emotionally neglected adoptee. Still, all along my forsaken detached journey with my emotionally dysfunctional parents, amply documented in my last two memoirs, I was never denied a roof over my head, fed, clothed, and schooled, despite never being held once on any of my parents' laps, or felt that self-assured sense of family belonging. It took me a while to figure out the real reason I was going to Miami and not to Waukegan, Illinois, to live with my adopted dad William, his new wife Ronnie, and my two younger siblings, Marie Marcelle and Jean Willy.

The two excuses given at first were that dad's new wife would not have felt safe for me to come live at her place, and next was their limited space and their meager disposable income. As I understood it later, my folks were going to a sort of informal divorce. Part of the agreed-upon arrangement was for my dad to take under his care his two older biological children while I, the adopted one, would go to Miami to live in the Fougères family's room and board. The latter was one of dad's close business associates from Les Cayes. The unsaid financial expectation behind the agreement was for me to become a lifeline income for those remaining behind in Port-au-Prince.

At this defining juncture, I could have exited the plane like many before me had done and never again looked back. But the forgiven child that I was, stood in solidarity by the sides of my mother, Yolle and my two younger siblings, Karl-Henry and Frantz. I remember those horrifying food rationing episodes when most of our Les Cayes businesses went belly up and later when the first anticipated monthly remittance check from Waukegan had taken three months before reaching us.

In solidarity, for having gone through such challenging, trying times with my family would have alone dissuaded me from turning my back on the folks left behind in Port-au-Prince to fend for themselves. I was resolute to do my utmost best not to deceive any members of my tribe, despite the unflattering treatment that I received growing up as an unloved and unwanted adoptee.

# PART I

Lyonel Gerdes

# Miami's Little Haiti's Nascent Years

My Pan Am flight finally landed at Miami International Airport in the mid-afternoon hour of that last Wednesday of July 1975. Besides my modest checked luggage, I carried with me a small bag with not much in it but a few personal items and documents like my protud journalist card from "Le Petit Samed Soir," my Haitian passport, Fougères' Miami address and my wallet with just one US $20 in it. Though I did not speak a word of English, I knew instinctively to follow the disembarking passengers on the path leading to the US Immigration Center. Luckily for me, the lady who processed my papers was friendly and spoke enough French to ease what could have been an otherwise maladroit experience.

At the end of the process, I was given a green card – an incalculable gift I would later learn to value and appreciate. I exited the Airport to look for a taxicab. Unable to communicate in English, I kept waving the wide paper with Fougères' address written in large print to the incoming taxicabs until one made a stop. I was instructed to ask the driver for the approximate cost of the ride, so after showing the address to him, I inquired about the ride's cost by making a money sign gesture to him with my five fingers. I only had $20 in my wallet, and I was warned that some dishonest taxicab drivers would undoubtedly take advantage of my inability to speak the language to take me for a real ride, all the while inflating the cost. Sitting in the back of the yellow cab, the I-95 cruising was quite a visual feast to my eyes. My overwhelming impression of Miami's busy highways, overpasses, and buildings on my way to Fougères, who lived in a house on 51$^{st}$, the Street between North-West first Avenue and North Miami Avenue, was simply ecstatic. The last time I felt so elated by a place was when I came to Port-au-Prince as an eight-year-old coming from Les Cayes, visiting with my mother for the first time, Haiti's capital.

I arrived safely at my destination, where I was warmly received by Fougères himself and the rest of his family, making me forget earlier apprehensions I had about an unwelcome Miami reception. In response, I generously bought ice cream for all three of Fougères' children from a passing musical truck on its regular afternoon ride. I was left with enough money in my wallet to put my last $10 in an envelope and send it back to my mother's Ruelle Titus' Port-au-Prince address. Except that in my eagerness to make a gesture of early financial commitment to the folks back home, I forgot to conceal the $10 in the envelope, as I learned later that it was never received, obviously stolen at the post office. Following a copious dinner with the family, I was told by Fougères that I would not be staying with them for now. I would temporarily be staying at another family's home not too far from his. It was Fougères' second home, and his mistress's name was Mirlande. She lived four to five blocks from his main legal home, as routinely done back home.

3

Some things never changed in the Haitian culture, not even at such an early stage of the Haitian diaspora in Miami. I was at first taken aback by the unexpected relocation change in my status stay, but I rolled with the punches.

The room I was supposed to stay in was occupied by Pierre Leger. The Leger family was well known in Les Cayes and had a store around the Iron Market square when I lived in the second house from my first memoir. I remember him well even though it had been several years since. We quickly warmed up toward one another in solidarity with our endearing, beloved city of Les Cayes. We joyfully reminisced over many of our collective memories. Later, I met Georges Gelin, who was a friend of Pierre. Both were taking English and vocational classes at downtown Lindsey Hopkins Technical College. All three of us were about the same age. Little did I know that we would soon become inseparable, as our chance meeting that afternoon was just the start of the celebrated appellation group of "Les Pépés."

As it was getting late, Fougères took me to that house off North Miami Avenue and 47th. Street, where his mistress Myrlande lived. She was a decent-looking, light skin Haitian lady. She was friendly. I was not so sure that she was from Les Cayes, as I never asked. She was expecting me as a permanent room and board tenant at her place. She showed me the tiny little square space where I would be sleeping. There was no privacy. It was an open, tiny area in the house with enough room for just a medium-size bed. With no window and no door, the only thing remotely private about my room was when it was bedtime, I could pull a hanging thick fabric held up by a mounting tread on each side of the walls for privacy. That was, for the record, my Miami's first night's sleep accommodation.

I could barely sleep that first night as I was reflecting on how fast things were developing around me. From the time I took off from Haiti's International Airport to my landing in Miami. The dizzying speed of events was too awry: One day, I was a journalist at one of the most respected weekly magazines in Port-au-Prince, and the following day, I was somewhat of a 'nobody.' As my host Fougères would later remind me, "Here, my friend, there's no philosophy but only mopology." It was his sarcastic way of contemptuously mocking those highly educated Haitians who had gone all the way to their philosophy classes back in Haiti but ended up at the end mopping floors here for a meager $3.35 hourly wage.

The Fougères I met in Miami was a completely changed man, not for the best. I recalled a loving, amicable Fougères who used to visit us often from Les Cayes in the aftermath of the family's internal migration to Port-au-Prince. I could always tell when fun times were back again in our Martissant home whenever he showed up to our doorstep, as he was bringing money monthly to my dad for the various businesses he had with him. However, rumors were running wild that, in the end, he was not an honest partner to my dad, as the garage business, along with other investments they had, were continually running in the red. Some even argued that he was able to migrate to Miami with his family, thanks in part to all his ill-gotten money stolen from his business partners, my dad included.

In Miami, he was doing exceptionally well as a top manager in a Hialeah factory and was living the decent life of a working-class family person in a nice neighborhood of Miami. He owned that four-bedroom family house and was among a handful of black families living there at the time. He had arrived and did not want to be reminded of his Les Cayes' humbling past. I knew from day one by his unfriendly attitude and contemptuous body language that it was only a matter of time before the two of us would come to a major confrontation. In the meantime, I would enjoy the honeymoon ride while it lasted. The following day was my twenty-first birthday. I made no mention of it to anyone. I just let it slide.

On my first Saturday, I met with Pierre and Georges at Fougères'. They decided to show me around town by taking me for my first downtown Miami tour. Both were in Miami on student visas and did not yet own a car. We took a bus ride, and within a few minutes, I was walking among the tallest Miami skyscraper buildings, which made an enormous impact on the 'just come' teenager that I was. Downtown Miami in the mid-seventies was majority non-Hispanic white, its suburbs included. The number of Hispanics and blacks who owned a downtown business was marginal. It would take another decade before the big white flight away from Miami began, following the massive migration of the Cuban Marielitos from Cuba and the infamous Haitian 'boat people' coming from Haiti, the Bahamas, and elsewhere.

Pierre and Georges took me to the only Haitian store in Downtown Miami at the time, named "Les Cousins," owned by a certain Viter Juste. It was a unique Haitian store in the heart of Miami's white downtown with a wide variety of books, French and Haitian music, plus an array of Haitian artifacts and primitive paintings. Viter Juste, a well-known activist and Haitian businessman, happened to be in his downtown store when the three of us went in. He knew my new friends by judging the way he greeted them. They were frequent visitors and part of his loyal few clientele. If one was homesick or had a dire longing for things Haitian, that was the weekend's spot for a stop. The ethnic Haitian music being played there alone would certainly do the trick to reconnect your longing mood.

I was introduced to the man whose name, years later, would be coined as the "Father of Little Haiti." Upon learning that I just arrived in Miami and that I was a journalist at "Le Petit Samedi Soir," he took a sudden interest in me. And Viter, being Viter, asked me right off the bat to help him edit and publish what would be the first-ever Haitian bi-weekly paper in Miami to inform and guide what was then a fledgling Haitian community in Miami following

7

the 1972 arrival of the first Haitian "boat people" in Pompano Beach. I agreed to lend my assistance to him, and that was the beginning of a long and enduring relationship with him. Three weeks went by, and many things have happened since. First, with the help of Georges and Pierre, who were already attending classes at Lindsay Hopkins Technical School, I signed up for English classes there. I knew from the onset that furthering my education was the only way out of the routine factory job trap career many educated Haitian immigrants got lured into. While attending day classes for English, I did some evening restaurant and janitorial work under pressure to send money to my family and to start paying for my room and board at Myrlande's.

In a nutshell, I dodged two significant bullets, thanks to the perfect timing of my arrival in the US: the first one was that America's Imperial war in Vietnam was over two years ago, and the US was in a war fatigue mode thus no need for Washington's war mongers to look for young canon folders like me coming from the impoverished land of Haiti. Second, I was a legal resident here, unlike many unfortunate compatriots of mine, who did not have their legal documents and were constantly worried about being picked up by an immigration agent and sent back home. With those two major concerns out of my hair, I was more than ready to face anything coming my way.

Thus, my willingness to try a few menial jobs here and there while looking for something more my speed. My first-ever job as a dishwasher lasted three days. I was hired for the 3-11 pm shift at a restaurant found in North Miami Beach, off 163rd Street and NE 18th Avenue. It was a high end restaurant frequented mostly by a well-off white clientele, and the management needed someone to work in the dishwasher room. From day one, I knew that I was simply not cut out for the task and duty at hand. I purposely spent my first two days on-the-job training, but on the third day, the manager cut up with my gimmick, and I was unceremoniously fired. My next gig was window washing at a fancy Miami Beach Resort Hotel. That job suited me more than the last one.

My first assignment was to clean all the windows surrounding the Resort's area pool. Working in the great outdoors, where I could see the vast blueness of the Atlantic Ocean, was by itself quite soothing to my eyes. I was also motivated by the atmosphere in and around the Olympic size pool, as there were so many white ladies in their bikinis swimming and tanning. Since I started to attend Lindsay Hopkins' lunch cafeteria, I was quite amazed at myself, catching myself shamelessly flirting with white girls. For some unknown reason, I began to find them both fascinating and mysterious. I was having a blast at my new window washing job. Two weeks went by at the Resort's gig, until one Saturday when I was working around the pool area, I was approached by a young and pretty blond girl with the most beautiful pair of blue eyes and an engaging smile. Her tanned skin made her look even more attractive in my eyes. She said hi to me and wanted to know where I came from as she heard me speak with an accent. With my limited English, I managed to tell her that I was from Haiti. She immediately made the connection that I must speak French and tried to tell me in her own broken French that she was visiting from Boston and was taking French classes at the University. She asked me if I could recommend a good dancing club on the Beach so she could go dancing tonight with her other traveling girlfriend pointing toward her direction. She was equally attractive and seeing the opportunity to meet later with both ladies at a club, I told her to leave me her room number so I could call her later with a recommendation.

That was my first close, awkward encounter with what I would later call "Les Filles de L'Oncle" [The Uncle's girls]. I never got a chance to get her room number, as I was suddenly interrupted by a supervisor asking me to report immediately to the front office. I was served a layoff notice an hour later. I suspected that the real reason behind my brutal dismissal was that I was too cozy and friendly with the pretty blond patron, even though she was the one who approached me. But to the managerial staff watching my encounter with her, I was the guilty party for forgetting my proper place and status.

The news of getting laid off and losing yet another job was

not so well received by Fougères' mistress, who was counting on my $100 room and board monthly payment. Because of my green card status, it was suggested that I immediately file for unemployment benefits and Food Stamps. I did not like at all the idea that I had just got here and was already acting like an indigent person leaning on the US Welfare State system begging for aid. I had some dignity and categorically rejected those suggestions. A friend of Myrlande who was visiting her had heard that I was looking for a job and told her that at Fort Myer's migrant farm, they were hiring and looking for Haitian workers, and the pay was very promising. Myrlande, who by now had begun to figure me out, did not even bother mentioning such an offer to me. Still, the pressure of finding a new job was mounting. I needed to make a payment for my room and board and send some money home. Out of despair, I, in some moment of cheerful insanity, contemplated the awful Fort Myers' farm work suggestion, despite the many horrific stories heard about the slave-like working conditions in those farms. And how the mostly Haitian farm workers were treated in utter contempt. The managerial farms up in Fort Myers knew that most of their Haitian workers had no formal legal papers and no work permits and, thus, were exposed to an array of abuses. They ranged from unpaid wages, refusal to pay for extra hours worked in overtime, and, to add insult to injury, the demand for an excessive production load before the Haitian farm workers could receive their slave wages at the end of their hellish workday.

The journalistic instinct in me wanted so much to investigate such alleged abuses occurring there, even for just one day. What better way to do that than to get up one early morning for the 3 a.m. pickup and get inside a crowded van or in the back of a huge truck for the almost 3-hour-long ride to Fort Myers? But deep inside, I knew I wouldn't last not even one hour and chickened out when taking into consideration the punishments involved in my intended farm working environment investigation, like long working hours under a hot sun, chemical exposures, and a host of other unpleasant things which would certainly remind me of my black Haitian ancestors' harrowing slave plantation days.

My meager two-week pay from the Hotel Resort added to my 3-day restaurant check, barely paid for what I owed Myrlande for my room and board. I still managed to send $150 money order check to my mother, hoping to find a steadier, more reliable job to begin sending her more money on a regular basis.

Meanwhile, the friendly chemistry between Georges and me was growing unbelievably well. He looked up to me more than he did his own half-older brother Jerry, who was also a half-brother to Tabou Combo's iconic singer Shoubou. We would later make good use of that Shoubou connection and his biological affiliation to Jerry to reinforce our "Pépé Gwo Flannè" image that we started developing among all the beautiful Haitian girls around the neighborhood, which would soon become Miami's little Haiti.

I started hanging out more in Georges' small efficiency room that he shared with his brother. They had a similar lodging and food agreement that I had with Fougères' mistress, Myrlande. Their mother, who lived in the Bahamas, was paying for her two boys' room and board, who were in Miami studying on student visas. They rented their room from Marie, a close friend of their mother. Georges' mom was what could be called a high-end 'Madan Sara' who purchased a variety of merchandise in Miami to take to her resale store in the Bahamas.

My dear friend Georges was also aware of the dire financial crisis I was in and suggested that I temporarily move with him and his brother until I found a job and got myself situated. I was so moved and humbled by his brotherly offer that I had teary eyes. Looking back at this specific moment in time, Georges was to me like a sent angel with a helping hand that tended to me when I most needed it. Following an unfortunate incident involving myself and Fougères, I decided to take on Georges' offer and moved out of Myrlande's place the same day to Georges' small efficiency room located on 52nd Street between Northwest 1st and Northwest 2nd Avenue, just one block shy of Fougères' legal home.

I was technically homeless, broke, not a penny to my name,

and desperately looking for a job which I could live with. Yet, despite all those life-changing events I was faced with, I remained stoic, sensing that it would all be all right and that I was for now in much better hands with the Gelins brothers. For the first time since my arrival here in Miami a few weeks ago, I did not have to put up with my host, Fougères' sarcasm. I could breathe a long sigh of relief as I felt that I was on the right path to recovery and was just waiting for a better time to come.

Linsey Hopkins' lunch hour at the school's Cafeteria was quite a social event and a gathering spectacle for the large student body there. All four of the original "Les Pépés" in the persons of Jerry, Georges, Pierre and I were all attending classes there, and we were all equally busy socializing. We met with the Devot sisters, Christiane and her older sibling and later Kettly. The latter was not a student at LHTC, but that did not make much of a difference, as she and her other gorgeous-looking sisters became the female faces of the group "Les Pépés." It was one good-looking gathering bunch. We formed a tight, cool circle of friends, caring for one another. From our regular daily routine Cafeteria meeting, we started to meet every weekend at many neighborhood parties or at the Devot sisters' family home, which was the group's informal headquarters weekend rendezvous.

What made our group gathering so special was the very fact that there were not too many cool looking Haitians like us in the

Miami area of the mid-70s. Ergo, each time we met, was an excuse for a celebration and an occasion to pop up the champagne bottle and the toasting glasses. It was never one boring moment in our group weekend hangouts, and we had such good, genuine, clean fun. The Devot's sisters' participation was a definite breath of fresh air, bringing a particular spark to the group's already glamorous silhouette and handsomeness. Several decades later, it was still a continuing life celebration affair whenever some of the group's surviving members happened to reconnect despite their changing lifestyle. Long live the vibe of that early Miami youth group popularly called "Les Pépés."

I landed a stream of odd jobs like the plaster cast sculpture factory at that assembly line in Hialeah, where I removed Greek and Roman carved statues and towers from their silicone rubber molds. It was my first ruthless assembly line experience. At day's end, I was useless and unpleasantly dirty, with white silicone plaster dust all over me and my work clothes. But I found a much cleaner job at a carton box-making factory around the 36th Street railway near the Airport. The work consisted of stacking strings of clean cardboard boxes coming from a machine. With this job, I could schedule my Miami Dade College classes during the day, as I had just started my associate degree studies in Social Science. One momentous advantage this job had, besides paying a little more than the starving $3.35 hourly minimum wage, was that the machine I worked on

15

periodically broke, allowing me to cover several pages from my school's reading assignments. I did not have a car yet and did not know how to drive one either, or so did the rest of the gang. Our only means of transportation was public buses or else getting rides from friends and acquaintances to go around. We walked almost everywhere, especially to one of our favorite spots, the not-so-nearby Morningside Park off 54$^{th}$ Street and Biscayne Blvd.

With my latest blue-collar job, I was able to contribute a little more to my room and board. My family in Haiti also saw an increase in their monthly remittances, and I began to relax and feel better about the future. While there were plenty of opportunities to meet with interesting girls, I was very wary of getting too involved with anyone that early in the game. The furthering of my education and my continuing financial support for my family in Haiti were my foremost preoccupations. Besides, a couple of Haitian girls showing some interest in me wanted to get married and have babies, way too fast for my taste. One girl even made a marriage business proposal to me in exchange for $3,000 after failing to lure me into marrying her for love. Obtaining a green card paper from me was her only motivation. I also met a couple of Black American girls at the then-popular Miami Elks Club Lodge off NW 65$^{th}$ Street and 18$^{th}$ Avenue, but that did not score well either. I suspected that my Frenchie attitude represented a classic clash of cultures with them. On the other hand, the rest of the gang was not as cautious.

Miami, Florida: A Sunshine State's Unauthorized And Unredacted Journey

They had a particular taste for black American girls or anything dark, foreign and exotic in skirts. One Saturday morning, while Pierre, Georges and I were at the NW 2$^{nd}$ Avenue bus stop near our homes, waiting for a downtown ride, a car suddenly made a sharp, noisy U-turn right in the middle of the road. It slowed down right by us. Two ladies were inside the vehicles. The oldest one, sitting in the driver's seat, offered us a ride to wherever we were going. Noticing that they were both attractive, Georges quickly jumped on that free ride offer, hoping that would lead to more than just a ride. We were all three sitting in the back of the car. Peggy was the name of the girl behind the wheel, while the youngest one on the front passenger side was Yvonne. Peggy, a beautiful black American woman born and raised in Miami, was slightly older than Pierre. She was just coming out of a painful divorce, and as was often the case for many women like her, she was ready for a consoling rebound relationship, and Pierre was her prime target from the get-go. Yvonne, in contrast, was more subdued. She was a light skin girl from Honduras and was closer to Georges' age, who was just 19th years old at the time. Both had instant love chemistry for one another, and they started dating, while Yvonne's friend Peggy had a hard time keeping her hands off Pierre.

Now that Pierre and Georges were seriously dating Peggy and Yvonne, they had some serious privacy issues they had to deal with. In Pierre's case, Fougères would not allow him to bring his

17

date to his family home. On our end, our efficiency room was already overcrowded for the three of us, and bringing Yvonne in was ruled out as an option. We all agreed to look for a 4-bedroom rental home where we could all lodge and contribute to the expenses. Georges and Yvonne would occupy the master bedroom, and Pierre, Jerry, and I would each have our separate rooms.

We were lucky to find just the right place not too far from where we were all living before. A house on a nice, quiet street off NE 3$^{rd}$ Avenue and 58$^{th}$ Street. Both Peggy and Yvonne moved to live with us in our newly rented place. Georges purchased his first used Thunderbird car, which made life a lot easier on our weekend activities. We all took turns learning how to drive in Georges' light blue T-bird car, and I was already looking to buy my own. The opportunity would soon arrive one Saturday when Georges had to take his car for a tune-up at a car repair garage on 71$^{st}$ Street and 2$^{nd}$ Avenue owned by Jean Gavot. Gavot, a Haitian businessman from Jeremie who could easily pass for white, recently moved his car repair business from New York to Miami. He was among the few Haitian entrepreneurs in this area at the time. Had he not addressed us in Creole by asking us how he could help us that day, we would not have known that he was one of our compatriots.

Adrien Besson was the name of the mechanic working on Georges's car. He was another white-looking Haitian from Jeremie, like his close relative and Boss, Jean Gavot. For some reason,

Adrien was quite intrigued by us. We exchanged phone numbers and
promised to stay in touch afterward. Upon hearing that I was looking
to buy a car, and he wanted to get rid of his old black Cadillac, he
offered to sell it to me for a mere $200. Even though I knew I would
be spending a pile of money on gas, I could not pass on that offer. It
was a big deal in the eyes of the poor Haitian immigrant who arrived
here not long ago with just $20 in his wallet! After all, it was a
Cadillac, and a Cadillac was a Cadillac regardless of its year and
condition.

I went to Adrien's House the following day to close out on
the car purchase deal. He was living in a house on 75 Street and
Northeast Second Avenue. There, I met for the first time his
beautiful mulatto wife, Michelle and his brother-in-law Philippe
Carrie, who also came from New York with his young, attractive
wife, Nadia. Those two couples had one thing in common: they had
enough of the fast-moving Big Apple's lifestyle and its fierce winter
seasons. Georges drove me there, and we were having so much fun
interacting with all these cool bunch of people that we ended up
spending a good amount of time chitchatting long after the Cadillac
sale was sealed.

My impressive black Cadillac was such a hit in the
neighborhood that Georges' brother Jerry bought himself one the
following month. Thus, with the two of us showing up at weekend
parties with our bourgeois Cadillac cars, it was just a matter of time

19

before everyone started calling us "Pépé Cadillac." Absent the materialist aspect of owning a Cadillac, one of the capitalistic symbols of the American dream, there was a certain irony in the pleasure that I sure took back then in driving a car that many viewed as a sign of success. Subsequently, because of the cars we were driving, we became even more popular not just with the girls but also with the guys. Mind you, that most of our friends did not own a car at the time and that many of them were still relied on public transportation like we once did to get around.

One of the most remarkable 'Pépé' ladies was Michelle Denerville, a.k.a Yolle. We met her at one of our frequent Saturday parties. She instantly became a bona fide member of our group because of her all-around outgoing personality, charm and intelligence. We met often at her place where she lived with her mother, a distinguished Haitian lady name Maria Belnau Denerville. The latter was another white Haitian lady of polish descent. She came from Haiti's Cazale community, known for its concentration of people from Polish ancestry, going back to nine generations who had made Haiti their adopted, beloved land. According to history, several Polish soldiers, around 5,000 or so, were sent by Napoleon Bonaparte to fight the slave uprising in France's richest colony at the time, Saint Domingue, modern-day Haiti. But they were so horrified by the heartless, genocidal mistreatments of the rebellious slaves in Haiti that around 400 Polish soldiers turned against their own legion commanders to join the fight on the side of the Haitian armies. The surviving Polish soldiers of Haiti's Independence, who fought on the side of the slaves, were given lands, financial help, and guaranteed constitutional protection in Haiti. Many of those Polish soldiers' descendants still live to this day in Cazale. I never could wrap my mind around such historical twist and turn!

Besides meeting Yolle's mother, I also met her older sister, Viviane Denerville Pluviose, who was an accomplished, famed dancer, choreographer and reciter in Haiti. She had once performed for the autocrat Papa Doc and often came to visit her family in Miami. Next door to the Denerville lived two equally interesting ladies, Toutoune and Violette. All three ladies were in their 50s, well-educated and sophisticated. Toutoune and Violette had a particular penchant for much younger men, so Georges and I were fair game to them. As cautious as I was back then on matters related to women and sex, I dove Toutoune's bullet. But I could not say the same for my younger pal Georges, who was a lot more adventurous than I was. Violette, the hottest of the two, had eyes for him. I would not have bet my last dollar that Georges did not respond in kind.

In this same circle of new acquaintances, I also met with the well-known playwright Limoné Joseph and his poet friend, Inavy Joseph, of the same last names, though not related. My meeting them was a motivation to go back to writing again following months of writer's block since my arrival here in Miami.

I assisted Limoné Joseph in his grand theatrical play, which was a first in Miami's early cultural activity. "À ta Santé L'Amour" was the play's title, and evening rehearsals were regularly scheduled at Miami Edison Middle School's Auditorium, where it was premiered. A certain Mrs. Jean Louis, spouse of Dr. Jean Louis, the latter a Miami educator, was involved in several cultural activities. Her husband was one of the first chairmen of HACAD, which stood for the Haitian American Community Association of Dade County. Limoné was able to use the Miami Edison Middle School's auditorium for the presentation of his play, thanks to his influence as he was one of the staff educators there. I became very close to Jean Louis, especially when I briefly stayed on 62$^{nd}$ Street behind the first Cayard grocery store in the Miami Haitian Diaspora.

I spent many hours helping and volunteering at HACAD, as in those days, there was no money in the budget to pay for employees, let alone for volunteers. The organization was doing all it could to assist with the mounting influx of the 'Haitian boat people' coming off the Florida Shores on leaking, unsafe wooden boats. All the HACAD volunteers and donors in the 70s were unsung heroes, as the Association could barely help the hundreds of Haitian refugees in need with the donations they were receiving from churches and charitable organizations.

I cultivated a very close friendship with Inavy Joseph, who lived on 43$^{rd}$ Street between Northeast Second and First Avenue with his wife and daughter. Near his home was a makeshift mini park with benches where we sat many afternoons to reminisce and "Parler de tout et de rien" [Chitchatting]. I would often talk about the not-so-distant exciting life I had as a member of Haiti's Independent Press. He seemed to be taking great interest in my brazing journalistic stories. I talked about the fear and the high risk of being killed or imprisoned as a journalist under the dictatorial rule of the Jean Claude regime.

I explained to him that one of the main reasons that my family worked so hard to rush me out of the country was for my own personal safety. I had to confess how much I really missed my pen colleagues, who were like family, and, of course, the celebrity-like status I had, working as the youngest journalist at the weekly magazine "Le Petit Samedi Soir." I told him about the unbreakable bond we, the young journalist team, the likes of Gasner Raymond, Dany Laferrière, Pierre Andre Clitandre, and others, had formed. And how we were convinced that only a free, independent Press could change the nation's political trajectory away from the abyss where it was headed. And how I felt, even after many months since my arrival here, as both an economic and political immigrant, a profound sentiment of guilt for leaving.

I was still coping with the insidious feeling that I had abandoned a noble cause for a free, independent Haiti. "We were like real brothers at the LPSS Redaction room," I said, talking to

Inavy. "Yet I did not have the courage to tell any of my LPSS brothers that I would soon be going AWOL." Though I broke my silence at the eleventh hour when Jean Dominique, a.k.a. JanDo, gave me that ride home on the eve of my departure to Miami, with Dany Laferrière sitting in the front passenger seat. I could not keep my scheduled incoming trip a secret any longer. I told them that I was leaving the country tomorrow for Miami.

Both were shocked, and I remember how I got lectured by my late great mentor JanDo, not to ever forget the truth seeker in me, regardless of where I ended up in the future. As for my pal Dany, he was simply too stunned to utter any word, for we were close buddies, and my sudden departure news was a bit too much for him to grasp. Years later, when we met again in Montreal before he moved to Miami to live with his family, he was the only one who thought of making copies of several of my published political essays, satires and existential poems from my publishing days at LPSS weekly magazine. Without this action of a true friend coming from Dany, many of those early works of mine could have been forgotten or irreversibly lost.

## Living With the Gelin's Brothers

Moving in with the Gelins had been the best decision I made when I was in serious trouble paying for my room and board. I remember the time when Georges, the brother with the heart of gold, had to split several of his dinner plates to share their halves with me. We were three to sleep in that small room, giving credence to early stereotypes about many Haitians living in small, confined spaces in Miami. We shared lots of things. I even borrowed some of his clothes, as we were about the same size. The only thing Georges would not share with me was his women. The handsome devil that he was, he wanted all the pretty ones and as many as he could have his hands on. Being the lady's man that he was, he had many successes with a few of the Pépé girls until he met Yvonne. He seemed to have been in an existential tight race with time. On my side of the spectrum, I was restrained by taking cover behind my seemingly nerdy ways about girls. Busy with my job, school, and voluntary work in the fledgling Haitian community, I felt in some reassuring way that time was on my side and that there was no need for me to rush into things like my dear brother Georges' zest for life.

The perfect chemistry existing between me and the Gelin brothers was nothing short of exceptional. I had no recollection of any fights among us during the time we all lived together. Of course, Georges, a highly opinionated fellow, smart and witty, enjoyed

25

many steamy arguments with me. But in the end, we both agreed to differ, and that was it. Though I remember showing him the door once at my Isidor's bachelor's pad, as he went way overboard in his argument. Of course, we made peace the following day when he called me to apologize. I later found out that he was going through a lot during that time, and that was his way to vent whatever existential anger and frustration he had in his heart. When I met for the first time the Gelins' mother, Aline, who lived in the Bahamas, I understood why her two boys came out the way they did. She was the proverbial apple tree, a very sweet, loving, soft-spoken lady in her early 40s. She adored her two boys to pieces, and she would do anything to see them both successful in life. The closeness I had with her two sons was effortlessly extended to her to such an extent that I surprised myself by calling her mom, too, like her two sons. The feeling was reciprocal on her side, for I became one of hers too, by extension, affiliation and affinity. We had since moved happily as roommates to three different places, all the while maintaining and sharing the cost-of-living in each home.

My days were spent driving in the morning to Miami-Dade College North Campus and then to my evening job. I was qualified to get student loans due to my limited income, which had helped significantly with the overall rising cost of school tuition and book purchases. I met with many students and colleagues on Campus, preferably Americans, to practice my English, which was still in a deplorable state. The mistake I made in the beginning, as the defensive Creolophone/Francophone that I was, was too much hanging out with my Creole and French-speaking buddies and acquaintances. This attitude of mine had, in essence, slowed down considerably my ability to learn and speak English, especially when I was not a foreign language wizard of the caliber of my late sister Marie Marcelle. I was certainly better at reading and understanding English than I was at speaking it. In fact, I often scored 100% in many of my Social Science tests, even though I tended to keep quiet in class's oral participation and discussion. All that out of fear that my heavy Creole/French accent would embarrass me, as I could never suffer the thought of not being understood and people asking me to repeat myself. But lately, I made the courageous decision to overcome my linguistic phobia and engage in more conversation with English-speaking students. And what faster way to learn a language than to either befriend or, better yet, date someone who spoke the language? There were several opportunities for me to meet with white American female students in many of my daily courses. I was simply waiting for the ideal, perfect timing to make a move.

What I learned so far from some encounters I had with white girls I met at parties and clubs was that they mainly looked for pure, genuine fun once they decided to go black against the grain. Not looking for security, marriage and having babies like the bulk of my conditioned country girls or my black American sisters. One more

27

benefit of dating white girls was that they did not mind going Dutch or better yet taking the whole tab. Such dating advantages were right up my alley, as I wanted to remain a bachelor for as long as I could without having to break the bank or run into sentimental dramas with girls. I wanted to finish my studies and embark on a career while taking care of my family in Haiti, who depended mainly on me. For all the above reasons, dating white girls was the ideal, aside from the exotic, exciting appeals of going after the forbidden fruit that they symbolized in my rebellious eyes.

Typically, after spending the morning hours on campus, I had to rush back home to go to an informal, homelike neighborhood restaurant to purchase some delicious, yummy Haitian food. Back then, I had a strictly Haitian diet. Only later, when I began dating white girls who were vegetarian and vegan, that I became aware of those alternative diets. I would change into my afternoon work clothes and hit the road in my big black Cadillac, cruising on the local 36th Street Road leading to the airport for my 3-11 pm shift in the carton/box factory across the railway.

Alix François, who lived off 51st Street and North Miami Avenue, had lately turned his house's large front yard the hangout spot for all the 'flannè' and 'flannèz' in the growing Pépé gathering group. There, many of the veteran members would meet with the latest cool-looking boys and girls joining the group. Members were briefed on the next evening's party gathering: the address, location, and the name of the host. We took turns staging the parties where everyone in our informal group expected to have a blast; as we all knew one another, then never a dull moment.

Meanwhile, Georges and I continued our friendship with Adrien and his wife, Michelle. We got very close and visited them often. Michelle, who was an incorrigible daddy's girl, would frequently travel to New York to spend time with her dad. And when that happened, Adrien would take Georges and me to some trendy Miami clubs. One was near the old area around the Greyhound Racetracks by the airport, which changed later to Jai-Alai. The other popular club was on Biscayne Blvd and 114th Street. The latter was the scene of the first astounding encounter I had with a classic, stereotypical blond girl, convincing me more and more that there was some mysterious sentimental connection between me and the uncle's daughters that both God and the Devil would rather stay out of it. That night upon entering the club with both Adrien and Georges, we went to the bar where Adrien ordered three beers. The place was super crowded. Georges and I were the only blacks there, while Adrien, due to his light, fair skin complexion and Caucasian features, effortlessly passed for white and blended in the crowd.

I would have started to feel quite uncomfortable if it were not for the two blond girls standing at the bar next to us who engaged us in a friendly chat. We soon learned that they were both on Spring break from the West Coast of California, visiting the Sunshine state for the first-time and were out looking for a good time in Miami. Minutes later, the next thing I remember was that Georges and I were pulled onto the stage by both girls. They were great dancers, especially the one that I was disco dancing with. She was the prettiest and the blondest of the two. What I did not see coming was when she locked me in a tight embrace with her arms and began kissing me. How was that for a shock and awe introduction, as a girl like her was typically coined in the racist white American culture, as the blond bombshell American dream! Coming from a conservative, Haitian background, I was quite taken aback by her spontaneous, brazing kissing act with me, being the only two black males in an all-white club. It took me a few seconds to regain my composure, and respond to her kissing, all the while looking over my shoulders in fear of any potential rogue retribution. I was sort of mesmerized by the whole thing. She did what she did with me on the dance floor because she could and felt empowered and entitled to, and the hell with all the white racist society's taboos.

When she was about to leave the club after causing such an uproar inside the bar, she asked me to accompany her to her car. While outside, leaning on the side of her vehicle, she again pulled me towards her and began making out with me in the parking lot. It was only after she left with her friend that I realized that I never had a chance to ask her for her name, nor did I get a number where she could be reached. I was simply too overwhelmed by the entire surreal episode involving me and the bombshell Cinderella to materialize it into the realm of reality! I came out convinced after that 'incident' that there seemed to exist an undeniable natural and mutual chemistry between me and the blond babes!

In "Little Haiti," the news of the popular Mini Jazz Tabou Combo coming to Miami very soon for a weekend extravaganza was making its rounds in the burgeoning Haitian community. Tabou Combo, since its creation in 1968 in the suburb of Pétion Ville by the likes of Albert Jr. Chancy, Herman Nau and others, had completely transformed itself into one mega international group. It has performed in several cities around the world. Never since Tabou Combo's meteoric rise at home, in the Haitian Diaspora and abroad had any home-grown musical band reached such a spectacular rise in global recognition. What Tabou Combo did for the musical genre of "Kompa Dirèk" [Compas Direct] was tantamount to what Bob Marley accomplished in putting Reggae on the global map. Following their many successful tours in Europe, Asia, the Caribbean, and South and North America, the group made Miami the next city to grace with their trendy, unique Konpa Dirèk style of music. Tabou Combo was at the peak of its now over half-a-century-old musical dominion. Fast-forwarding to 2023, they are now one of the longest-surviving Haitian bands alongside Septentrional and Tropicana D'Haiti.

The Haitian Diaspora in Miami, battling against a barrage

of racially motivated bad presses constantly portraying the striving community as nothing more than an agglomeration of boat people swimming to Florida's shores, was looking forward to Tabou Combo's visit to refurbish its somewhat battered image. All the PéPés were overly excited by the coming musical shodown. Several of them purchased advanced tickets, making sure that they would not be missing in action when the day arrived. The fact that they knew that Jerry, one of the original Pépés, was the half-brother of Shoubou himself, the band's larger-than-life singer alongside Fanfan, added extra momentum to their motivation and excitement. One could easily see the portrayal resemblance to Shoubou by just looking at my roommate friend Jerry. The Tabou Combo dancing soiree was scheduled at a Grand Miami Downtown hotel, which is no longer in existence today, as developers had used the space to extend road access to and out of Downtown, Brickell Avenue and I-95. On the eve of the event, Jerry took his brother Georges and me to the hotel to meet with his famed half-brother. We were all mesmerized by the charismatic Shoubou. He could not spend too much time with us as he was getting himself ready for one last rehearsal with the band before tomorrow night's big soiree. He gave us three VIP passes for the incoming event. If anything, Tabou Combo's Miami visit had done was to force a whole class of well-to-do Haitians to come out of the woodwork. I was always under the impression that most Haitians living in Miami were all

confined within those three to four miles long areas from
Northwest second Avenue to Northeast 2$^{nd}$ Avenue and from 45$^{th}$
Street to 79$^{th}$ Street, but I was wrong. The bulk of Tabou Combo's
fans who showed up that night for the event came from a wide
range of places, and I never suspected there were that many
Haitians living in them. People were coming down from as far as
Homestead, Kendall, and South Miami and as far north as West
Palm, Pompano Beach, Delray, and Fort Lauderdale. They seemed
to be coming from different walks of life and layers of the Haitian
diaspora living in Florida. The event was a formidable success to
such an extent that the band promised to come back to play again
and entertain their South Florida Haitian fan base soon.

As for the Pépés' reputation, that went up tremendously
thanks to this event, as people saw Shoubou himself coming to our
table on more than one occasion to exchange pleasantries and a few
jokes with his half-brother Jerry and us. Fast-forwarding to 2023, a
YouTube video by Fanfan, Tabou's other famed singer, about
Shoubou went viral throughout the Haitian Diaspora, as an answer
to an earlier one that also went viral depicting the larger-than-life
Shoubou in a pitiful state sitting in a wheelchair in a nursing home.
Fanfan explained that when Shoubou lost his beloved wife to
COVID, he dove into a deep depression. He did not know how to
deal with such unbelievable pain. He voluntarily bedridden himself
out of depression for over a year.

The Haitian Mike Jagger, Shoubou, had a death wish. By the time the rest of the band, who were themselves going through hard times during the Coronavirus pandemic, caught up with the singer, Shoubou's condition was critical. He had to be hospitalized immediately and relearn how to walk again. He was on the road to recovery at that nursing home, continued Fanfan when a video of him was taken while he was casually singing with no fancies and fanfare on his wheelchair, unbeknownst that a video of him would soon be going viral on social media. In all, Fanfan was confident in reassuring us that Shoubou was doing well and improving. He is expected to join the group for a family reunion on their next-December tour. Back to where I left off, I had to acknowledge that our group, aside from making many new friends and acquaintances, also made many envious and jealous. Chief among them was an obscure newcomer in the Miami Haitian Community named Bob Lecorps. He came with a sullied reputation of being a cocaine drug dealer, constantly in trouble with the Miami Police. No one in our group wanted anything to do with him, and he did not take that snubby rejection well.

The irony with Bob was that he had two brothers who were the exact opposites of him. They were so cool that they naturally joined our group and were invited to many of our weekend gatherings. They had even distanced themselves from their own blood brother. However, because we were such a tight, small community and everyone knew where the next gathering event would be held, Bob Lecorps always showed up uninvited to our parties. He could not suffer the group's snub, despite his repeated futile attempts to impress and coerce some of the Pépés girls with his expensive car, flashy display of his gross collection of gold chains and jewelry, not to mention his waving of brand-new rolls of hundreds of US dollar bills. He had a personal, vindictive beef with Georges, Jerry and me, as he rightly suspected that we were among the most popular ones in the group. When he met us at some public venue, he would always come as close as he could to the group for a provocation. Having the "tapageur" [street fighter] reputation he had among some circle of questionable friends, he would throw insult after insult at us, hoping to incite a reaction from one of us, which could lead to a fight. He never succeeded in such desperate attempts, as we would just ignore his insults and simply move away from him for as long as he cautiously kept his hands to himself. We would not, for the life of us, stand at the despicable level that the man was at.

Behind Bob's intimidating loudmouth, he was known not to be much of a true, real fighter. In fact, he was a pussycat, fearful fighter acting in a bullying way. He took advantage of illegal Haitians who avoided going into a fight with him out of fear that would cause a running into the police and immigration officers. Some were simply scared of the unfounded rumors of him being a trigger-happy lunatic. But many a time, he ran into some Haitians who were much crazier than him and had his ass handed to him. And when that happened, he often ran away from the bloody fight, pretending to go for his machine gun in his car's trunk, but never came back. As the old saying goes, when the going gets tough, the tough get going.

He was, according to his entourage, a classic undiagnosed mental case who should have been on medication, supervision, or in jail. He was an alcoholic, high on cocaine 24/seven. By the time Bob made it to the venue, he was so wasted that he was in no condition to fight. This was the primary reason why he had to rely on his loudmouth and bullying tactic to intimidate a fighter to win any fight for his minion fans. Thus giving them something to talk about the next day, desperately hoping to elevate his ill repute urban legend image. Bob's mental obsession was to be Miami's reenactment of Haiti's proverbial street fighter and "tapageur" extraordinaire. Except that here in the State, the urban legend's character hero, when caught by the police, ended up in jail after the fight.

The last time I ran into Bob was at Aux Palmistes, a trendy Haitian Bar/Restaurant owned by the late Yvon St. Albain, located on 68th Street and Northeast second Avenue. It was the time when Miami's Top Vice was in its early formation days. As expected, Bob, being Bob, was there running his mouth again. But late Ramon Flores, who happened to be around at the club that night, reassured me not to worry a bit about Bob, that he got my back. Ramon was a tall, muscular, skilled fighter and a fierce trained boxer who often came to our gatherings, making him a full fledge member of our group. He appeared that he had some old scores to settle with Bob. "Let him run his mouth," said Ramon, "He's just a coward, and we're just waiting for him to make one move on you, and we'll take him down real fast."

Ramon knew about Bob Lecorps' long rap sheet with fighting, bullying, and some encounters with the Miami Police, for he worked with the Law Enforcement bureau as a private investigator and a bond officer. Twice, he came to our table just to send a clear, unequivocal message to Bob and his minions to just chill out. Bob obviously got the message, as it was the last time I was ever provoked or heard of him until the news of his sudden, brutal murder in Haiti had hit the radios' air waves in the community. He was a fugitive on the run, hiding in Haiti after he shot his wife, whom he accused of stealing large sums of his drug money. Miami Police investigators were looking for him everywhere as a person of interest. But he escaped from Miami by boat to avoid getting caught by law enforcement and sent to prison. Not long after his escape, Bob's lifeless body was found, murdered execution-style with a bullet in the back of his skull, most likely in a drug deal going bad.

# Gasner Raymond Was No Longer With Us

Tuesday, June 1st., 1976, was one of the worst days of my life when the news of my beloved pen brother Gasner Raymond's death reached me in Miami, where I had been living for months. The explosive effect of Gasner's passing was tantamount to the paralyzing numbness I experienced as an eleven-year-old living in Les Cayes, Haiti, upon hearing on the radio of JFK's Dallas assassination.

In the same way, I clearly remember to this day where I was and what I was doing at the time of JFK's planned Deep State assassination; I also remember equally well where I was when the news of Gasner's killing blew me away. The only difference this time was that my numbness seemed to have been tenfold, as I personally knew him, who was a genuine friend, a brother, and a colleague. We shared the same passion, vision and dream of a Haitian homeland that would be one day free and independent from Washington's clutches, itself acting under strict orders from the Global Money Empire's evil doers. I had not one iota of doubt that the decision to neutralize him came from way above the pay grades of those who murdered him by strangulation, to then dispose of his lifeless body on a remote, isolated roadside between Haiti's capital city and the nearby Léogâne suburb.

The initial reaction in Haiti and throughout the Haitian

diaspora living in the States, Canada, France, and elsewhere was total dismay and outrage. The rumors on the street were that Gasner Raymond's support for the "Cement D'Haiti" strike caused his untimely death, for he crossed a redline that the so-called liberal regime of Jean Claude Duvalier could not allow a journalist from the rising Independent Press to cross. However, upon a more in-depth observation and investigation, it was later revealed that aside from Gasner's full support for the overly exploited Haitian workers at the Cement D'Haiti plant, he was also working on a much bigger target, a more treacherous dossier concerning shameless corruption at the highest level of government. If the power that be would allow such a dossier on corruption to see the light of day, there could be no telling how many heads in Jean Claude's regime could be rolling. Hence, the urgent imperative for Gasner Raymond to be silenced.

Internal political observers, as well as external ones, were keenly aware of the power struggle within the Haitian government opposing the regime's old guard, resisting the tides of change, with the implicit support of Mama Duvalier, versus the more liberal branch championed by Jean Claude with Washington's blessings. The young president knew as he was tipped off by the US State Department on the rampant corruption at the Reggie du Tabac by none other than its director, Henry Siclait. Jean Claude was also told that for as long as Siclait kept siphoning off such huge sums of money, he would never be able to implement meaningful

39

fundamental reform and tackle for real the systemic, institutional corruption in Haiti.

But to oust strongman Siclait at the helm of Regie Tabac was no small task, as explained by that quote from one political observer: "Siclait, through his control of non-fiscalized taxes collected by the Regie on a broad range of commodities, was the power behind the throne, a notoriously corrupt and shadowy Machiavellian eminence whose influence was pervasive and whose ambitions in recent times may have extended to the Presidency itself." Thus, Jean Claude, as he had been doing since the onset of his apparent liberal regime, had used the newly emerging Independent Media outlets in his fight against the old guard. He was a huge fan of Marcus Garcia's popular radio show and the controversial weekly magazine "Le Petit Samedi Soir." Both were in the business of speaking truth to power. It was a strange, odd alliance in the treacherous fight against Haiti's entrenched institutional corruption. Yes, Washington wanted to oust Siclait; we got that, but to what end? Was it for the betterment of the average living standard of Haitians, or was it simply a case of preparing the ground for an even more vicious neo-liberal agenda favoring Wall Street's vultures? In short, it was yet again the classic case of getting rid of one bad act to replace it with another.

Henri Siclait had to go, but it had to be done cleverly, as he wheeled so much influence due to the power of the purse that he controlled. He had the entire old guard behind him, including the

President's own mother. Many politicians and officers were also on his informal payroll list, buying their loyalties. That was how he knew about the ploy involving the Independent weekly magazine "Le Petit Samedi Soir" working on a corruption dossier to force him out of power. He knew that the US embassy in Port-au-Prince was giving inculpating documents against him to the magazine. He also learned that Gasner Raymond was the reporter assigned to prepare that corruption dossier, then sealing the fate of my endearing friend and colleague.

The corruption dossier that Gasner was working on before his lifeless body was found was what really caused his untimely death more so than his support of the Cement D'Haiti's strike. The sad reality was that our innocent, unsuspected friend was simply caught between the two rival political factions within the regime's infighting and was unceremoniously used as a disposable cannon folder by both. First, by Jean Claude's liberal branch aimed to expose Henry Siclait's corruption and greed as a first clever step to oust him from his strongman perch, second by Siclait himself sending an unequivocal intimidating message to his foes.

Gasner obviously knew that the direction his investigative, journalistic work was heading would increase the stake and de facto place him in mortal physical danger, but the love of his homeland and the truth seeker that he was would never allow fear to get in the way of his pursuit of the true. June 1st, 1976 was quite a date of

41

infamy for Haiti's striving Independent Press. By murdering him, his killers had turned him into a larger-than-life journalistic figure. In fact, he became one of the unquestionable symbolic faces of Press Freedom in Haiti by his martyrdom.

At his informal public funeral, thousands of Haitians, among them students, journalists, writers, artists, and mourners from all walks of life, showed up in anger, sorrow, and solidarity for this young 23-years-old dead journalist who had been martyred by the regime's sbires. Gasner Raymond's death was a forerunner of what was to come four years later for Press Freedom in Haiti when the regime of Jean Claude Duvalier's fake liberal mask literally fell off its face.

The time of using and manipulating the Independent Press was slowly running out of its course. The existential battle opposing the old guard to the new was won by the latter since strongman Henry Siclait, representing the old Duvalierist clan, was sent packing in exile, followed by Simone Ovide Duvalier, her daughters, and several of their close supporters. One thing was for certain: Gasner Raymond did not die in vain, as his life sacrifice had inspired many more like him to come out and continue with his fight legacy for a free Press, and prosperous Haiti for all.

# The Start of My Bachelor Pad Days

Georges and Jerry's mom decided to buy a home in Miami for her two sons to live in. Until now, she had been paying a considerable amount of rent money. Money that could never again be recovered. Gone. A Real Estate agent found them a nice three-bedroom family home in a North Miami suburb that they purchased. They offered me the chance to move with them, as had been the case since my arrival here in Miami.

However, I felt that it was about time for me to take off from the Gelin's nest and be on my own for a change. I would never appreciate enough how helpful and supportive my co-living experience with the Gelins brothers was. They would forever be a part of me.

I found a rental studio apartment in the same vicinity where I landed when I first arrived here. The two-story corner lot apartment building was off 43$^{rd}$ Street and Northeast 1$^{st}$ Court. There were three studio rooms on the top floor, and the last unoccupied unit had just been taken by me. I would later meet with my two interesting second-floor neighbors. The studio room next to mine was rented by none other than Pierre Mendes Alcindor, a.k.a. Dada, who had just arrived in Miami from Haiti. He would later earn a doctoral degree and became one of Miami's most renown personalities in Little Haiti's Radio Broadcasting. In the studio room next to Dada was a

43

truly nice fellow named Jean Anduze, who moved to Miami from New York. We three had immediately formed a bond which would last for years.

As the "Just Come" that we three were at the time, we were simply living in a state of pure survival. We three worked odd jobs just to survive while going to school. Pierre Mendes remembered reading my articles in the LPSS weekly magazine and held me in very high esteem. In fact, he was very proud of being my next-door neighbor, as I was one of his idols for my journalistic contribution to Haiti's Independent Press. Now, thanks to such a chance meeting at this apartment building, we both seemed to embark on a common destiny ride together. Later, when he became a community activist and a radio personality, he published in a literary magazine that he founded in association with Lucie Tondreau, my highly controversial poem "Les Exilés De Nul Pays" [Exiled from Nowhere] that had graced the pages of the famed LPSS magazine, few days before leaving my homeland.

From the onset, Pierre displayed a unique urge to change his current situational condition. He was a go-getter who would not sit and take it without a fight. He briefly came to work with me in the Carton factory as he was looking for work. It was a time that brought back interesting memories, as one of the cornerstones' chapters in my Miami journey. I was on my own for the very first time. Living all by myself and independent at last. I was no one else's roommate.

However, I should confess that Jean, who was a good, genuine friend from the beginning, happened to be also a good cook who occasionally took great culinary care of us many a time. He was dating a beautiful, black American woman called Helen, who had an infant son named Daniel. Every now and then, she would come to visit Jean's studio room, and each time that happened, she would change the entire chemistry of the entire second floor.

The building was owned by a white American lady in her 40s who was dating a black Haitian male, said to be a business partner of hers. He was not particularly friendly with us. The rules were very strict. Could not have parties. Noise had to be kept at a minimum, especially at night. The $100 rent money was due on the 1$^{st}$ of every month, with no exception. The owners wanted to keep a certain image of a respectable family home. We began to suspect that behind all the strict house rules was a wary Haitian lover who was suspicious that his flirtatious business partner could find one of us too cute to resist, as we learned that he was married to another woman, and she was just his mistress. We followed the house's rules, as the rooms were nicely furnished, the building location and presentation were excellent, and we did not want to be kicked out from such an ideal, low-rental place. Besides, I was proud to live at one of the few superbly made structures acknowledged by the city itself to be historical in a neighborhood which was becoming Little Haiti as more and more Haitians were moving in.

I missed the Gelins brothers, especially Georges, the one that I was the closest to. But we kept in touch with one another. I went to visit them regularly at their new beautiful North Miami home, and they came often to visit me in my new bachelor's pad. Georges spent more time hanging out with me at my place than he spent in his bourgeois suburban home. I sometimes felt that he was slightly jealous of my newfound bachelor pad's lifestyle, especially when it turned out later to be a hangout spot for the new generation of Pépés.

My neighbor friend Jean next door had been in the habit of smoking marijuana especially on weekends when his gorgeous black American girl friend, Helen, would visit him at his place. Both had been unsuccessfully trying to introduce me to the recreational use of the herb, but I always found some excuses not to go along with their try-out offer. Coming from the conservative provincial background I was raised; I had a litany of preconceived negative stereotypes about the use of any drug. But one day out of cheer curiosity I decided to take two innocent puffs out of the passing joint. Then, what happened next would be one pivotal happenstance in my entire life journey. I began to feel that I was about to lose my mind. And that I was on one roller coaster ride where no one came back the same at the end.

I was not in control of my thought processing. I had to quickly excuse myself when I felt that I was about to faint and collapse. I rushed into my studio room, and as soon as I got through

46

the door, I literally threw myself onto the bed, turned on my back, facing the room's ceiling. I did not know what exactly was happening. Everything around me was spinning incredulously fast, and my eyes seemed to be spinning along with the ceiling and everything else around me. It was one heck of a harrowing introduction to Cannabis. It scared the living hell out of me. Frightened to death, I went into a near panic shock, where I really felt that things were not looking good. And that the likelihood of me coming out of this ganja experience unhurt was very slim. I honestly thought that my moment of reckoning had finally arrived!

Fortunately for me, after about a two hours' time, laying on my back with my head still spinning, things started to settle a bit around me. The initial fast-speeding spin in my head began to slowly subside, to later be replaced by one overwhelming state of mind and awareness that I never thought existed before in the realm of the human consciousness.

I always had in my room a recorded cassette with a cool collection of French chansonnette songs that I grew up listening to my entire life. But when Francoise Hardy's hit songs, "Des Ronds dans L'Eau" [Circles in the Water], came up, I was blown away by the surreal sound coming out of the recording. Hardy's voice, the lyrics, and the melody were all out of this world. I heard that tune a hundred times before, but this time, it sounded a million times sweeter, as if it was the very first time I ever heard it.

Lyonel Gerdes

Obviously one of the effects of smoking resulting from the cannabis psychoactive THC ingredient was to heighten one's senses when smoked, thus making colors seem brighter and sound much clearer. In my case, I felt that my experience with the herb, past my first psychotic trip, opened unsuspected windows for me to look into, with a multitude of incredible panoramic angles, valleys' contours and forms, and avenues of wonder I never thought existed around me before. One sure thing weed did for me was to lower considerably my chronic social inhibitions, as it awakened that area in my brain responsive to relaxation, euphoria and that feel-good sensation. Since that initial faux pas experiment with ganja, a one puff recreational ganja like my one-drink alcohol habit when partying with friends became the protocol.

Jean, Helen and Dada never suspected that I came that close to suffering a serious cannabis-related breakdown. But in the end, I had recovered remarkably well. I was simply grateful that I came back fine and survived the ordeal. A no-weekday smoking pot was a definite must for me, as I anticipated that it would interfere with my evening job and would also negatively impact the quality of my academic school work. Speaking of school, I just successfully completed my associate degree in arts at Miami-Dade College North Campus. I started taking a preparation course to help me pass the SAT required test to be admitted into the FIU's undergraduate sociology program. I was delighted when I passed the entrance exam and was accepted into the bachelor's degree program there.

My studio room finally got its first baptism when the attractive, elegant spouse of an eminent personality in the Haitian community came one evening to visit. She was in her 40s and was very involved in socio-cultural activities in Little Haiti. Her family name would not be revealed here out of respect for her and her relatives. She was certainly one safe discretionary sexual escapade for me, thanks first to her marital status and second to our age gap difference. She was a safe ride against the phobic fear I had for any kind of committed involvement with a woman. I trusted that she would not interfere with any of my grand academic plans to earn a doctoral degree in International Relations, to better my life status here, support my family financially and eventually bring them to the States. Then, despite the moral ethic violation implied by her visit to my bachelor pad, I sort of play down the guilt that I was conditioned to feel when crossing such established social taboo of having sex with a married woman. She was a highly respected lady who had no intention to divorce her successful husband and was very discreet in her sexcapade. She was simply bored in her long, failed marriage and needed just a sidekick romantic distraction from a much younger lover. She did not need any money from me. No marriage commitment, no babies, and no green card. I so happened to have been around at a few socio-cultural venues that she attended in the community and had caught her fancy.

Lyonel Gerdes

Our nameless socialite reminded me so much of a lady named Tante Paulette that I had an epic crush on right before I migrated to Miami. Both were in their early 40s, had the same voluptuous built, grace and sophistication. Her striking resemblance to Tante Paulette was what really picked my interest. And when I had her that first time in my bed, it was the closest I came to feel what it could have been like had I had such lucky opportunity with my beloved Tante Paulette, alas! We met twice more, but I had so much respect for her distinguished husband that I could not possibly live with the guilt and discontinued the affair.

Since I began to take classes for my undergraduate studies at FIU Tamiami Campus, I had to readjust everything to fit in with my loaded, heavy schedule. FIU's South Campus was nothing like the close by Miami Dade College North Campus that I attended for months. It took a journey to make it there, and I was beginning to feel the gas pinch effect at the pump with my already skinny wallet, driving with my big old black Cadillac. I had to reschedule my hours in such a way as to allow enough transitional time for me to squeeze things in so I could attend to other things like my evening job.

I was getting student loan money, but they were never generous enough for me to quit my evening job and become a career professional student. Though, I would be later called one by a frustrated girlfriend of mine, tired of my constant preoccupation with schoolwork and academia while not spending enough time with

50

her. Besides, all the checks received from the student loan department, starting with those from Miami Dade College to FIU, were all deposited into a special savings account. This fund was not to be touched under any circumstances except in the case of an urgent, extreme emergency occurring either back home in Haiti or if I happened to be in an accident and was not able to work and provide for myself. In addition, I was always wary about the Trojan horse deception of the student's loan money being given to me.

In my mind, there was nothing benevolent or generous about the entire student loan program. It was what it was, a sneaky dept entrapment scheme on the upcoming new generation of workers. Thus, one more reason for me not to abuse the program or take advantage of it, thinking that it was free helicopter money that I would never have to repay.

With that in mind, I watched carefully how I spent the hard-earned money I was making from my blue-collar work and never considered my student loan money as part of my yearly income budget. Hence, my tendency to constantly look for bargaining deals on about everything, such as food, clothing, cheap and affordable rent, you named it. I was never sold by the daily dose of what was being portrayed and displayed on my TV screen as the ultimate American Dream, meaning the big suburban house and the brand-new car, to name just a few.

51

## Lyonel Gerdes

I managed for many years to resist the bourgeois charm of godless materialism and consumerism while saving as much money as I could to later invest wisely in things that would help build a secure economic foundation to better my life, not just in material advancement through investments, but also in spiritual gains. Ironically, I received many criticisms for my low-cost, anti-consumerist lifestyle from friends and foes and family alike. However, when that sort of criticism came from one of my dear half-brothers for whom, in parts, all my material sacrifices had been made to begin with, it really broke my heart.

But 1 would set the record straight on this tiny, inconsequential family controversy by arguing that had I bought headlong into the prevailing American consumerist cliché with the little paycheck money I was still making back then, there would have been many food rationing days for him, and the rest of the family members left behind in Port-au-Prince. I would have to send a lot, lot less money than I was routinely sending to them every first of the month so I could pay for the sizable mortgage of my suburban Miami home and for the cost of the fancy new car, too.

The irony at the end of such a family meme struck a telling acknowledgment chord with many members, for there came a time when my misguided sibling brother needed an emergency $30,000 to be deposited in an account, and the money was nowhere to be found. It was a collateral fund demanded by the US Immigration office to finalize his official green card papers, with a rapidly approaching deadline. And in the middle of a nearly chaotic situation, guess who came to the rescue at the eleventh hour, the wrongly accused penny-pinching brother, me. The emergency discretionary fund saved throughout the years of accumulation from all my student loan checks was finally put to good use and for a noble common family cause at last.

# Fast Forward To 2024
# Miami and an America in Decline

Miami is no longer the same city that I landed in nearly half a century ago. The white population's flight away from the city had been achieved and completed some three decades earlier. The current Miami population is, in large part, a Hispanic majority, one with a low percentage of other races and ethnicities. Its political, social, and cultural landscapes had gone through so many fundamental changes and transformations that many astute observers labeled the city as just another banana republic except for its world-class buildings in the downtown area, Brickell Avenue, and its landmark I-95 highways. The Little Haiti enclave, where I lived for months when I first arrived here in the mid-70s, was no longer called by its old name, as many Haitians had long moved out the old neighborhood to look for jobs elsewhere in Florida.

There are still huge conglomerations of Haitians living in North Miami, Miramar and in several suburban areas, where they had their own elected commissioners and mayors, a political feast which could only be dreamt of some five decades ago. While so much progress was made by many Haitians, many more of our compatriots living in Miami and elsewhere in the States were still struggling to make ends meet. It was no rocket science to figure out why life in general seemed to be getting harder and harder, not just for minority immigrants but also for the average white Americans in the US. Frankly, the state of the union is in dire trouble.

The declining American Empire fell into the same historical traps that the Roman Empire had fallen when the latter expanded its legionary forces so far out that it left unprotected its own national territorial borders. They were invaded and, over time, ransacked and decimated by the surrounding tribes of barbarians. There's not a place on the earth's map where there are rare earths, minerals, and resources to be pillaged and plundered that you won't find American military bases nearby, while their own respective borders with Mexico and Canada are known to be open and unprotected. One can only guess how America's sworn enemies had been quietly using the US open border situation to infiltrate and install many of their dormant cells, and terrorist assets waiting to be activated on marching orders for the final take down of the American Empire.

The opioid and meth epidemic in the US could not be that widespread had both the Mexican and Canadian borders with the US been seriously checked, controlled, and surveilled by the Department of Homeland Security. Aside from the destabilizing risks of illegal drugs coming from countries like China, Southeast Asia, and South America, to name just a few, entering through the same border channels, it would not be preposterous that materials to make a dirty bomb could also find its way here. Notice that we're not even talking about the possibility, thanks to the US' proxy

Ukrainian war and the weapon proliferation resulting from it, that a portable javelin or stinger missile could one day find its way back home in the wrong hand. And when that happened, the nation's Civil Aviation overall safety would be at much greater risk. And the drug cartel warlords in Mexico have now more weapons of war in their arsenal to fight US border law officers.

An open border is not the only thing contributing to America's power decline in the world. The US proxy war in Ukraine had amply demonstrated that America's overall weaponry system performance paled in comparison to that of its Russian counterparts. Since Alexander the Great, it has been shown that superior weapons in battle were the decisive crux to defeat and subjugate your enemies. Bigger and better guns had allowed the white colonial power elites of Europe to exploit and control first their own European mass land, to then move on to other continents such as Africa, Asia, and North and South America, dominating them for centuries. Now, with the latest hypersonic weapons in the hands of Russia, China, North Korea and now Iran, while the collective West is falling behind and playing catch-up, for how much longer will the imperialist, neocolonial powers' global dominance last? And for how much longer will they continue to feel entitled to their eternal free lunch claim at the world's food counter?

The imperial West, with America's leadership role, had been eating everyone else's breakfast, lunch, and dinner from the Global

South while holding them down under the barrel of their guns. Now what will the future be like with the BRICS nations taking a courageous stand against the biased arrangement of the international rules-based order of the West. They had been working since to put an end to the US dollar domination and its bullying militaristic hegemon, which had allowed America the longest economic free ride it had enjoyed for over ¾ of a century. BRICS nations had been working tirelessly to put in place a currency backed up by gold as an alternative to the US petrodollar. And when and if they succeed at doing that, it will be the death knell of the dollar hegemony. In the meantime, the bulk of their heavy trading occurred within their own respective national currencies, thus bypassing the US dollar.

America had been living overly large beyond its means, forcing all the countries using the dollar-dominated SWIFT Payment system to absorb its mountainous, untenable trade deficit. But the gargantuan percentage pie of the world's economy that the US once enjoyed unchallenged had been considerably shrinking due to the competitive economies from the rising Global South nations such as China, India, Brazil and now Russia. Consequently, because America's political elite's foremost loyalty is to its billionaire's master class first, its bottom working classes were thrown under the bus, making them the fall guys for the US's shrinking pie.

US' decline can also be seen through its overall crumbling infrastructures like the increase in train derailments, fallen bridges, unkept roads and schools. Added to that was America's mass shooting epidemic, unemployment, opioid crisis, crystal meth addictions, and homelessness had left parts of many major American cities, such as Los Angeles, New York, Seattle, Phoenix, Denver, San Francisco, and Detroit, looking like a Fourth World countries. And the number of US cities joining the list keeps growing. How did America, once the shining city on the hill, the beacon of light and hope for the Global North as well as the Global South, end up in such a pathetic state? Simple, America's elite billionaire class, by extension the Global Money Empire, controlled not just the three branches of the US government but also owned its Fourth Estate, America's Mainstream media. With all the check and balance institutions in their pocket, it was easy for the elite class to embark on the total deindustrialization of America for more profit abroad.

I wonder how much Marx's theory of capitalism's inherent contradictions had foreseen that late capitalism could have gone through an even much quicker self-destruct process through the offshoring and outsourcing of all its major production lines and services for the sake of mounting, insane profits. Access to China's huge market and the exploitation of its low slave labor cost were the bate for the globalists without them realizing that China had many hidden cards up its sleeve. Indeed, sending all their factory bases along with their know-how technology sharing to China, Southeast Asia, and other parts of the world had rendered America weak and

China strong. Specifically, China insisted on a must-share technology as a pre-condition for US Capitalism to exploit its cheap, large pool of labor and access its astronomical consumer base.

Decades later, since the start of Globalization 3.0 started under Clinton, China had learned to outsmart US Capitalism at its own game. The elite billionaire class in the US, through its unchecked greed, had contributed to the complete impoverishment of the once-striving American middle class. An American middle class that was once the envy of the world but had found itself on life support for several years now.

When I first migrated here in the mid-70s, things were not as prosperous as they once were during and after the Second World War for America's working class, but I could tell by so many observable indications that wealth distribution to a certain degree was much fairer back then than it is in today's America. The schools were functioning well. The highways were well maintained. Downtown Miami was flourishing with international trade, businesses, and tourism. The Port of Miami, a major seaport located in Biscayne Bay at the mouth of the Miami River, was exploding and raking billions as the largest passenger port in the world and among one of the top 10 largest cargo ports in the States.

Money was being invested and spent in maintaining the nation's major infrastructure, like its bridges, roads, schools, highways, and public transportation. I remember the time I used to take the public bus; it was running more efficiently than it is today. I did not have to wait that long to catch a ride downtown or to my first restaurant gig in North Miami Beach. Speaking of that first restaurant job, I was back then in utter disbelief at the amount of leftover food I was being directed to throw into the large waste container. Coming from an impoverished island, where hundreds of thousands of Haitians were being starved and gone to bed hungry, and millions of Haitian children suffering from malnutrition, I could not stomach discarding whole untouched meals sent back by the patrons. I knew then that America was one filthy rich country, and the proof was in the way its white, affluent middle-class could afford to come to a fancy restaurant, order expensive meals, barely touch them, return them, and still pay the restaurant bill.

Such flattering portrayal of the American middle-class' throw-away consumerist attitude occurred, of course, some five decades ago when the billionaire elite class was still being restrained by some rules of decency. They had not started yet to rage their all-out economic war against America's bottom classes.

In the mid-70s, following the big Vietnam debacles, America's military-industrial complex and the shadowy behind them, meaning the banksters, decided that it was perhaps a perfect moment for a pause from the systemic plundering of the nation's tax base revenues and its national treasure. Noting that all during the

Miami, Florida: A Sunshine State's Unauthorized And Unredacted Journey

Vietnam War's eleven years of unnecessary mass killings, over half of the country's tax base annual collection was going into the proverbial Pentagon's rabbit hole war budget, where the bulk of the money could never be found and accounted for through any audit.

This time-out break offered to America's middle classes' apparent rise in living standard was nothing but a clever strategy by the Global Money Empire in charge of both "The City of London" and Wall Street asking them to go back to their drawing board to ploy yet their biggest, lethal anti-working-class programs to ever be implemented by the global elite against not only America's own national economy but also to the entire world's economy. Neoliberalism, a euphemism for corporate fascism on wheels and on steroids, was luring at the gate and its harsh and cruel economic policies would take a few years' time before coming to full fruition in the US and in the United Kingdom. Its ugly heads would simultaneously appear in the early 1980s under Ronald Reagan's conservative, Republican administration and in the U.K. with his partner in crime, British Prime Minister Margaret Thatcher. Both were minions and assets owned, bought, and paid for by the Global Money Empire. Neoliberalism's true hidden agenda in its core economic austerity for the poor, but not for the rich, is a deceptive tactic allowing unlimited wealth transfer from the bottom classes to the top global elite class. And its vague promise that some of that vast transfer of wealth will perhaps, in due time, trickle down to the

61

bottom poor was an oxymoron.

The economic premises and policies of neoliberalism as applied and implemented by Reaganomics in the US, and Thatcherism in the UK, and throughout the vassalized nations of the world, were nothing but a systematic plundering scheme of most countries' national economies, treasures, and resources. The working-class workers in both the Global South and the Global North were being robbed blind and literally taken to the cleaner.

The display of wealth that I witnessed from an affluent, striving American Middle-class at my first dishwasher job, was now a thing of the past. Neoliberalism is still alive and well despite its utter failures to deliver on its promise to raise everyone's standard of living along with the rising wealth of the one-percenter class. Perhaps help to take America's bottom classes off their life-support ventilator may come where they least expected.

It's clear that the existential battle in the current Ukrainian proxy war, being waged against Russia by the Global Money Empire hiding behind NATO, is to maintain at all costs its unipolar, globalist, and neoliberal hegemonic world versus the BRICS nation's promises of a better, multipolar world. More and more nations from the Global South, Africa chief among them, seem to be tempted by the economic development prospects offered by China's Belt and Road Initiatives, with the icing on the cake that they get to remain free and independent by maintaining their culture and national sovereignty. All that in sharp contrast to what the Global Money Empire offers through its IMF and World Bank's debt peonage loans and the collective West's genocidal war of extermination, terrorism, and color revolution against them. The collective South is tired of getting tired, used, humiliated, and exploited by the Imperial powers of Europe and North America.

Russia's courageous fight not to allow the West's evildoers from balkanizing their country for one end alone, to pillage and plunder its vast natural resources, stood not just for the sovereignty of Russia's motherland, but also for the rest of the entire planet that had been living in one form or in another in total and quasi servitude for centuries with their sore neck under the fierce, relentless knees of the Global Money Empire, where no one country in the current world's unipolar scam is free including America itself.

Lyonel Gerdes

# My Rental Apartment
# At Isidor's Family Home

All three of us on the apartment's second floor were looking for a place to move, as the owners of the building where we were staying sold their property and gave us two weeks' advance notice to vacate our rooms. One lucky day, while driving on Biscayne Blvd, a rental sign advertising for a studio and an efficiency caught my attention. I turned around quickly and asked my friend Georges, who was in the car with me at the time, to write down the phone number on the cardboard sign. I later called and talked to a lady who sounded very nice on the phone. I let her know that I was interested in seeing the efficiency room I saw being advertised. We agreed on a time for me to come check out the place.

As soon as I entered the Isidor building, I sensed the positive, welcoming vibe at the lobby entrance. It was an old solid concrete structure built in the 1920s. Mr. Isidor, after I rang the house front bell, came to open the door. He was an old, affable gentleman. An Italian American man in his 70s who moved down to Miami from Jersey City with his wife Catherine some years earlier. They purchased this six-unit property, using a portion of their pension funds as a down payment, with the intent to turn it into a rental property business to supplement their retirement income.

I was introduced to Mrs. Isidor, also in her 70s, who was

chatty and friendly, which made me feel welcome and at home. Next, her husband proceeded to show me the rental apartment that was vacant. It was the first one on the right as soon as you entered the building. He opened the door and gestured for me to go in. The studio/efficiency was a furnished one with a kitchenette in the middle as a cooking space with a small oven, a tiny table for two, a faucet sink, and a window. Next to it on the left side as you entered the apartment, was a sizable bath shower tub in it.

The sleeping quarter, which was to the right of the kitchenette, was the largest space in the entire unit. The room had glass windows all around giving it access to more sunlight from the outside. It contained two medium-sized beds against on both sides of the room's outer walls. The sleeping quarter also came with a tall cabinet closet and a small buffet where a TV could be placed on top. There was enough space on top of the closet cabinet to install my stereo system. The rent was $125 a month, with water and electricity included. I instantly adored the three separate spaces of the unit layout, which made the efficiency apartment appear much bigger than it really was. I let Mr. Isidor know that I was pleased with the unit's design and that I would take it.

House rules were made clear to me on the dos and don'ts. $ 250 was due immediately for me to move in and seal the contract. Half of the initial $250 checks I signed that day would be held as a security deposit. I could not be any happier with what I just accomplished. I was moving to a new place in an exciting location just walking distance from downtown Miami. The ocean was only half a block away from the new apartment. All I had to do was a leisurely walk in the direction of the waves to meet with the mighty Atlantic. A relaxing activity I have done countless times in the nearly ten years I lived at Isidor's rental bachelor pad.

One excellent advantage of furnished property rentals was that all you had to do was turn in your keys and collect your security deposits, as there was no need for a moving truck to transport a load of furniture from one place to the next. I moved out the following week from the 43$^{rd}$ Street building to begin a whole new chapter of my Miami's journey. One notable thing worth mentioning in passing was the sad fact that for the first time since I arrived here in Miami, I would be living outside the familiar neighborhood space which was now frequently referred to as "Little Haiti."

I quietly installed myself in my new bachelor pad off Biscayne Blvd. and 25$^{th}$ Street. I set my stereo system on top of the tall closet in the sleeping room and my TV on top of the smaller buffet furniture used by me to store extra pieces of clothing that I could not find space to store in the larger one. The sleeping quarter's bottom floor was about eight meters below the rest of the efficiency's, giving the impression of a makeshift New York basement. The basement-like effect with the room's surrounding tall glass windows created a spontaneous, inviting mood for any newcomer. That inviting, cozy charm was not just unique to the sleeping quarter but was also extended to the rest of the efficiency. I kept my new charming place as neat as possible. It was not, after all, such a big space to clean.

I barely used the kitchenette, for I mostly ate out, as cooking time for my busy schedule was an unaffordable luxury. Books and music were my top hobbies. I started to purchase the English translations of many of the old classic books that I read in French back in my growing-up days in Haiti. I was now reading the English version, a way to ease my challenging grasp of the English language. I also began to amass a great vinyl records collection of the music and songs that had immensely impacted my life. I still have, to this day, many of my old music collections, except for a few that I lost because of friends who borrowed some and never gave them back.

My first new neighborhood excursion came the following day. I went straight down in the direction of the water. I could not believe how close my new apartment was to the sea. I felt that it was a cheap, affordable privilege to just walk down passed a few apartments whenever I had the urge to feel humble and experience the grandiosity and the mighty beauty of the waves.

After spending nearly an hour contemplating the Atlantic Ocean's mystifying vastness and looking at a few passing motorboats, I walked down to Biscayne Blvd. and crossed it to enter the House of Pancakes, a chain restaurant known to serve breakfast all day on Sunday. It had a dark blue triangular rooftop, which was its signature design. You could never miss that structure as it stood out. It changed its original name to something else over the years. After breakfast, I continued with my neighborhood exploration by walking south on the boulevard toward the new Omni International Shopping Mall, which had just opened its doors.

Omni's mall was Miami's biggest, latest sensation. The forerunner before the widespread, burgeoning Miami mall culture. It was an architectural marvel in all its newness. There was the Omni Hotel lodged inside of it, a movie theater, several big brand name stores, boutiques, and restaurants. Its Carousel was a definite twist of entertainment for kids and adults alike.

People watching as I was into its visual euphoria was one bonus attraction for me. Built as a major tourist hub, the International Omni Mall attracted both domestic visitors and international ones from Europe and South America. It was a relocation bonanza to know that I lived so close to Miami's downtown, the ocean, and the happening Omni Mall. I lived less than a ten-minute walk from such sites, and in no time, I was in my new bachelor pad's warm and cozy bed.

Despite living somewhat outside of "Little Haiti," I managed to spend many hours there, in the old neighborhood. To paraphrase the old saying, "You can take me out of Little Haiti, but you cannot take Little Haiti out of me." Alix François' fifty-first Street front yard was still one of the favorite meeting places for the new generation of "Pépés". Friday afternoon was the meeting time where everyone in the group would come to reconnect and meet with new friends and found out where the next party house would be the next day. Gregory Carré and Eddy Fabien, two new members of the group, took on a special liking for me, and both ended up spending time in my new bachelor's pad, smoking and listening to British classic rock like The Rolling Stones, Led Zeppelin, Super Tramp, and The Pet Shop Boys among others. Pink Floyd's two hit albums, "The Dark Side of the Moon" and "The Wall" were our favorites.

Pierre Mendez Alcindor and Jean Anduze, my two last co-tenant pals, stayed in close contact with me. The latter, before he moved out of Florida, briefly lived in the room across mine. It was like reliving the good old days all over again. It was during his stay there, that my new bachelor pad was marvelously baptized with my first ever three-some act with his gorgeous, voluptuous black American girlfriend. It was the first in a stream of sexcapades during my nearly decade-long stay at the Isidor's apartment complex. If only those bachelor's pad walls could speak!

On a visit by my old roommate friend Dada, I learned about a new job opportunity that paid more than the standard minimum wage. The place was a huge printing shop company owned by

Harvey Mordoff, an American Jewish man of middle age, who was in urgent need of hiring a half-dozen workers for a big printing job contract his company had just signed. I followed through with Dada's advice, and I was hired on the spot.

The new printing shop was a significant job upgrade for me in so many different ways. First, the pay was so much better than I had been getting so far from any of my past years' gigs. Second, it required the use of more grey matter in setting up the printing job. The shop's location was in the mid-section of the industrialized zone in downtown Miami, which was booming with business. Harvey Moldoff, the owner, a self-made millionaire, was very proud of his successful financial accomplishment. He prided himself in the tell-tale of how he made so many sacrifices to arrive where he was today. Coming out of the Army, he was penniless and had to take odd jobs like anyone else to make ends meet and stay in small efficiency rooms to save money. The old family's printing shop that he owned now was not doing that well before.

As a family business, it was badly mismanaged by his dad, with whom he had no lost love. The shop was in dire financial crisis and near bankruptcy when he took it over. He was able to obtain a VA loan to purchase the building and became his dad's business associate. He swiftly transformed his family's printing business and turned it into an efficient, profitable enterprise. Though he made the bulk of his fortune in Real Estate and the Market, the printing shop was more of a sentimental, family affair to him. He treated all his employees with respect and kindness, and as soon as you were hired, you became part of his large working family. He had no children and wife; thus, the printing shop's working environment was a prime substitute for him to the family life he did not have. For Harvey, it had to be the right chemistry at first sight, and in my case, the chemistry was perfect.

He was moved by my story of coming to Miami with only $20 in my possession, working odd jobs, and managing to put myself into college and university. But Harvey was only the tip of the iceberg of what was really happening at the printing shop. Whether it occurred by accident or by design, there was quite an eclectic group of characters working there. The first among them was Michael Jarvis, a.k.a. Jack, with whom I started a friendship which lasted until today. He became, over the years, a fiction writer currently working on his fourth fiction book. Jack, who lived in Coconut Grove, was the one who first introduced me to the Village-type atmosphere residing in that upscale neighborhood of Miami with inviting sidewalks, outdoor cafes, restaurants, and chic boutiques. I immediately felt for the Grove's festive charm and ambiance, which to many was Miami's modest but nevertheless charming answer to Manhattan's Greenwich Village.

Next was a group of five workers, all were 'premis' who worshiped an Indian spiritual master named Guru Maharaj Ji. They claimed to have received from him the ancient knowledge of the inner self and the divine light. Three among the five stood out: Georges Fisherman, a girl named Lynn, and a stunning-looking Australian beauty named Kathy. She was by far better looking than Nicole Kidman. She needed no makeup, blessed with a flawless porcelain skin, long blond hair, blue eyes, and the sweetest smile to ever grace a girl's face. I joked upon seeing her that if all the girls in the land down under were like her, I would migrate to Australia.

Every eligible bachelor in the printing shop had eyes for Kathy; not even Harvey, the big boss, could not help falling under her mystifying beauty spell. Working around Kathy, along with her other beautiful 'premis' friends, was like being transported in a euphoric state of bliss. I barely noticed the passing time. Work, what work! I was simply cruising and floating throughout the 8-hour shift, fascinated by the overall energy of inner peace and love emanating from this group. I said yes to an invitation made by Georges to attend the group's next Satsang at a gathering place in Coral Way. I remember how excited I was behind the wheels of my big black Cadillac to pick up Georges on my way to the meeting.

I thought that the intriguing spiritual feast I had with the 'premis' at the Printing Shop could never be surpassed, but was I wrong? The minute that I entered the hallway where the meeting was happening, it was as if I was thrusted into a colossal vacuum of what some experts would have qualified it as a mass formation psychosis. The feel-good vibe, the loving energy, and the immense feeling of inner tranquility in the room were hyped a hundredfold. A soft-talking beautiful lady named Margee made the evening's welcoming message to the seating audience. Next, a TV screen lit up, and the spiritual leader, Guru Maharaj Ji, himself appeared in a video addressing a huge audience of his followers.

Coming from a journalistic, secular background, that old instinct was kicking inside of me despite all the smiling pretty faces and the contagious feel-good vibe in the crowd. I shall admit that one of the prime motivations for me being there in the first place, besides the intriguing spiritual vibe, was my secret hope to meet with a girl like the Australian Kathy at work. So, I was very cautious to give myself time not to rush into any decision to join the group. I did not meet any Kathy that evening, but instead I started a friendship with Margee, the presenter, who approached me in a conversation at the end of the Satsang. She was one of the few individuals trained by the spiritual leader himself to reveal to the willing devotees the ancient knowledge of the inner self and the divine light within.

She was in her late 20s and was a force of nature, charming and charismatic. For some obscure reasons that I could never explain, Margee has taken quite a genuine, spontaneous liking to me. We talked for a long time that evening following the end of the program and exchanged phone numbers. To my surprise, she was the first one to call. She invited me to accompany her to a Satsang program at the International Omni Mall close to where I lived. First, I had to pick her up at the Miami Beach Resort hotel, where she worked as a massage therapist, then go for a bite to eat at the mall where the Satsang was being held.

That was the start of an intriguing non-sexual dating pattern I had with Margee, which lasted for months. It never once occurred to me to make an unwanted pass at her and vice versa. It was not that she was not one desirable woman, but for me, just being in her shining presence alone was a form of conquest. We had so much fun in each other's company that the thought of ruining all that genuine chemistry by one misguided pass on my part never crossed my mind. Even though I had ample opportunities to do just that when I took her to my bachelor's pad by the water to introduce her to my collection of books and music. Of course, there's no doubt in my mind, had she herself made a move on me; I would not have put her in her place. Not in a million years! I figured out early in the game that she was too fulfilled and taken by her spiritual love for her guru to fathom any sexual relationship with me. Despite the non-physical hanky-panky between me and the beautiful Maggie, something as strange and mysterious was occurring among us regardless. The closest I could come to describe the feeling and the experience was a deep, penetrating type of ongoing spiritual lovemaking in both our minds each time we met.

Miami, Florida: A Sunshine State's Unauthorized And Unredacted Journey

It appeared to me now in hindsight that she might have given me, either willingly or inadvertently, the ancient knowledge of the inner self, thus allowing me to experience the divine Light on my own without ever having to kneel and ask her to receive it. I could not help feeling myself right up there with her and feeling as shiny as she was. I began to experience that formidable rise in internal peace and joy that I never felt before my entire life, and I also felt that urging sensation to make others around me feel the same exact way that I was feeling. Was it possible that Maggie had turned me into a non-worshipping 'premis' without me knowing? If that were the case, I welcomed it wholeheartedly, for I began to witness a profound spiritual transformation within me and the tremendous impact that I began to have on people around me, especially girls.

A new shiny me was emerging at work, in school, and at the party scenes. I started to make people feel more relaxed in my presence and more accepting of me. My bachelor pad, which used to house mainly boys on weekends and holidays before, started to welcome in its already limited space the company of beautiful young ladies who suddenly found me charmingly attractive and irresistible despite my proverbial nerdy look. They did not seem to care about my not-so-hot non-JQ appearance, nor did they care about my bachelor pad's limited space. On the contrary, something utterly transcendental seemed to have been the ultimate turn-on element!

It was no exaggeration that on any given Saturday evening,

75

an unannounced visitor entering my sleeping quarter would have found one or two beautiful young ladies friends of mine having a near-psychedelic experience, aided and abetted by the smoking of cannabis with the soothing, mellow sound of Supertramp, The Moody Blues, The Pet Shop Boys, and Pink Floyd in the background. If it was true that knowledge of the inner self and the divine light within were given to me willfully or inadvertently by Margee as a gift, it was by far a more precious gift than any sex I could have had with her, as I began to reap the benefits and rewards that came with the changed person that I became overnight.

One good-looking mixed couple, Tony and Cindy, became regular in hanging out with me on weekends. Tony, a light-skinned black man from one of the British Virgin Islands, was a classic charming freeloader. He was literally living off Cindy, who was one of the top managers of the only Marriott Hotel in downtown Miami at the time. A stunning-looking 6-foot-tall white American woman from Arizona with quite a lustful body on her. I began to sense that she started looking at me lately with such intense, desiring eyes, making me feel a bit uncomfortable, especially in front of her adoring boyfriend, Tony. I suspected that they were either timid closet swingers but were not so sure yet where I stood on 'Ménage à Trois' [Threesome] to reveal themselves to me, or worst-case scenario, she would rather be with me altogether instead of being with her handsome beau Tony. Judging by the intensity of her adoring eyes when looking at me, I started to panic and worry about what was really going on with her. Sure, had she not been Tony's main squeeze, I had no doubt in my mind that I would have been all over that piece of you know what, but again I had some pudor and was not about to risk my friendship with both or my life over such damning temptation. Again, rule number one: No major piece of 'derriere,' no matter how formidable that was, was worth dying over. So, I instinctively took Cindy's tease and opened advances with a grain of salt by playing them down and not acting on them. I even pretended that I was so out-to-lunch and disconnected that I had no clues of what they met.

On many an occasion, when we were all three sitting in the front of my now iconic black Cadillac going to an event, Cindy's place would always be in the middle. Then, all through the ride, she would appear to lean more on my side than on Tony's. She never stopped praising me right in front of him for my hard work, and resiliency. How I came here all alone with no money and not much support and managed to keep my head afloat was in Cindy's eyes, nothing short of remarkable. While her handsome gigolo Tony, despite her full emotional and financial support to him, refused to get a job or continue with his studies. He would rather be a stay-at-home boyfriend, responsible for cooking, the laundry and the overall house's upkeep and miscellaneous.

It was at a Haitian dance event organized by a member of the group 'Les PéPés' that Cindy's wild physical attraction to me went unchecked on the dance floor. Under the false, convenient pretext of teaching her the steps of the Haitian national dance 'Compas Direct', she hurled me to the dance floor with her. She pulled me so tightly close to her voluminous chest, that I knew then how deep in crisis land I was with her. I have been there many a time before and was quite familiar with the inevitable outcome, and according to my track record, nothing good ever came out of it but trouble. Despite that unexpected turn-on erection that her hot, sexy embrace provoked in me; I had the decency to pull myself away from her just in time to prevent the situation from deteriorating any further in uncharted territory. By exercising such willful restraint despite my own obvious physical attraction to Cindy, I avoided making a fool out of myself and publicly embarrassing my fellow black brother, Tony. Cindy, a natural dirty blond, born and raised in an all-white middle-class Arizona town, had never been exposed to any of the black American experience until she was transferred to Miami by her Marriott employer. She was well-educated and a career-driven woman. Blessed with beauty, intelligence, and, above all, whiteness in a world dominated by her kind, she could not help feeling absolutely entitled to all things good. Cindy's wishes were, in many respects, Uncle Sam's command, as she epitomized the proverbial "Fille de L'Oncle" [Uncle's Daughter] all-around image. Tony, whom she met at one of Marriott's organized functions, was the first black male lover she ever had.

Apparently, she did not take my dance floor's rain check stand that easily, as it was beyond her comprehension. How many males in their right mind, white or black, would not have jumped at such a golden opportunity to cozy up with her on that dance floor? Instead, she doubled down on her pursuit of me, as she was too puzzled at this stage of her pursuit to give up on me. Dirty blond Cindy in this context scenario fit to the tee 19th Century French writer and poet, Alfred de Musset, in one of his many observations of women when he was quoted as saying that "Une femme est comme votre ombre, courez après, elle vous fuit; fuyez-la, elle vous court après!" [Woman is like your shadow; run after, she will flee, retreat from her, she'll run after you].

Cindy's next opportunity to solve the enigma behind me resisting her advances despite my obvious physical attraction to her came in handy when one weekend in July, Tony had to go out of town for three days to attend the funeral services of a deceased family member. She cooked up a brazing scheme, imploring me to come to spend Saturday night at her guest apartment's room, claiming to be scared to sleep alone in that big apartment of hers located in Sabal Palm, an exclusive, high-end set of buildings along 54th Street, between Northeast second to Northeast Fifth Avenue, not far from where I used to live in the day.

Lyonel Gerdes

Speaking of Cindy and Tony's apartment building in Sabal Palm, it would be worth mentioning that one month earlier I had one of my most traumatizing experiences with America's institutional racist machine as a young black Haitian male while visiting Tony and Cindy. The frightening, ugly head of America's bigotry had shown up unexpectedly to take a huge first bite at me. Recently it has been reported on the Chanel 10's Evening News that there was an uptick in house burglary around the Sabal Palm's Apartment Complex. Of course, the almost all-white Sabal Palm's residents blamed all the reported housebreakings on the latest influx of the 'Haitians Boat People' in nearby 'Little Haiti'.

I was at a routine, relaxing evening at Cindy and Tony's. As always, we three would share a joint, have some pizza delivered, and listen to some cool Reggae music. We were so stunned and having a swelled time that not one of us had any clue of what was happening beyond the walls of the apartment where we were. Cindy had even rolled a joint for me to take home upon leaving her house.

However, the sooner I stepped outside the building's main entrance door, I ran into a Police Force hostage-like barricade. There was at least a half-dozen cops, all lined up with their weapons drawn, aiming at me ready to shoot, with their blinding flashlights and their loudspeakers ordering me to surrender to the police by slowly turning around with my hands up over my head, facing the building's high wall. I instinctively threw the joint off my hands in the middle of all that brouhaha, wondering to myself if I were just in the middle of a police drug bust, or did I just find myself victim of a gross mistaken identity by the police? I was cautiously approached by two uniformed white Police officers, a male and a female with their guns drawn and ready to shout had I made any sudden move. Both put me in handcuffs and placed me under arrest in the back seat of one of their police cars, as I was not offering any resistance for them to go for a police takedown. I assumed that they never saw the joint flying out of my hand, as the arresting officers made no mention of marijuana possession by me to build their case. With the driver's license I provided to them, they ran it through their system to check for any criminal record but could not find any. I had a clean citizen record to fit the Police narrative they already had in mind for me. After repeatedly ignoring my question of why I was in handcuffs and sitting in the back of a police car for having committed no crimes, the white male officer finally admitted that an old white lady at the apartment above Cindy and Tony who saw me entering the building an hour earlier called 911 to report a home invasion and that a thief was on the loose in the building. He also admitted that there was no evidence of breaking in any of the four units connected with this entrance; thus, once again, it was a big nothing burger. The Police had once again wasted taxpayers' money over nothing. I asked both officers who made the arrest for their badge numbers to file a major complaint against them now that I knew for certain that they had not one iota of evidence against me, not even the marijuana joint I had in my possession. What really annoyed me was how they played down Cindy and Tony, who came out to tell the Police that I was their invited guest and that I spent the entire time with them when the so-called housebreaking was supposed to have occurred. In addition, I also displayed two important documents to them: my FIU Tamiami Campus student identity card and my HRS card as a state employee. None of that seemed to have convinced them of my innocence, especially on the part of that nasty, tomboy white female cop with a fish merchant mouth. No pieces of evidence would have convinced her that I was a clean, honest, taxpayer contributing to her salary and offered me an apology. Instead, she was convinced that I happened to be very lucky changing my mind before committing the criminal activities I set out to do that night.

I kept my cool during this nasty, ugly episode with the Police, knowing fully well about the criminal inclinations of many dishonest cops who made up evidence to fit the crimes of their arrested subjects. I did not resist arrest, nor did I throw any insult back at the officers. I took both officers' names and badge numbers to file the following week a major complaint with the Bureau of Miami Police Investigation for violation of my civil rights, and unlawful police detention, as I was kept for nearly half an hour before being released and taken off the Police's handcuffs.

Miami, Florida: A Sunshine State's Unauthorized And Unredacted Journey

Again, back to where I left off, I finally caved into Cindy's persistence to come to her apartment to stay the night, as that would make her feel so much safer with me sleeping next door to her room. Tony was out of town for the entire weekend, so I was told. I took a few light items. The situation was quite awkward, as she knew that I was aware by now of her feelings toward me and that even though I found her very attractive, I did not feel right betraying the friendship I had with Tony. I barely survived the harrowing temptation, as it was one of the worst sleepless nights for me ever. Cindy, for some peculiar reason, did not lock the master bedroom door. Instead, she kept it wide open all through the entire night. It was certainly an oddity for someone who was afraid of a potential intruder in her apartment. Sure, her unit was on the first floor, and her Living Room apartment's window was exposed to the increasingly busy 54$^{th}$ Street Road, where most of the housebreakings were being reported. Except, of course, that might have been a calculated move by Cindy luring me in and hoping that I would have, at last, overcome my fear of betraying Tony by joining her in bed. I did not have to knock or force myself through any door, as her bedroom was wide open for me, the invited guest, to come in and do whatever I wished to do with her that night.

I also assumed there would have been no screams for help coming out of her if only I had some mega balls to go into her room that night and jungle F her in ways that no one had ever done before, not even her beastly gigolo boy Tony. Of course, all that was mere wishful thinking on my part, as I spent a great portion of the night in the guestroom bed next-door, pondering on the do or die decision of the moment: "Shall I or shall I not go to her."

The following day was a bright, sunny Sunday, when Cindy's sweet voice woke me up to join her for breakfast. She did not appear to have been sleepless; on the contrary, she looked refreshed and had never been more attractive and sexier than that morning. Had she spent hours like me on her bed pondering whether I was coming or not to keep her company, the signs of her sleepless night were not apparent to me. I kept away from Cindy for the next two weeks out of guilt. There was no denying that I was attracted to her, and she was woman enough to sense that. One more reason for her to be puzzled by me for not jumping yet again on a missed occasion to make love to her at her when Tony was out of town. She began to wonder about what would it take for me to let go of all my bourgeois inhibitions and simply embark on the joy ride she was incessantly offering me. I was starting to worry about Cindy's frustration which could get her to go rogue on me for what she might perceive as a classic rejection. As Alfred de Musset keenly observed "Une femme pardonne tout, excepté qu'on ne veuille pas d'elle" [A woman can be forgiven, except when she is rejected and not wanted]

Cindy became so worrisome about my whereabouts, as I had not visited her and Tony for days since the night I stayed over. For some unexplained reason, she had begun to develop a fetish-like fixation over me. In her insane admiration for me, she saw a resilient man who managed to keep a frugal lifestyle to provide for his family left behind in Haiti. A hard-working Haitian immigrant working long hours at work and on school Campus to improve his plight in life. She also was convinced that I needed a good, loving woman behind me, and that she was the one. She appeared to understand better than anyone who had been into my life so far that there was more to me than meet the eyes. She suspected that behind all the parties, the ganja, the music, the laughter, and the weekend's euphoria that I was capable to inspire to others, in my inner self, I was living a depressing but stoic life. In the end, Cindy's mission, like the old white man's burden, was to save a lonely, poor black Haitian fellow by rescuing him from loneliness, lovelessness, and ultimately from himself. In short, she felt that I needed a good, loving, strong woman behind me and that she was the one destined to fulfill that empty space in my life. Cindy was that close to unveil a fundamental love and hate confusing enigma I had in me for women in general. For those who read my last two memoirs, they are fully aware of how I grew up in a loveless family home with a mother incapable of love, or to express any motherly feeling toward me. And how I became highly suspicious of any woman showing sincere affection for me, trusting that if my own biological mother could not unconditionally love me, who else could!

When I did not return any of Cindy's calls, she went into panic. She pressured her own lover Tony to come to my place to make sure that I was safe and okay, and that I was not dying a lonely, painful death in my bachelor's pad all alone. Poor Tony! He was so humbled by the whole thing upon realizing the unusual, shameless attraction that his otherwise cool, and collected high-end girlfriend Cindy had for such an unassuming nerdy-looking guy like me. In that respect, we were both on the same page, as I could not possibly fathom what she saw in me!

The pressure on Tony was such that he showed up at my place one evening to beg me to please talk to Cindy. He conceded, despite his huge male ego, that his girlfriend was literally sick and not feeling well, following my obvious snub of ignoring her calls.

I contacted Cindy the following day. She was so excited to hear my voice that she went speechless for a few seconds. She wanted to apologize for anything she might have inadvertently said or done. I cut her short by letting her know that she owed me no apology, as I was simply very busy between my day job and schoolwork's term papers. She was relieved at once that she did not offend me in any way and that we were back as the good old-time friends that we were. The reconciliatory call occurred on a Tuesday evening, and at the end of it, we made plans to meet the coming weekend for a kiss and make up reunion.

However, little did I anticipate that the grand meeting celebration Cindy and I had arranged over the phone would come sooner than I ever imagined, the following night.

Weekdays were no hanging out or party time at the bachelor pad. I had to wake up early every day to begin a long, arduous journey between work and school. All my friends knew that and respected my request not to be disturbed in my busy weekday schedule. So, when I suddenly heard a timid knock at my door, I wondered who that could be at this late, unholy weekday hour. I opened the door and guessed who was behind it, dirty blonde Cindy herself with a bottle of red wine in her hand. I was even more shocked upon realizing that she did not bring Tony with her. She apologized for showing up like that at my place unannounced. She said she could not wait that long to see me. And that she was going insane and had to see me in person. She needed to talk to me, feel me, be around me, and hear my music. In short, she missed being in my room except this time she wanted to be alone with me without her boyfriend, Tony. My first question to her out of an abundance of caution was: "Is Tony aware of your visit here?" to which she replied, "Yes." She even added that her solo visit was even suggested by Tony himself and that he was ok with whatever happened here during it.

Useless to say that I started to breathe a lot, lot easier after Cindy's candid confession, confirming the earlier suspicion that they were in a somewhat open relationship. I knew for sure that Tony was no Mr. Faithful himself and that he had asked me to use my bachelor pad on at least two occasions and had even once shared one of his female conquests with me. I assumed that was the lifestyle both had chosen to live, and who was I to judge them? I also assumed that Tony was doing all that with perhaps Cindy's approval and that she was a happy camper herself.

Regardless, a threesome 'menage-a-trois' with Cindy was where Tony drew the line. The mere thought of sharing Cindy, his prize jewel woman, his bread and butter with me that nerdy, Frenchy guy from Haiti with an attitude, was a definite non-starter. And for him to finally resign himself with such fait accompli that his girl Cindy had such naughty sexual desire for me, was mind-boggling.

In the meantime, Cindy was making herself comfortably at home in the inviting sleeping quarter portion of my bachelor pad where the light was instantly dimmed to create a relaxing, surreal atmosphere. It was in this scenery that she chose to lay her majestic, 6-feet long bombshell body onto the bed next to the Entertainment center. We shared a whole joint together, some red wine, and were both semi-wasted, and laughing hysterically over the slightest, and silliest comments out of our mouths.

I could not help Looking at how serene Cindy was, just to be with me in that cozy room of mine. I figured that Margee, the Guru

## Miami, Florida: A Sunshine State's Unauthorized And Unredacted Journey

Maharaj Ji's priestess, might have not only given me knowledge but had allowed me to share it with whomever I fancied. And Cindy was one of the ladies that I happened to fancy. I could not help reflecting that any of Cindy's Marriott suite was undoubtedly twice the size of my humble bachelor's pad, and yet I was under the impression that she would not have traded off the current spot she was now for any of her executive suite, nor for her Sabal Palm's high-priced condo.

She excused herself to go into the toilet, and after a few minutes, reentered the sleeping quarter, but this time, totally nude to my shocking surprise! In a soft but commanding voice, she ordered me to do the same. I tried to utter a word, but she quickly shushed me with a forefinger on my lips, all the while helping me unbutton my shirt. Soon after I was done freeing myself from my clothes, she began kissing me all over with such voracity that I had a hard time catching up with my breath. Next, she proceeded to do just the unthinkable by giving me one stunning oral sex moment while her gigantic pair of melons were bouncing all over my trembling lap.

She had the softest porcelain skin, and my feverish fingers were delighted in caressing its surfaces. She, so far, had been the lead initiator; now it was my turn to start taking the initiative by asking her to lay down, relax, and enjoy what was about to be delivered to her. She was so hot and steamy by just having the full length of my tool inside her mouth that when I started to make my own descent with my tongue into her steamy, wet bottom, I was under the impression that the entire Miami River had just overflowed its bank straight out of her. The whole bed was soaking wet with her body fluid, as she was from a rare breed of fountain women. We had to move for comfort's sake onto the other bed for the final crossing. I made sure this time that extra towels were placed on the bed to absorb all the liquid fluid coming out of her. Amid all the ongoing excitement for the big bang, I put on my rubber condom to be on the safe side.

The awesome body chemistry between Cindy and I was so instrumentally intense that upon my full-fledged penetration of her, she was well on her way to a gasping, choking climax in just a few minutes-time. And it was only the start of a cavalcade of them to follow non-stop. Multiple orgasms seemed to come as part of her fountain woman status, as she left me absolutely speechless when, in one violent convulsion of her voluptuous body, a jet stream of liquid shot up high out of her with such startling velocity. It was the pee fountain display of Cindy's last explosive orgasm.

In her self-indulgent, hedonistic pleasure, Cindy was a loud, unapologetic screamer all throughout our sex act. Any sidewalk passersby near my bachelor pad could have heard her astounding screams to fairly concluded that some lucky lady in that little annexed room was having too much of a wild, decadent time! My worst fear back then was having my place swarmed by a S.W.A.T team responding to another unanimous call from a frustrated racist, sex-starved neighbor, reporting that a young, innocent white American female was being scalped, if not tortured alive, not by a surviving Miami tribe Indian, but by an ingrateful Haitian migrant.

Cindy was so exhausted, dehydrated, and kaput that she literally collapsed onto the bed and slept till the wee hours of the following day. One thing was for certain: when she finally left my bachelor's pad, she went home to Tony with the largest smile ever on her pretty face. She appeared to have just been reborn and graced by something out of this world.

That was not the last I have heard or seen of Cindy. She was on a quiet agenda to kick Tony out of her apartment and replace him with me. But I made that clear to her that I did not want any part of that planned scenario of hers. I did not want to be the one tearing up what I saw as an interesting living arrangement for them both. She gave up after many unsuccessful attempts at coercing me into becoming her official main squeeze and agreed to keep our sexual escapades discreet and under wraps. Cindy represented the first real challenge in a long line of challenges to my entrenched independent lifestyle. She came charging like a bull for a full-frontal assault against what I was already turning myself into, meaning that incorrigible, convinced bachelor.

I dodged Cindy's bullet by avoiding falling from her constant charm offensive. In hindsight, I could have easily fallen into her traps, as she had all the major cards in her hands to win. How I managed not to turn myself into a cowed, domesticated, and inconsequential proverbial husband to her, with the typical suburban house, the two-family cars, and an army of beautiful mixed children, was beyond me. And nothing short of divine providence seemed to have protected me. Over the years, I lost all contacts with both Tony and Cindy. I missed them so much, as both were so much a part of my early Miami years. Just hearing 10CC's 'I'm Not in Love,' Gary Wright's 'Dream Weaver,' or Eric Carmen's 'All by Myself,' reminded me of Cindy's memorable smile. I kept among my most valued album collection, The Moody Blues' 'Nights in White Satin', as it was one of Cindy's precious gifts to me, for knowing how much love I had for music.

## Coconut Grove's Village Inn:
## A Bar/Restaurant for The Ages

Mike Jarvis, a.k.a. Jack, whom I met at Harvey's Printing Shop, who lived in the heart of the Grove area, invited me to join him at the annual celebration of the Art Festival there. It was Miami's largest, outdoor festival, with music, food and a multitude of vendors displaying their artifacts and paintings. The ambiance of chic boutiques and outdoor cafes there was unique to the Grove. If you were addicted to people-watching, you could not find a much better spot to indulge yourself in doing just that. All the best-looking people in South Florida, Europe, South America, and elsewhere seemed to answer the call for that annual glamorous catwalk show of force at Coconut Grove's last-weekend Art show.

It was a time when the only action in town was there. South Beach's golden age had to wait for yet another decade before it could seriously offer a significant alternative to the Grove's unmatched dominance of South Miami's party scene, outdoor activities, and sidewalk cafes. I met with Jack as scheduled, and off we went for the much-anticipated out-of-this-world ambiance. The relaxing, familiar hippie groove there was at its most magnificent display ever, with many of the pretty ladies from all ages strolling by in their long casual multi-colored dresses, wearing sandals, necklaces, ornaments, and, yes, flowers in their hair. The long-hair hippie men were also out in force that day, vowing not to let their lady counterparts make complete umbrage of them in the ongoing street parade of good looks, styles, and competing fashion statements. The main park in the heart of the Grove where Jefferson Airplane, the legendary San Francisco psychedelic rock band, once performed, had a lineup of high-profile rock bands grace the Park's stage on the last days of the Art Festival.

My Sunday afternoon discovery highlight of the day, came when Jack and I chose the Village Inn Restaurant/Bar for a quick bite to eat. With an unassuming, quasi-uninviting entrance, the last thing I expected was to be swept off my feet upon entering the place. The home's signature brick walls inside created a welcoming cozy atmosphere like that of a second home away from home. On the right side of the restaurant, where the bar was located, was a whole different ambiance. There, was a live Reggae band playing on a small stage back in the rear of the Bar. Several Reggae classic hit songs were superbly renditioned. The band's name was Roots Uprising, and to listen to their awesome renditions of Bob Marley, Jimmy Cliff, Peter Tosh, Dennis Brown, and Third World to name just a few, made a profound, everlasting impression on me.

I would never again listen to Reggae music the way I used to in my bachelor pad. It was a major musical awakening for me that Sunday afternoon. Like a musical rebirth, Reggae had suddenly become a unique, formidable outlet of soul expression to me.

## Miami, Florida: A Sunshine State's Unauthorized And Unredacted Journey

Reggae's relentless soothing beat, rhythm, lyrics, and melodies were all-encompassing to fill in a vacuum within that I did not know existed before. In all, Reggae was my all-time spiritual, musical awakening, and the birthplace where such a prodigious feast occurred was at the Village Inn's Sunday afternoon Reggae extravaganza. The awesome mixed crowd assembled inside the dimmed-lit Bar and on its small, overcrowded dance floor in front of the band's stage was a definite touch of cosmic harmony on a heavenly scale among the various races and ethnicities. Nowhere in Miami could one find such a genuine, earthly ambiance. I never saw so many black and white couples dancing together and having such a swell time with no fear of being stared at, judged, labeled, or even attacked and assaulted in many parts of Florida and the States. It was my newfound religious experience, a golden existential refuge for me. To illustrate my point, I brought along dirty blond Cindy with me to the Village Inn the following Sunday for a first major, grand entrance into the Sunday Reggae afternoon scenery there. She fell for the place in the same dumbfounded fashion it happened to me the Sunday before. If the inside bar scene were so out of this world, the outside ambiance was even tenfold more awesome, with the most beautiful gathering group of people all around the parking lot enjoying Coconut Grove's great outdoors. Everyone seemed to be minding their own business: young mixed couples were making out right in the open, and two or more Rastafarian brothers were discretely smoking a joint. When the band was on its first break break, I took bombshell-looking Cindy for a royal walk into some of the cute narrow roads off Coconut Grove's Grand Avenue, and she really enjoyed the 'see and be seen' atmosphere that Coconut Grove was most iconically known for.

We went back inside the bar and onto the small, limited space to resume our dancing hysteria. Cindy's impressive stature, her good look and the manner she was dancing with me, was undoubtedly a bonanza treat to the number of voyeuristic men and women there who worked out a visual turn-on by watching beautiful mixed-race couples getting it on, right on the Village Inn's sinful dance floor, aided and abetted by the conspiratorial, liberating Reggae music of the uniquely talented Roots Uprising band. At the end of the Sunday matinee.

Following my first inaugural introduction with the hot-looking Cindy at the Village Inn, I went on a shameless rampage by bringing along with me a new date every other week. All my dates had one thing in common: they were all blonds, and it did not matter whether they were natural or bottle blondes. I'm embarrassed to admit it today on how hopelessly puerile I acted back then. I earned a notorious, infamous image of a womanizer on the prowl, dating and seducing many uncle's daughters I managed to put my voodoo Haitian spell on. I was picking girls up everywhere I went, from the workplace, on the school Campus ground at FIU, or at the club scenes in the Grove on Friday and Saturday nights. My strategy was to lure as many white girls as possible to the Village Inn's Sunday Reggae matinee and let the mind-blowing atmosphere do the rest. Armed with my newfound confidence in my wild seductive power, and convincing charm, I was able to successfully appear at the Village Inn with several different dates. Two of my early dates were Kathy, the drop-dead gorgeous Australian beauty who worked at Harvey's Printing Shop and Margee.

I was not able to convince Kathy to go home with me that night. But the idea of being seen in the company of such an array of good-looking ladies, played a tremendous effect in the psyche of other beautiful women watching, as the natural tendency in humans tended to often reward winners over losers. The more successful you appeared to be with the ladies, the more other ladies seemed to desire you. A repeat of the classic scheme of the rich getting richer and the poor poorer amid the eternal, sexual dialectic of the sexes. The ladies looking for a wild time with a lover with no strings attached would seek me out first before going with a guy who had yet to be seen with a hot date. Ergo, despite the not-so-clean womanizer reputation I rightly earned at the Village Inn, I was shocked to see some ladies who, despite knowing that I was a badass, still made passes at me. On some occasions when I did not bring a date with me, I managed to convince a few of the regulars to follow me home. They would later confess that curiosity was what, in the end, killed the cats in them. In short, I was a puzzle for them, as they could not figure out how I managed to have so many different hot dates with me all the time. From what they could visually attest, I was no Mr. America and no Mr. JQ either. They wanted at any cost to experience the magical, mystical spell I seemed to have on women, even if they had to sleep with me to find out what was all the fuss about!

The first one in the bunch was an attractive-looking French girl called Brigitte. I called her Brigitte Bardot in a teasing way, as she had Bardot's spicy, vivacious look, flawless skin, build, and hair. She even had a slight resemblance to the 60s sex symbol icon who ruled France and the rest of the world for decades. Brigitte and I hooked it up more nicely than she ever expected. She revealed that there was a certain "Ce je ne sais quoi" about me that, despite all the women she saw me with, had picked her interest. Her gut feeling told her that there was more to me than the womanizing image. She was dying to get to know me intimately, but the opportunity never presented itself, as I always had someone or an entourage of friends around me. I ambushed her while she was coming out from the ladies' restroom. I took hold of her hand with such commanding authority and took her right in the middle of the dance floor. By not pulling her hand away from mine and following me onto the dance floor was her way to tacitly consent that she was ready for that wild ride of getting to know me at last. The physical sparks between me and Brigitte were so darn intense that within minutes of dancing with her, we ended up in one of the longest French kisses I had in a long time with a woman. Mind you, I was yet to know her name and vice versa.

We both had no clues of what was really happening on that dance floor. Our heads were spinning, and we simply let ourselves descend into the ecstasy of the moment. We stayed on the dance floor as if we were glued to it until Roots Uprising took their routine break. We went into my car, usually parked in the adjacent outside parking lot, to light up a joint and get to know each other more. Brigitte was a Parisian, born and raised in a well-to-do French middle-class family. Living here on a student visa, she was taking undergraduate classes in business administration at the University of Miami and was in the final quarter to graduate. I also learned that she was officially engaged to a Parisian fiancé with a plan to marry him upon returning to Paris.

We had a good laugh and joked about all the plans we made as humans for the future, while in the end, what really mattered were the moment and the now. Hence, we resumed with the making out, which started earlier on the dance floor in the back seat of my black Cadillac. My French-Creole accent was a big turn-on to her and was also impressed that I was taking undergraduate courses for a BS degree in Sociology and was a poet and former journalist. She laughed hysterically at the fact that I almost had her fooled by my deceptive, projecting image of a walking penis hitting on every piece of white ass on sight. We went back inside the Village Inn to resume our dancing feast. She later followed me to my bachelor's pad and ended up spending the night with me.

We had so much fun with one another, more so than we ever thought possible. It was a good thing that she set aside her prior arrested biases and prejudices she initially had against me by opening herself up to have with me such a memorable time. She came down to spend the following weekend. I paraded her almost everywhere. I even took her to a visit at Tony and Cindy's Sabal Palm apartment. While Cindy was obviously not too jumpy and welcoming with my latest conquest, her boyfriend Tony's eyes, on the other hand, were all over Brigitte, the lusty pig that he was.

I dated Brigitte exclusively for the last two months she had left to finish her studies before returning to the other life awaiting her back home in Paris. She spent her last night in Miami at my bachelor's pad and took her to the Airport the following day. When the last call for her flight's departure came through the loudspeakers, Brigitte was so inconsolable that she put me into tears, too. That was the longest time I ever dated anyone else but Brigitte. Even my Haitian connection down at the Village Inn, the likes of Ti Harold, Edwing, Chilov Lafond, and Patrick Duperval, who were in the same bachelor's confirmed mode that I was, were beginning to worry about me becoming dulled and inconsequential.

## Miami, Florida: A Sunshine State's Unauthorized And Unredacted Journey

My adopted dad William, a.k.a. Pappy Will, whom I have not seen for nearly a decade since he migrated to Waukegan, Illinois, visited me. It was one telling moment for both of us. I described the emotional aspect of my dad's stay in my bachelor pad in ample detail in the second tome of my trilogy memoir entitled "Port-au-Prince, Haiti..." At first, it was an awkward situation for the two of us, as there had never been a genuine, close father/son established bond between us. But as time elapsed, during Papy Will's five-day visit, we made genuine attempts at amending whatever malaise existed in our father/adopted son relationship, now that I have become a grown, changed person and that he himself had considerably changed since I last saw him leaving us that somber afternoon at Port-au-Prince's airport.

He was living on painkiller medicine as he suffered from an unnamed, uncured disease that he purportedly contracted in the wood of Aux Cayes, according to his private Waukegan physician. I showed my dad all around town to make him feel as welcoming as possible. He came down during the time I was seeing the Parisian bombshell blond a.k.a Brigitte Bardot. She was fond of him, and we both took dad for a stroll at the pleasant Coconut Grove hot spot. How delighted the old man was to watch all this parade of beautiful people while sitting and dinning at an outdoor café! Dad was totally sold on Brigitte's beauty and sweetness. He advised me that she was a good girl and she would make a very good wife for me. Dad's trip had established a bond that was never built between us. I got to see him as a more jovial, and engaging dad. The kind of Pappy Will I wished was there for me throughout my turbulent childhood days.

As if my dad's visit were a scouting one evaluating the Miami environment for someone else's eventual move, I received a call within days from Jean Willy, one of my three younger half-brothers, still living with my dad in Illinois. In the call, my brother told me about his plan to move to Miami in two week and planned to stay with me until he got himself situated. I welcomed his move and picked him up at the Airport as scheduled. I casually mentioned to Harvey Moldoff, the printing shop's owner where I worked, about Willy's arrival. Harvey quickly acted on the news by telling me that he had a job for him. He would start him off the Monday following his arrival. Speaking of luck, I wish I had such darn good one when I first arrived here in Miami. Willy was well received. For Harvey, it got to be love at first sight. My brother was trained for a new position and after completing the training, he took on the manager position. It was in that managerial role that weeks later he would be in the envious privilege of meeting with the legendary Reggae superstar Bob Marley himself. The iconic singer of "No Woman, No Cry," who contracted Harvey's printing shop to make flyers and bumper stickers for his upcoming eleventh "Survival" album. He came incognito there to take one last look before the printing process began. Due to privacy and security concerns, not everyone working at the shop was aware of Bob Marley's presence at the shop. To start with, he drove in a low-key, average-looking car, and his larger-than-life dreadlocks seen live on stage and in his videos were mostly hidden under a Rastafarian hat. Though I was able to catch a glimpse of Bob Marley when he was leaving the shop talking with Harvey, I did not make much of it. It was only after his departure that I was told that the Rastafarian dude I saw leaving earlier and talking to the boss was none other than the one and only Bob Marley. My brother Jean Willy, who was working on Bob Marley's project and who met with the legendary Jamaican singer, gave me a full, honest account of his brief, glorious encounter with the icon.

According to Willy, he lost it when told that Bob Marley himself was coming to his work section to check on the final setting of the job. He was starstruck beyond belief and made a complete fool of himself upon meeting with him. Thanks to him, Marley, who by now was used to the devastating, humbling power of his fame on his fans, understood what my brother Willy was going through at the time and handled it graciously well.

Bob was wearing a T-shirt with his name and picture on it; still, my brother uttered that silly remark at him like: "You sure looked like Bob Marley...?", thinking perhaps that someone at the shop was pulling his leg, which, of course, brought everyone around to a non-stop laughter. The next silly thing out of Willy's mouth was when he asked Bob how he managed to grow such a huge pile of dread locks, to which the legend wisely replied: "By the grace of god, my brother". Following Bob Marley's visit, we became a lot more captivated by the man's aura and persona and also by the outward militant aspect of his towering Reggae music.

At FIU's Tamiami Campus, where I was still attending classes five times a week, my academic commitment had begun to take on a life of its own. I spent lots of time there between the library doing research and the cafeteria, where I would regularly meet with my beautiful colleague friend, Joanne Biondi, not to mention my frequent Campus bar scene visits, hoping to meet some new girls for my next Sunday afternoon showdown at the Village Inn. The Sociology Department staff back then was one of the best in the country with the likes of such distinguished tenured professors such as Dr. Anthony Maingot, a native of Trinidad, Dr. Alex Stepick, a researcher with whom I worked on an extensive survey about the newly emerging Little Haiti's informal market economy. Also, on the list was the stunning-looking Dr. Shearon Lowery, with whom I could not help having an embarrassing crush, reminding me of a similar one I had with my Lindsay Hopkins' first English teacher. Finally, Dr. Jerry Brown, whose course on the use of mushrooms and hallucinogenic drugs throughout human history and religions was quite an eye-opener for me, making me feel lots less guilty about my non-abusive, moderate use of the herb. With Dr. Brown, the connection I had with him was immediate and long-lasting till today. He was the first professor in the Sociology Department who encouraged me to make an oral presentation of my first English-written essay on Haiti to an intimidating FIU audience. My reticence from making the oral exposé was due to my thick French accent, believed by me to be an impediment. All that despite having been told on repeated occasions by the ladies that my accent was quite lovely and, above all, comprehensible. However, Dr. Brown would not buy my accent argument and scheduled me for my first ever oral presentation in English. It was a good thing that I did, as the whole thing went better than I ever expected it would. It was particularly exciting in the Q and A part following the presentation.

What made those staff members so special was their downright down-to-earth attitude despite their prestigious academic tenures. I remember attending parties at Dr. Maingot's beautiful home, who had one of the most stunning looking wives for a scholar. I also remember the gathering parties at the stunning-looking Dr. Lowery, where I painfully found out that she was a lesbian, de facto, dimming out any hope I had to make a sentimental impression on her. And, of course, the fantastic parties at Dr. Jerry Brown, where I met his lovely-looking wife, Julie Brown. The first time I ever heard The Rolling Stones' tune, "You Can't Always Get What You Want," was at one of his parties, a musical hit that has made an ever-lasting impact on me. This was also the time Claude Wells, a handsome-looking black American brother who was taking the same undergraduate classes as me, became a remarkably close friend and was at every one of those parties.

The excellent opportunity to go to New York for the first time presented itself to me in such unexpected fashion when late Roland Chatelain, a friend of Philippe Carrie, who lived in Long Island, New York, who drove from there to Miami, needed a return road companion to help him with the driving. He even offered me an incentive to pay for my Airline's return ticket, plus I could stay at his Long Island place for as long as I wanted. I was, since I migrated to the State, fascinated by the thought of visiting one day the Big Apple, but the cost of such a visit was always the discouraging factor. With such a generous offer from Roland, I would finally make my dream visit to New York come true without breaking the bank.

I accepted his offer, and one early Friday morning, Roland picked me up from my bachelor's pad with enough clothing packed in a mid-size suitcase for one week, and off we went on the I-95 highway. Roland, unfortunately, is no longer with us, but what a cool dude he was. The man just had a heart of gold. It was the smoothest driving journey I was ever on, as I did the Miami-New York stretch for at least three more times with a friend named Eddy Perodin before realizing the discouraging, punishing aspect of the tedious, long hours trip. But on this first driving adventure to New York, the tedious, long hours were the last thing in my mind to worry about. I was simply too eager to explore, discover, and drive through many different border states and to appreciate their beauties and many differences.

We made frequent stops along the way, stayed the night once at one important border crossing and got back early on the road the following morning. We arrived at Roland's Long Island residence the same day at around midnight hour. Making it to New York in the middle of the night did rob me somehow of the major shock and awe effect that I was expecting to get hit with. Still, I could tell that I was in for one major, mega-city treat that the Western industrialized world had ever built. I would have to wait the following day for my true shock and awe moment, when following the bus instructions from my host Roland I ended up in the heart of Manhattan's massive concrete jungle. Roland returned the following day to his job at JFK Airport. My daily schedule was to get up every day and ride with him to the Airport. From there, I would take a bus to Manhattan's Port Authority and do the same in reverse in the evening to meet back with him at his job to return to Long Island.

My first sincere impression of being in the middle of Manhattan's tallest skyscraper buildings was more of shock than awe. I could not help feeling so small and totally intimidated by such grandiosity. The dizzying, spinning spell I brutally felt in looking up at the top of such a monstrosity of a city's overwhelming concrete build-up did not help in any way my biblical discomfort. I felt as if the tops of all the skyscrapers were in motion and that it was just a matter of time before they would all come crashing down into one another, spelling the end of everyone on the ground, including myself. In short, the correct account of my first exposure to New York's concrete jungle was mostly of fear, if not a borderline claustrophobic reaction to feeling frightfully small and inconsequential among the crowd's unbelievable vastness on Fifth Avenue, Times Square and everywhere else, added with the suffocating immensity of the concrete skyscrapers around me. It would take me some struggling hours before I could get over such feelings of mental discomfort I always found myself gripping at the beginning of my arrival at Manhattan's Port Authority Bus Terminal. I realized that one soothing way for me to calm my nerves down a bit was to spend a relaxing, quiet time in Central Park's endless, soothing green space. From there, I learned through breathing and calming exercises to reconcile myself with the mystifying island of Manhattan and get on par with what the late Haitian poet René Philoctète rightfully called "Ces Iles Qui Marchent" [Those Walking Islands]. The sooner I could get past those early moments of confusion and intimidation, the faster I could go on about the business of exploring Manhattan, an otherwise marvelous, most interesting place for one to visit.

Once upon a time, the most common wishes from people the world over was to wish not to leave this life until after they saw

## Miami, Florida: A Sunshine State's Unauthorized And Unredacted Journey

Paris, the city of lights per excellence, for just once during their lifetime. But by the last quarter of the 20th century, Manhattan had replaced Paris with a commanding lead as the shiniest mega city on the hill that everyone wished to one day visit before they die.

I had a busy daily schedule of things to do and places to visit during my week's stay in New York. I knew that, realistically, I needed more than a week to be able to cover a significant portion of the top ten hot spots there, but with the little time I had available to me, I tried my best to prioritize and explore as much as I could. Yesterday, I visited The Empire State building and went all the way to the top floor for an aerial view of New York's phenomenal skyline. From the Empire State Building, I hopped off the Macy's two-block-long, huge shopping store as both were in such proximity to one another.

My plan for today was to venture into Greenwich Village's reputed decadent zone, one of the most talked about places to visit. I was determined and readied to experience the remnants of whatever was left from the 60s rebellious youth culture there. I was quite pleased by the enchanted atmosphere when I arrived at the famed square. It was a whole different scene and décor altogether from anything I have seen so far since my arrival at the Big Apple. There were several drumming sections, musicians, artists, roller skaters, tourists, and onlookers all around the park. The people-watching visual parade was anything that I had never seen anywhere else in my entire life.

You could easily make a clear distinction between the visiting tourist crowd there from the hard-core, diehard park regulars by the marked difference in their respective dress code alone. Fashion warfare was an understatement to describe the various displays of stylish clothing parading around. The prevailing aroma of ganja reigned supreme in many of the park's sections. With a fast-moving scenery all throughout, there was no room for boredom or dullness. While sitting on one of the crowded benches at the park with my eyes and my mouth's jaw-dropping to the ground, I wondered what life would've been like here as an activist during those impassioned, querulous days of the 60s.

If only a magical hand could turn the time machine back to those days of youth rebellion in that exact location where I was, I would have found myself amidst one of humanity's most awakening cultural and spiritual moments of make love, not war. I made a point since then to always come by for a Greenwich Village visit every time I happened to be in New York, just out of respect and in honor of the non-conformist atmosphere which could still be felt and experienced at the park long after nearly two decades later.

My next major visit was to go to the top of Manhattan's Twin Towers the next day. I arrived around mid-day in Lower Manhattan's Financial District, and I made a stop first at Bryant

Park, located behind the New York Public Library building, for a bite to eat. I enjoyed having lunch there, for it was one of the Park's busiest hours, besides its weekend's hours and their popular open-air Monday evening movie showing. Several office bureaucrats in the nearby surroundings would casually walk by with their lunch bags, looking for vacant spots to enjoy a leisurely lunch break in the great, greenish Bryant Park outdoors. I had the excitement to people-watch two distinct groups of people: The white-collar folks working for various corporations and companies around the park in their dark proverbial suits and ties, while at a much lower speed, a relaxed group of mostly local sunbathers, lying their bodies on that football size green grass in the middle of the park for a suntan.

I could never get over the interesting comparison of the two distinctive groups of New Yorkers co-existing with each other in such a limited, confined green space at Bryant Park's midday lunch break. As much as I wanted to stay a little longer at my observation spot, I had to move onto my next New York adventure.

The line at the World Trade Center was discouragingly long when I arrived there. It was as if a multitude of people wanted to experience what it was like to be closer to God and heaven, while others were using the Towers' vertiginous height hoping to at last conquer their atrocious feeling of vertigo and acrophobia. After an hour of waiting and standing in line, I finally made it to one of the Twin Towers' tallest observation floors. You could walk around to get different aerial views and angles of the entire Manhattan-packed concrete jungle's panoramic skyline. Except this time, it was much less intimidating as it was way below me, who was at 1,368 feet high, and looking through the thick, clear, protective surrounding glass windows.

Everything from up there looked so small and reduced on the streets below. I could not positively identify the gender of any of the street walkers below going about their daily businesses, nor could I tell the passing cars' makes and models, for things simply appeared so minuscule and too minute for me to make any identification of any sort. Here I was perched on top of one of the tallest buildings in the world at the time, enjoying a breathtaking surreal view, but I could never back then have foreseen the fate awaiting the Towers' monumental structures along with 2,996 people dead on 9/11 within and outside their walls. Fast forwarding to the present, most Americans by now rejected the mainstream media's dulled narrative, nor did they accept the official Commission Report of what really occurred that day in Lower Manhattan. To start with, historically, buildings had been known to be burned for days and weeks, but they never went down as the towers did within minutes of burning and in straight demolition style following the fire from the planes allegedly blamed for causing their collapse.

So called conspiracy theories exploded on social media following the event of the decade. Several of them argued that 9-11 was an inside job and dismissed the entire official narrative that a few numbers of al Qaeda terrorists who had little to no training in flying planes were able to penetrate the most expensive air defense system in the world to accomplish such highly skilled flying feast by hitting the two Towers and the Pentagon's building the way they did. In support of their inside job theory, they argued that many people knew that something big was about to happen that day. Some were given dire early warning not to show up for work in the buildings that day under any circumstances. Others argued that weeks before the Twin Towers' destruction, the insurance coverage on them increased considerably. For many days before that fateful day, no unauthorized person was allowed to access some critical sections of the building's basement foundation under the excuse that renovation and construction works were being done. Many found the weeks long, no trespassing signs highly convenient, as they allowed the 9-11 conspirators plenty of time to set undisturbed the odious crime of the decade.

Dr. Judy Wood, in her book "Where Did the Towers Go," made a remarkable analysis of the use of directed-energy weapons in the taking down of the Twin Towers. She presented evidence suggesting the use of secret technology that turned metal and most of the Towers to dust. The expected mountain high of piles of rubbles from all the collapsing structures was nowhere to be seen and found, as everything, steel columns, aluminum, and tons of concrete, had been almost entirely dustified and turned to dust.

"To whom the crimes profit," was the $64,000 question for anyone to ask when looking for answers. Thus, by following the money, all the usual suspects surfaced like the Central banking banksters, the warmongering Globalist neocons, and the merchants of death who ended up raking in billions from America's fake forever war against terror worldwide. Many sovereign countries known not to submit to the collective West's rules based international order were falsely accused of supporting and harboring terrorism, ergo marked for destruction by the American Empire's speedy, overblown response following 9/11. The subsequent invasions of Iraq, Afghanistan, Libya, Syria, Yemen, and several of America's undisclosed proxy wars in Africa, Southeast Asia, and elsewhere in the world only contributed to filling up the coffers of Lockheed Martin, Boeing, Northrop Grumman, Raytheon, and General Dynamics, and by extension the Global Money Empire behind the financing of all the above players and unrestrained invasions. America is not any safer today than it was before 9/11 despite billions spent in its war against terror. It had been fully documented that the dirty business of being an Empire made strange bedfellows with the terrorists we claimed to be at war with. Sorry, but the terrorists were and are to this day, our own creation. And to put it bluntly, we are the terrorists.

By some twisted scenario of truth stranger than fiction,

several of America's Deep State usual suspects involved in the Kennedy brothers' assassinations, Martin Luther King, and America's fake moon landing, with their subsequent cover-ups, were again at the rendezvous in the concocted 9-11 final solution project to save the US' waning, declining Empire.

Again, little did I know in my first World Trade Center visit that its iconic complex tower structures would have one day turned to dust in the wind, and with them, the nearly 3,000 people who were cold-bloodedly murdered that day by the power that be. And we are not even talking about the tens of millions of people killed by the post-9/11 collective West's raging wars against humanity, while they were simply wars of looting and plunder: banksters' wars.

It was Friday afternoon, my remaining last hours at the big apple, before flying back home on the next day. I was sitting and savoring one more 'bain de foule' [crowd's shower], and cool people-watching across the Rockefeller Center on the Avenue of the Americas in Midtown Manhattan. At this time of the hour, many of New York's white as well as blue collar workers were caught in the routine rush hour meme, outpacing one another on their way back home to begin a well-deserved weekend of rest. One could never miss the bloody neon lights of the famed Radio City Music Hall sign from where I was when unexpectedly I saw Richard, Philippe Carrie's younger brother whom I met in Miami and who lived in New York, walking on the sidewalk, coming my way. The odd of bumping into anyone one knew on an overcrowded Manhattan rush hour sidewalk was one to a billion. Yet, for some unexplained reason, we both just beat the odds. That was how I managed to spend one unforgettable evening at the Carrie's family home in Jamaica, Queens. We both arrived at a full, crowded house at the Carrie's. I was warned by Philippe, the family's elder son who now lived in Miami, that starting Friday afternoon, it was happy hour and a celebration of life gathering at his dad's house where friends and family members came to hang out. Michelle, the beautiful oldest sibling daughter, also the spouse of Adrien Besson, my friend, and only car's caretaker, was on one of her routine, spontaneous visits back home in New York. For the first time, I was introduced to the rest of the family whom I had not yet met, like Peter, the second oldest son, and Gina, the youngest and equally pretty daughter of the Carries. Gina had just started dating her would-be future handsome beau, Roger Biambi, who would become one of the movers and shakers in the Haitian Diaspora's Miami politics of the 1980s. When I thought that was it and there could be no more surprises on the evening agenda for me, I was dead wrong when someone rang the house entrance bell.

Guess who that person was. It was Maurice Sixto himself. It was a definite evening of surprises on top of surprises. Sixto, who was an old enduring friend of the Carrie family from way back in Pè Carrié's growing-up days in Gonaives, Haiti. He made it a duty to always visit his old friend Pierre, a.k.a. Pè Carrie whenever he was on in New York from Philadelphia where he had taken up residency. For many of my non-Haitian readers who have never heard of Maurice Sixto, he was a Haitian icon in his own right, as the chief architect behind a mass appeal oral literary genre, proverbially known as "Lodyans" [storytelling]. Lodyans was a type of oral story telling with a humoristic message tainted with sarcasm with a moral lesson at the end of the story. Though Sixto had not invented this popular, traditional storytelling genre found in the general Haitian culture, he had, however, perfected it and taken it to a whole other dimension. His satirical voice and the delivery tone of his telltale lodyans were quite an anathema to many from his own bourgeois middle-class Haitian compatriots.

He revealed and exposed the Haitian elite's greed, class, and color prejudices, all the while sending every one of his listeners rolling to the floor with unadulterated laughter. It was a delightful treat to have met him in person at Carrie's family home. What a grand finale for my New York week to finish it in the company of the famed author and "Grand diseur" [Gifted reciter] of "Lea Kokoyé" and "J'ai Vengé la Race" to name just a few from the six published volumes of his highly popular Lodyans workload.

On the plane taking me back to Miami, I could not help reflecting on my first-ever visit to New York City and how, despite my initial discomfort, I managed to turn things around and enjoyed the ride. Because of Manhattan's mega size and intimidating concrete skyscrapers, it was understandable for many first-time visitors to experience a temporary claustrophobic reaction due to a feeling of smallness and powerlessness inherent in many first timers. I also could see that once those irrational fears were no longer an issue, one could easily become addicted to the monstrosity of the mega city vibe, charm, and dizzying ambiance.

It was not easy for me to go back to my normal, regular routine Miami life, as the New York's state of mind was still alive and well and kicking in my head. But slowly and surely, I had to readjust myself to blend into the much slower pace of life here in Miami. Still, for many days, I struggled over the monumental impact made on me by New York's unmatched hustle and bustle, where things seemed to go on and on non-stop, earning it its well-deserved appellation of "A City That Never Sleeps." Deep inside, I had a natural sense of belonging to many aspects of New York city life. An existential connecting vibe, perhaps from another prior existential life. In any case, I promised myself that my first and recent visit to the big apple would not be my last.

I had just gotten off the plane at Miami International airport on a late Saturday afternoon flight, and I was already making plans to hit Coconut Grove's bar scene area the same night in search of a hot, new date for my next Village Inn's Satsang like experience. After my fabulous week in New York, only the Grove's bar scene ambiance could come close enough to offer me a soothing transition. I went off track a bit from my usual two-week-dating stand in the two months that I dated Brigitte, the closest I got to dating a Brigitte Bardot look-alike straight from the city of lights. This self-imposed dating time limit on myself, though cynical as it may sound to many, was in reaction to an equally heartbreaking realization that there were too many good-looking blond babes out there in the bar scenes and way too little time for poor me or anyone else to render justice to every one of them. I was your typical wonder child who ended up in that chocolate store to realize that I could try as many samples as possible at no financial and emotional cost to me.

The bulk of the young ladies in the bar scenes were equally adventurous. They mostly came for a wild, unforgettable time in the Grove's club scene's free love culture with no expectation of any string attached to follow suit. They came from North and South America and Europe. Some could be traced all the way to New Zealand or the land down under. The few locals who lived in the Grove's vicinity or in South Miami and the Gables were spoiled, trust fund babes looking equally for the forbidden jungle fever-like experiences with a black dude without the dangers and potentially high cost of traveling all the way to Africa or to a remote Caribbean Island to have their sexual fantasy fix. All they had to do was to drive their parents' fancy bourgeois cars just a few miles down to one of the Grove's local bars to find the forbidden, low hanging fruits ripe and ready to eat.

I began early with my bar's hoping routine strategy, starting at the Tavern, Hungry Sailor, and my last stop was at the Taurus bar near the historic Coconut Grove Playhouse Theater. There, I got lucky when I approached a fairly good-looking, long, curly, red-haired girl who was standing alone at the bar all by herself. Her name was Peggy and that she was in Miami for the very first time, visiting from England. She was staying with a girlfriend for the duration of her visit. She lived a mere walking distance from Coconut Grove's tourist hub and outdoor cafes. Though she was reserved and shy at first, I managed to make her feel relaxed. We did well in our pleasant exchange of words despite the countering loud and noisy background of the local Rock band playing there at the time. Her lovely British accent was a definite turn-on for me. I had never dated a Brit before, and I was determined to make her my first. The conquest of one of the Queen's charming royal subjects would be a considerable added trophy for moi.

Peggy was very deep on the spiritual side. She had that sultry Mona Lisa mysterious-like smile and some smooth, inviting facial cheekbones gracing her face. She was about my height and appeared to have a nice lean figure, though I could not confirm that, as she wore hippie baggy clothes, preventing me from telling for sure all the hidden treasures underneath her long dress-attire. The only thing missing to complete the perfect image of the Aquarian flower girl, was to place a set of flowers on top of her long, luxurious red hair. We stepped outside of the club's parking lot for some fresh Coconut Grove evening breeze away from the cigarette-polluted air inside the Taurus bar. We sat on one of the outside benches to continue with our mutually engaging conversation.

The physical and spiritual attractions were undeniably reciprocal and intense between us. A certain feel-good momentum seemed to envelop us, as I became so confident in my wild animal magnetism and hypnotic vibe to make Peggy feel so sexually turned on that she would want to have it right there on that bench. We both were caught in that sensual, ethereal love dance and we knew exactly where it would inevitably lead us. She invited me to her place, which was just two blocks from the Taurus, for chamomile tea and to share a joint with her.

I responded positively to Peggy's offer and found myself surprisingly walking alongside her hand in hand on the narrow Grove's Street until we arrived at a house that appeared to be buried under several luxurious trees, typical of many homes in the area. She told me to make myself comfortable, reassuring me that the house was hers for the entire night, as her roommate would be sleeping at her boyfriend's. That was her way of sending me a coded message that she was ready and open for anything and that time and space were both on our side tonight. After filling up two glasses of cold chamomile tea to toast to the occasion, she allowed me to light the joint that was in her hand. We both took turns puffing on it. The stunning effect was quick, as we were both tripping to high heaven in the cozy living room, where she started burning some incense to counter the foul, pungent ganja smell.

At one point, she spontaneously leaned her full body on me, and ordered me to slightly open my mouth. Next, she took a long hit from the weed, held the smoke in her mouth, and commandingly pressed her amazing pair of lips on mine to send a full load of the smoke inside my mouth. I had given and received many shotguns before, but hers was one hot, steamy opening act as it naturally turned into a long, passionate shotgun kiss. After we kissed, she asked me to follow her to her bedroom. There, she let her entire lustrous long hair down, loose, and free, by shaking her head in a wild, sensuous way. Next, she started to slowly take all her clothes off in a rhythmic, choreographic motion while looking at me in a teasy, provocative manner.

What I saw coming out under the pile of her baggy clothes was simply beyond anything that I ever anticipated to see. She had, to start with, the perfect tan I had not seen in a long time on a woman's nude body. The next surprising revelation was her breathtaking killer curves, topped with a well-rounded, sizable pair of teats gracing her chest. Finally, the coup de grace came in the formidable piece of ass she was blessed with, which would have made Beyonce envious. To think that all those jewels of hers were kept so nicely hidden and tucked away under her deceptive baggy gowns made me think twice to never again judge a book by its cover.

With her long, fiery red hair now freely hanging along her near-perfect figure, Peggy had instantly turned into a surreal creature in my bewildered hungry eyes. How could one even begin to make love to a creature like her without running the elevated risk of making a fool out of oneself? I was so turned on by Peggy that when she helped me out of my own set of clothes, to then sit her lustful bottom on top of my erected penis, disaster stroke. It was one of the fastest, most humiliating orgasmic discharges I had to endure in my entire life. In the classical Haitian jargon of premature ejaculation, what I had just done was a "Bonjou Pwèl," meaning a disastrous half-second fuck. Lucky for me, Peggy was not the type of girl who would let an annoying quicky incident ruin her entire evening, not after sizing up the length and width of my cock. She apparently was accustomed to seeing men humbled themselves within seconds following vaginal penetration with her. So, unphased by what just happened, she reassured me through her caresses that the night was still young and that the evening had just begun. Then slowly but surely, the old warrior in me recovered and rose to the occasion to serve Peggy, the visiting Queen's subject, with one majestic royal fuck leaving her shaking, and begging for more. To paraphrase one famed General, "I might have lost the first round of battle with her, but I did not lose the war, as I made a brazen, mendacious return to win and reign over her decisively."

The following day, I introduced Peggy to the Village Inn's Reggae afternoon Satsang. She naturally fell in love with the Village Inn's magical ambiance: the place, the people, and the music. Because of her organic nature, Peggy effortlessly melted into the overall chemistry of the Village Inn's atmosphere. Since my weeklong trip to New York, I had not been seen at my favorite Reggae spot for at least two Sundays in a row. The few rare Sundays that I had not been seen in action on that dance floor. And oh boy, had I made a triumphant return to the scene of the crime, arms in arms with my latest bombshell conquest from the UK.

Unfortunately, the red hair beauty went back home. But we promised to stay in touch with one another. The physical and spiritual connections we had going between us were too unique and transcendental to let all that that go to waste. What we had, though brief, was simply beyond borders, cultures, races, languages, and free from the limited human concept of time and space. Though we talked about her returning in a year or so for another visit or me visiting her in London, the only contact line with her was broken. I never saw or heard from Peggy again, but one thing was certain: she would always be a part of that life journey of mine. Then, despite my numerous affairs with women, before and after her, whereas most would never grace the pages of my Miami memoir, however, Peggy like Kathy, Cindy, and Brigitte made her mark on me.

## Miami, Florida: A Sunshine State's Unauthorized And Unredacted Journey

I finally got rid of my old black Cadillac to replace it with a much newer version keeping up with my old Pépé Cadillac image. But because of the mounting cost of fuel, driving back and forth to FIU's Tamiami South Campus five days a week was taking a toll on my wallet. I purchased a six-cylinder car which was an old Chevy model, from Gregory Carré, who was a friend of mine. I would drive my old chevy to work and to school during weekdays and used my newly bought fancy Cadillac on weekends in line of the bourgeois American materialist culture.

On the home front, things could not get any better. I continued unabated with my commitment to sending money home each month and was impatiently waiting for the five-year requirement needed for a green card resident to apply for US citizenship. By becoming an American citizen, I could be able to legally file for green card requests for my mother and my two half-siblings left behind in Haiti. Jean Willy, who recently moved to Miami from Waukegan, was still sharing my already space-starved bachelor's pad. Now, he had just moved into the rental unit across from mine after signing a contract with our landlord. It was about time and quite a relief, as there had been many awkward situations of privacy with the visiting ladies for both Willy and me.

Many of the couples that I was friends with were not doing well. My dear brother Georges was now separated from his long-time love, Yvonne, after giving birth to two beautiful young girls.

Philippe Carrie was divorced from his beautiful wife Nadia, with her keeping legal custody of his two daughters. I just learned that Adrien and Michelle were not doing well either in their marriage. All this unwelcome news about separations and divorces was, if anything, but an encouragement for me to double down on the enduring contempt I had against the legal institution of marriage. Long live the bachelor's life!

The surprising phone call I received in a long time came from my old friend Nènè, with whom I grew up when I was living in Martissant. He told me that he was moving to Miami as early as next week and that the rented house they planned to live in would not be ready until three days after they arrived in Miami next week. He asked me if he and his family could stay with me for those three days. He was moving to Miami with his wife Rosy and their five-year-old son to start afresh. It would be one crowded bachelor's pad, but they were members of my tribe. Besides, I already had in mind an emergency contingency plan to go stay across with my brother Willy and leave the entire place to them. They came in the following week, and it was one big family reunion for old-time sake. I offered them to stay for as long as they needed to, as I would be right next door staying with my brother Willy in case they needed any help.

Those who read my second book memoir could recall that both the Manigats and the Perodins were like extended family members to me. I grew up with Rosy from her Manigat family home where her father was like another adopted dad to me, and she was like a sister to me. In fact, I was the one who first introduced both Rosy and Nènè to each other back in the day. The week after they stayed in my pad, I helped them move to their new Miami home and was there to aid them in every feasible way I could.

I needed a well-deserved break from all that was happening around me recently. And when Sunday afternoon came for my routine Village Inn's escapade, I was already on the road cruising South on US-1 toward the Grove, behind the wheels of my brand-new purchased Cadillac. As soon as I was done paying the $3 entrance fee and got passed the entrance door, it was as if I were in an enchanted space where all my daily, burdensome worries dissipated. All the invisible loaded weight that I had on my back was taken off by a magical hand and left outside the bar's side door. Thus, this incredible sense of renewal of the self, a sort of lightness of being one could never fail to experience each time by simply being inside the bar's protective walls. Roots Uprising had never sounded so perfect in a few of their original songs and in many of their latest hit Reggae renditions and adaptations. Songs like Bob Marley's Bad Card, Dennis Brown's Should I, or The Police's The Bed's Too Big Without You sounded even better than the originals.

The beautiful mixed crowd's awesome chemistry and its near decadent "Joie De Vivre" zest for living life to its fullest were the integral parts of that heavenly package deal, which made the

Village Inn's afternoon Reggae extravaganza a unique gathering exception for its time.

I was in the middle of a conversation with the two handsome buggers Ti Harold and Patrick, the two usual suspects of Village Inns' top "Blond killers," titles they earned in terms of their high success rate in seducing blond babes at the bar. But I was interrupted by a feisty four feet five tall looking blond asking me for matches to light her cigarette. Gentleman obliged. I helped her with her request, and that was the icebreaker needed to start a conversation with her. Her name was Gil, and she was living in one of those multi-million-dollar mansions with her rich parents. She was the typical trust fund babe I talked about earlier. Her folk's mansion was on that main, exclusive road leading to the Fairchild Tropical Botanic Garden. I could tell by a mile the 'Miss entitled' energy coming out of her despite her clear charming, humbling smile. Her "What Gil wants, Gil gets" vibe could be cut with a knife, and for some wild reason, I was what Gil wanted in the here and now. She caught right through the chase by telling me that she had been watching my dancing style for the longest time, and she found me quite adorable with all my sensuous Reggae moves.

I was flattered by her compliment, and before I could even say thank you, I was pulled to the dance floor by Gil, the spoiled trust fund babe. She was having the time of her life dancing with me as I was doing my signature dancing moves with her, which she claimed she was so fond of. One interesting quality about Gil was her zest to immerse herself in the moment, and she did that with her disarming candid smile, revealing a genuine sense of charming naivety. We danced for hours. She would not let me out of her sight, nor would she let go of me on and off the dance floor. I was her POW. At the end of the soiree, she proposed to me to follow her to her folk's home, reassuring me not to worry about them, as they were away in Europe for three long weeks visiting friends in London. Gil managed to pick my interest in such an unexpected way. Suffice it to say that when she suggested that I follow her home, I did not let her repeat the invitation twice.

When I made it to her place, I was totally bewildered by her parents' rich estate. I knew the high value of all the properties within this zip code once she told me the street name where she lived. Going through the main entrance, two large doors, was as if I was entering a luxurious mini castle. The Mansion's Living Room high ceiling architecture was flattering to the eyes. I was a little tense and nervous, not too comfortable being in the middle of so much display of wealth. And yet Gil, the feisty, voluptuous, attractive 5-feet blond, appeared so unphased by the whole thing and seemed so comfortable and completely at ease and at home in it. Looking at the Living Room's voluminous space alone, I knew for sure that at least three of my bachelor pads would easily fit into its space. Gil offered me a drink, went to her room, and returned with two large, patted bed sheets to spread them onto the Living Room's inviting floor. She laid on them and asked me to join her.

I knew what her intention was when she invited me to her home. I knew it was not to impress me with her family's wealth but to screw my brain out. But I had some pudor and some degree of male dignity still left in me to resist her a bit, despite realizing that I was suffering from a mild case of sex addiction yet to be diagnosed. I did not want to appear cheap and too easy a lay in her eyes, even though there was something about her that I was dying to screw to oblivion. It was a subconscious desire in me to go after what Gil represented in my eyes: an embodiment of wealth, privilege, and status. In either case, I decided to play a little hard-to-get with Ms. Entitle. I laid myself near her but managed to keep a clear distance from her. She pulled me toward her and tried to kiss me, but I gently and slowly pulled away from her.

Obviously, Gil's compass was totally out of wrack, as she was not used, not to be wanted and desired by men, especially by a black man. She was simply too hot and too rich for rejection. In a worrisome voice, she asked me, "What's wrong?". I answered there was nothing wrong except, – I told her a made-up story – that I just came out of a failed, hurtful relationship with a girl, and I was wary not to jump too quickly onto another one, too soon. I could tell that Gil was puzzled by the whole thing and she did not know how to deal with the current developing situation. She thought that I was too tense and invited me to smoke yet another joint with her to relax and chill out. Gil was a jazz freak and chose one of her favorite albums to play in the background. It was Mark Kramer's latest hit album with a smooth collection of instrumental jazz. It so happened that Gil's interventions paid off, as I was no longer in the mood to play any more games. I was the one this time making a move on her by starting to undress her while kissing her all over her voluptuous figure. She responded wholeheartedly to my caresses. When she could not hold back anymore, as she was burning with unchained desires, she reversed her prior bodily position, which was under me, to get on top. She mounted me and went straight for the kill, meaning unrestrained vaginal penetration. Being the domineering type, she loved being in the top position, and I could tell that there was nothing amateurish about her skillful performance.

She knew exactly all the right angles, the twist and turns, giving her such upper hand in her ability to completely engulf at will the entire full length of my penis and in no time pleasure herself to no end. I was somehow pleasantly amazed to hear her exciting, still shaky voice thanking me so much for the wild orgasm she just had on top of me. Though in all fairness, I believed that she did most of the arduous work. All I did was resist the immense temptation of coming by holding back long enough to allow her enough time to pleasure herself. Now that the mansion's heiress was one happy woman, it was my turn to have my fix and the way I wanted it was the doggy style affording me the deepest vaginal penetration of her.

When I told her about my favorite lovemaking position, she, at once, rolled over, got herself on all fours, and opened herself wide to receive the full length of my thick, eight-inch-long tool. I rammed it through her relentlessly and following a few minutes of interminable sexual arousal and sensuous pleasures from both of us, one monstrous deafening orgasmic scream came out of Gil's throat, making dirty blond Cindy's loudest screams pale in comparison to that I just witnessed and heard.

Gil had been regularly crashing into my bachelor pad especially since her millionaire folks had returned from their City of London vacation. I did not feel right being there at her family's mansion. At first, I was a little self-conscious about inviting her to my modest bachelor's pad, but to my surprise, she felt completely at home at my place. She was overwhelmed by my pad's wall-to-wall smallness and coziness. Gil, who worked the evening shift waitressing at the popular Monty Trainer bar/restaurant for fun and out of pure boredom, would drive to my place straight from work in the insane wee morning hours as she began developing what appeared to be a mild case of sex addiction with me. As soon as she entered my room, I found myself under immediate sexual 'assault' by her. And the fact that I did not seem to mind Gil's crazed sexual addiction over me was quite alarming. Wearing loose bottom clothes and always pantyless, I only had time to wear a protective rubber before Ms. Entitled sat straight on it and relieved herself soon after.

That was only the start of a long five-course dinner menu with her, as she loved to have it for hours and everywhere in my bachelor's pad. It was as if she wanted to mark the entire place off with her scent, turning it into a no-trespassing zone to scare off potential other females. Gil was one wild creature and one of the most creative sexual partners I so far had, as she would insist on having it everywhere: in the shower, on the kitchen sink countertop, on the toilet seat, on the oven's top, and even on the small, unstable dining table in the kitchenette. She would wake me up in the middle of my sleep to go right back at it for yet another round of sex. She belonged to a rare group of women who enjoyed hard, rough intercourse. So, she would wholeheartedly welcome a couple of hard hits on her fantastic 'derriere' and pinches on her two nipples, which always seemed to add more explosive sparks to her orgasmic experience with me.

It took me some time before I realized that with Gil, I was perhaps dealing with a true sex-addicted woman at best and, at worst, a mild case of a nymphomaniac woman with an ongoing, non-stop sexual urges. I simply could not keep up with her constant sex impulses and her weekdays' wee hours morning interferences. I was a full-time worker and student with a busy daily schedule, and I needed to sleep and rest. Though Gil was taking Art classes on a part-time basis at the UM, she only worked 3 nights at Monty's, giving her plenty of time to recover from her addictive sex life. That was not the case for me. I did not have such luxury and the reliable cushion of a wealthy family to fall back on as she had. Besides, I started to feel that she was a trojan horse of sorts on a stealthy mission to alter my lifestyle and change it from its core.

She was not in it just for the sex, as I began to suspect. She wanted the total experience, meaning the spiritual and emotional elements she felt should also come with the sexual package. In short, she wanted me to fall absolutely and irreversibly in love with her and become a sexual slave to her. I had been exceptionally skilled and lucky at not mixing both the sexual and emotional components of all my sexcapades so far, and I was not about to change what was proven to work amazingly well for me. The natural survival instinct of the incorrigible bachelor in me started to kick in, and because I was not the confrontational type, I made use of my old passive-aggressive ways to protect and fend for myself.

I deliberately and purposely started seeing less and less of Gil, finding all sorts of excuses as part of a brilliant strategy not to fall into her traps and under her spell. The message was slowly but surely received by her. And the last time I saw Gil, she was in the arms of a handsome, muscular calypso drummer who had a weeknight gig at Monty Trainer, where she worked.

The three months I dated, Gil were another big challenge I

faced to maintain the integrity of my bachelor's cherished lifestyle with its philosophy of total freedom, consisting of not having to answer to any woman and the liberty to date and be with any girl I wanted. Next time, I promised myself to be more vigilant and not to let my guard down like I did with Gil. But little did I know that just within a three-week time, I got myself in yet another hot, steamy adventure with no fault of my own. I was just having a good time people-watching inside the International Omni Mall when I realized that I had to rush to my bank located right across the mall on the other side of Biscayne Blvd. It would be closed in the next 15 minutes. The bank's name back then was the 'Dade County School Employees Federal Credit Union.' I remember it to be the place where I had one of my early odd cleaning jobs. Peter, one of the original Pépés, was the first one hired to be the Bank office's janitor. I remember him bringing me along with him as they needed to hire one more person to complete the evening clean-up crew. Though that gig lasted a few days, I still felt funny every time I was there to make a banking transaction.

This time around, however, it was different, as someone standing in the line in front of me had all but captivated my attention. She was the physical sosie, if not the physical reincarnation of two memorable Haitian ladies I wrote intensely about in both of my last two memoirs. The first one was a lady named Michaelle, a high-end Cayes' courtesan. The second lady was also a high-class escort from

135

the time I lived in the second-family home in Martissant. The latter had a much less of a storyline than the former, but still influential enough to make a notable impression on me. I called her nameless, for she never allowed anyone near her to get to know her name. Both heroine ladies from my memoirs shared one thing in common: they were heavenly made, gorgeous, and beyond beautiful. They were the absolute embodiments of the Haitian black swans. Famed Haitian poet Oswald Duran wrote a panoply of romantic verses immortalizing black Haitian women like them. And the young black lady standing in the line in front of me happened to be the exact cloning version of them both. She had the height, the perfect build, the stunning perfect facial features, the soft, ebony skin, and the long, natural, straight black hair.

Her type was the absolute dominant black female beauty in many of my mid-teens wet dream reveries. The ideal black woman to marry when I grew up. Though recently, I have been a bit reluctant to go on any dates, not just with my Haitian counterpart women, but also with any black woman in general, following a handful of unpleasant incidents of entrapments. However, at the sight of such a stunning-looking creature, our black swan beauty, I seemed to quickly lean toward waving the current embargo I had on dating black women. Perhaps just to satisfy a long-craving, teenager's old fantasy of what it would be like to make love to a woman like her, a creature so perfectly made by Mother Nature.

Miami, Florida: A Sunshine State's Unauthorized And Unredacted
Journey

Hence, my hypnotic charm was in plain full gear deployment aiming at her. To this day, I have no recollection of what was the initial storyline I used to engage her in a conversation with me. Regardless, she appeared to have been kind of hooked on whatever feel-good vibe I fed her with. A sign that I was doing right by her was when she was willingly waiting for me at the bank's lobby after I suggested to her to go to the International Omni mall across from the bank for happy hour. The black swan beauty's name was Teressa, and she came from the windy city of Chicago, which opened a whole other line of conversation for me, as my relatives who lived in Waukegan, Illinois, for many years were not too far from the place where she was born and raised. Aside from being the knockout-looking black lady that Teressa was, she had one more trait in her arsenal of beauty: her unusual natural pair of light green eyes, contrasting amazingly well with her dark, smooth, ebony skin.

We were the last two customers to walk out of the Credit Union bank. We crossed the boulevard to enter the mall, where we found a chic happy hour place for a couple of relaxing drinks while getting to know one another some more. She learned a lot from me and vice versa. Mother nature had even gone beyond its over-the-top physical gifts to Teressa to also bless her with great charm and intelligence. She had a refined, sophisticated mind and was a highly educated person, making her a delightful conversationalist. She could go on and on for hours on any topic of conversation, as she

137

was very well-read and informed.

The physical and intellectual attractions between us were so utterly flawless that later in the evening, she offered no resistance to follow me to my place for what was in both our minds the anticipated grand conclusion of an amazing evening. As soon as we entered my pad, I moved on quickly to create a romantic atmosphere by turning on the music and lighting some candles and incense. I served her some red wine, and we once more raised our glasses to one another. I could tell that Teressa was making herself comfortably at ease with the cozy, relaxing ambiance known to my place. She was so at home that she asked me if I had some weed, to which I answered, "I thought you would never ask." A nicely rolled joint was handed to her. "It had been sometimes since I last smoked some..." she said, and she was bracing herself for a phenomenal high. Her wish came through sooner than expected when the immediate weed effect on her senses relaxed her even more. Next, she threw her shoes off and laid in a sexy posture, the full length of her majestic black swan figure on the sister bed across. Whenever such an unspoken, coded gesture was made by a lady guest in my sleeping quarter, it was always seen by me as a call for action.

With the complicity of the low, soothing sound of the background music, I joined her and began to caress her softly. She responded to my touches by reciprocating with more of her own, as she started to unbutton my shirt and unzip my pants. I followed suit by helping to free up what I could see was too perfect for words. And what a sight and an absolute delight to the eyes that was! I wanted to take it slowly with her. No reason for me to be in any rush. Teressa's type was the object of my wildest teenage fantasy to one day experience the euphoria-like sensation of having sex with a wonder creature like her. My dream was well on the way to become soon a reality, and I did not want to mess it up.

I started her up with a long French kiss while slowly using my known devilish fingers to stimulate the voluptuous pair of boobs that a generous nature had yet again blessed her chest with. Teressa's perfect black swan figure was set ablaze when I began to strike her clitoris gently and patiently with my insinuating, relentless tongue. The windy city girl was spacing out somewhere in the realm of the earth's stratosphere. After giving her one convulsive, earth-shaking orgasm, it was now her turn to reciprocate by giving me one of my most memorable blow jobs ever.

I could not get enough of her body's soft, ebony skin and its emanating sexual chemistry. The feeling was reciprocal judging by her own feverish responses to the touch of my soft brown skin. Following a quick break, we jumped right back to where we left off with the same intense body touches, caresses, and stimulations displayed earlier. Except this time, it was an all-or-nothing, total war between us. She could no longer wait for the ultimate fireworks that I seemed to have implanted in her head through my hypnotic, flirtatious brown eyes the moment I began making my move on her.

Our lovemaking heated up so high that Teressa lost all her sophistication, finesse, and pudor by begging me to go straight for the jugular, as she had her hand on my well-erected member. I responded to her frenetic demand by first wearing a protective rubber and knowing how vulnerable I was from both the missionary and the doggy style positions; I insisted for Teressa to go on top of me while I lay on my back. She went for the ultimate takedown over my sizable 8-inch tool. The refined, sophisticated lady that I met hours earlier at my bank, went through a total transformation where she became completely unrecognizable. Sex had turned her into a wild beast, though still hot and sexy. Her loud moaning screams and the language coming out of her mouth were ovewhelming.

Sensing that she was on her way to climax, I changed the tempo by taking her in the doggy-style position, to begin with the last stage of the grand finale. Her moaning screams got even louder, and so was her unladylike curses as I was getting harder and deeper into her and hitting all corners and angles inside the vagina's walls. The harder my cock was getting in its relentless pounding of her vagina, the loudest the Windy City lady was begging me while on all fours to fuck her harder and harder. The timing could not have been more perfect as we both climaxed together. Teressa's orgasm this time around was anything that I had ever seen with any of the women I had intercourse with before and long after her. Hers was an all-out-of-body experience. Her soul appeared to have suddenly vacated her uncontrollably shaken body and was somewhere floating near the ceiling in suspended levitation mode. From her detached levitating position, she was eagerly directing me on how best to ravage and finish her off.

I could not wait to take Teressa to the Village Inn's Satsang's experience to show her off. She enjoyed all the attention there, as she was being hit on by men as well as women. The mostly mixed crowd there was where one could come to see every Sunday the various wonders of mixed-race offspring display. Several among them were so puzzled by Teressa's contrasting natural pair of beautiful green eyes with her dark, silky, ebony skin.

My Haitian partners in crimes at the Village Inn, though a bit flirtatious with Teressa, were a little worried about me abandoning the avenging fun mission that we were engaged in with the collective West's Uncles' daughters. That was the first time they ever saw me with a black date at the scene, making them ponder about the possibility that Teressa's charm and beauty might trigger in me a 'return home' to my black woman. I reassured them that was not the case and that I was still on the avenging mission.

Speaking of Maurice Sixto's "J'ai Vengé la Race" [I Avenged the Race] popular story, where he entertained us with his humorous voice about his sexual encounter with a white lady. And how upon satisfying her sexually, he exclaimed victoriously that he, at last, avenged his black race in response to the white colonizers' systematic raping of countless black females on the slave plantations. It was at the Village Inn that Sixto's sweet revenge was being kept alive and well. He would have been so impressed to see its actual realization of his 'avenging the black race' in real-time on the Village Inn's dancing floor, where Rastafarian and other black brothers were with their white conquests, fearlessly making out with them right in the open. It was one thing when the seductions of the uncles' daughters were happening on a faraway African continent or on some isolated Caribbean islands, giving plausible deniability to the white racist Western propaganda machine. But that was not the case here at Coconut Grove's popular tourist hub, which was an international rendezvous spot where the entire world could see, watch, and witness the changing paradigm and the reversal of fortune.

The next place I took Teressa was to Cindy and Tony's Sabal Palm home. It was love at first sight for Cindy and Tony. Even their latest roommate Elsie, a drop-dead gorgeous-looking mulatto girl, was cozying up to her as well. I had been highly suspicious for some time that those three were living a secretive threesome lifestyle. And that Tony, being the sexual beast that he was, might have even gone behind Cindy's back to have a little unauthorized affair with Elsie on the side. How did I know that for sure, you would ask? The answer was that Tony had asked me to use my bachelor's pad on at least two occasions, and I presumed that it was to take Elsie there without Cindy's consent. Teressa was enamored by the charming reception she had there, especially by Tony, who was salivating all over her.

So, it was no great surprise to me when, a week later, Tony invited both of us to a special Saturday evening gathering at their Sabal Palm's estate, with the five of us only. He emphasized the party's dominant theme of 'Anything goes,' which was a euphemism for a fivesome orgy. I was at first taken aback by the whole thing, as I had never participated before in any such large sexual gathering. The closest I came to an orgy was when I was twice a participant in a threesome, first with my old friend Jean and his girlfriend, and the last one I was in was with two visiting girls from Quebec, Canada. Though they were both experimental in nature, my recollection of them was not all that glimmery, as both elements of sexual privacy and intimacy were openly sacrificed. I had some reservations following the sex experiments' aftereffects on romance and its overall demystifying impact. I assumed that in a fivesome, the sexual demystification would be even greater. Regardless, it was the 70s and still the age of free love, free sex, and daring sexual experiments, so I was open to trying that. What could possibly go wrong in a worst-case scenario, I asked myself, and I could find none. I extended the invitation to Teressa by asking her

143

what she thought of a fivesome orgy with Elsie, Tony, and Cindy this coming Saturday at their house. To my surprise, she responded positively to the idea and even appeared all excited by it.

And that was how all five of us ended up meeting at the Saturday evening rendezvous. I could not help feeling morbidly nervous as my old religious Cayes' background of "Ne fais pas ça enfant, tu vas tomber" [Do not do that, child, you are going to get hurt] swung into high gear. Lots of what-ifs came into my mind following Tony's orgy proposal. What if all four, including Teressa, were bisexuals, and I was the only heterosexual among them, with no desire to try what it would be like on the other side of the pond?

A large enough space in the middle of the house's Living Room was cleared, indicating where obviously all the actions would later be taking place. Drinks and rolling joints were being served and passed on. I needed more than my usual one puff of weed effects this time for me to relax and calm my nerves down. Both Elsie and Cindy were wearing hot, sexy lingerie with their low cleavage braless tops, yet another sure signs where the evening was irreversibly heading.

All the Living Room lights were intentionally kept dimmed to encourage as little inhibition as possible from all five of the participants. Elsie, the hot, voluptuous mulatto roommate, who was enamored with Motown's top 60s and 70s R&B tower of songs, made sure that a prerecorded cassette of old-school soul music was playing in the background. It was a stream of classic hits from the Temptation, Earth, Wind & Fire, The Commodores to Billy Paul's 'Me and Mrs. Jones', Manhattan's 'Kiss, and Say Goodbye', Teddy Pendergrass' 'Turn Off the Lights', and Marvin Gaye's 'Sexual Healing', setting the evening mode.

When Marvin Gaye's provocative hit song "Let's Get It On" came up from Elsie's selection, hot, dirty blond Cindy took it upon herself, as the lady host, to break the ice by asking me to dance. An offer I could not refuse, as everyone in the room was right up there in synch with brother Marvin. Cindy and I started slow dancing together, and because of the skimpy, braless top she had on, I instantly rose to the occasion with an erection. Before I knew it, I found myself pleasantly sandwiched by her roommate Elsie, who joined in the action while Tony was dancing with Teressa. The Living Room's temperature was hot and steamy when Tony, the sexual beast that he was known for, was all over Teressa making out with her. And judging from her responses, she did not appear to mind that at all. In one nanosecond, we had all but failed the dress code civility and were shamelessly circulating buck-naked around the room. Cindy left me with Elsie to go join both Tony and Teressa, who were making out on the Living Room couch. Large pieces of soft, thick fabric sheets were used to cover the floor.

Elsie and I were the first ones to lie on the floor to continue with our lovemaking, which started soon after Cindy left us by ourselves. Making love to Elsie had its own momentous flair of newness and freshness, as I already had sex with the other two other ladies in the room, Teressa and Cindy. It was not to negate anything about having intercourse with them, as they both were amazingly awesome, terrific lovers that I was so glad and privileged to have been with. However, the first-time element of having sex with anyone had its own magical impact, which could never be denied. And I could tell right off the bat that Elsie had so far amply demonstrated all the skills needed to make her an ideal, perfect sex partner. And she happened to have a true, genuine, natural penchant for sex to make anyone's time with her worthwhile and unforgettable, assuming, of course, that the physical attraction and the body chemistry were there. Obviously, there was no such issue with us, as we both lay down on that Living Room floor to foreplay and pleasure ourselves.

When both of us were sexually aroused, Elsie handed me a condom, as protective sex was one of the two only rules governing our fivesome – the second was that any of the participants could ask to stop anytime they chose - Elsie assumed the top position, as it was her favorite, by spreading her two muscular legs over my lean body to receive within her private parts my fully erected penis. She went on and on, perhaps on one of the longest mounting sex rides she had ever been on, while candidly pleasuring herself interminably. Elsie was so skilled at rotating and turning her wet, juicy bottom all around and over my tool that I struggled a lot not to shortchange her by using all the mental techniques I learned along the way. Or else she would not be having that long a ride with me lying there on the bottom. Elsie's long lamenting sexual moaning finally caught Cindy's attention, who apparently was on one side of the floor making love to Teressa while Tony was having intercourse with her from behind.

Cindy came to my rescue motivated by pure selfish impulse that the man-eater reputation that her mulatto roommate had with men would have worn me down before she could ever get to me. The clever way she used to save me from Elsie's nonstop joy ride on me was when she began to stimulate Elsie's clitoris. She was able to have easy access to it as her roommate had her back to me, facing away the entire time. Elsie, following Cindy's clitoris stimulation, finally came crashing down in one epic climax, thanks in part to Cindy. Elsie rolled over, completely exhausted, also suspecting that her roommate wanted her off me so she could have her turn, at last. Dirty blond Cindy started at a slow making-out pace, allowing time for me to recharge.

Mind you, Cindy was the first of three fountain women experiences I had with the ladies, the night she came alone without Tony in my bachelor pad. So, I was quite in familiar territory when she came to me with a dripping wet bottom from being sexually aroused alone. We had to use plenty of handy towels not just to dry herself up but to place some under her bottom part in anticipation of the incoming floodgate, which was her sexual legacy to no fault of her own. Far from looking at Cindy's fountain woman phenomenon as an outlier, I saw it as undeniable proof of how much I turned her on. Elsie, who seemed to have recovered faster than I expected, joined Tony and Teressa at the right time when he had just given her an orgasm. Soon, Elsie was on all fours, receiving Tony's still erect nine-inch-long penis on her to her next evening orgasmic bang, while Teressa still confused and disoriented from the wild climax she just had with Tony the beast, was still catching up her breath. I was slowly but surely coming along with Cindy's foreplay. There was something incredibly genuine about the existing chemistry between me and her. She just had it for me, and nothing, not even her handsome beau Tony, could interfere with that natural physical chemistry she had with me. She would even go as far as to candidly admit one day, after sex, that intercourse with me was better for her than with Tony. Her contention was on the ground that her beau's tool, though impressively long, was too skinny for her while maintaining that mine, though not long as Tony's, had, however, the precious advantage of thickness, which was in her eyes a far better stimulant for her, as I filled her up in ways Tony could never dream of. I was under the impression that Tony's oversized ego was hurt because of Cindy's difficulty in hiding her sexual preferences for me, and that was the reason that Tony was all over Teressa as a payback time of sorts. In the meantime, Cindy's tongue stimulation of my penis paid off royally as it came to an impressive, decisive stand, ready once more to deliver a knocked-out punch to anything standing in its way.

Cindy knew that her time for a treat was up, as she came right on top by traversing me, all the while spreading herself wide open to engulf my member completely and irreversibly within her soaked, overly wet sex. Cindy, opposite her roommate Elsie, enjoyed being on top while facing me for all the extra stimulations she routinely got with my fingers' gentle rubbing of her clitoris and from licking her overly sensitive large nipples. I tended to last much longer being on the bottom than in any other sexual postures. It was only after my sex partner fully climaxed or was on her way to a full orgasm that I would think of changing to a more vulnerable position.

Cindy, fully aware of those sexual rewards of me being on the bottom, was gleefully cruising back and forth, nonchalantly exploring all corners and angles connecting to her G-spot, as she was in full control of the situation. However, her moaning screams were getting louder and louder in the room, as she was, one could recall, one incorrigible screamer while having intercourse, especially with me. Even Tony, still in the middle of his doggie-style business with his roommate Elsie, seemed to be sidetracked, if not annoyed, by Cindy's uncanny loud moaning screams. When she was on her way to explode in yet another bloody orgasm, her euphoric loud screams, this time around, had a surprising, uncontrollable effect on me by taking me down right along with her to wherever she was heading to orgasmic oblivion. For the first time since we had been having sex in Catimini behind Tony's back, we had climaxed together, cementing that physical connection I always had with her.

Then, something strange and unusual happened to me after climaxing with Cindy. Either I passed out or fell asleep unconscious from exhaustion following my wild, sexual encounters with both Elsie and Cindy. Regardless, one thing was for certain: I woke up just in time to witness the most mystifying sex acts ever between a man and a woman, to be more precise, between Tony and Teressa. Tony's sexual beast reputation was about to explode and go rogue when I saw him placing both of Teressa's legs up on each side of his muscular shoulders all the while positioning two pillows under her buttock as to give it a lift.

In the sexual jargon's terms, this position was the coup de grace allowing the male sexual organ unrestricted access to the whole of the vagina. He then began a near half-hour of pure and adulterated sexual banging of Teressa. I suspected that he was using some sexual enhancement pill in preparation for the planned fivesome, as he was able to maintain his erect penis for hours. In the meantime, Teressa was the full recipient of Tony's relentless pounding. Honestly, I did not know what to make of the screams coming out of her throat. I could not tell in absolute certainty what they really were. Were they screams of pleasure, pain, or both? I would never know the answer, as I never again had the opportunity to ask Teressa for the truth. I reasoned that if they were screams of pain, she could have asked Tony to stop, as it was one of the established rules that we all had agreed to before taking part in the fivesome orgy.

Not once during that interminable scene of Teressa being jungle fucked to smithereens that I see her pushing Tony off her. Instead, what I saw and heard was a highly cooperative sex partner begging her sexual partner for more. At one point, she literally appeared to have detached herself completely from her own vagina, as she did with me in repeated occasions by denying it and despising it as hers by siding with Tony's dismantlement of her vagina. She, in her own words, was inciting him to wreck it beyond repair. It was, to my ears, the ultimate vagina betrayal that I heard coming from a woman's mouth in my lifetime. I would leave that to the sex expert to explain the mindset behind Teressa's odd sexual response to Tony's plain rough sex-making. There was no love in what I witnessed. Not even a genuine liking of sex for the sake of sex.

Tony's oversized ego following Cindy's noisy performance in the room, might have done a number on his head. He had long suspected that Cindy was sneakily fucking me behind his back. He just never could catch us in the act, as I would meet with her in other places, like at one of her free Marriot's executive suites, just to be on the safe side. Now, the cat was out of the bag when hearing and watching his main squeeze in a live sex act; having so much unrestrained pleasure was simply too much for him to handle. Hence, he had to at once avenge what was, in his mind, a public humiliation. And because Teressa was officially my date, thus my woman, he purposely targeted her for one degrading finish with the hope of humbling me back.

Again, what if I was dead wrong and that Teressa was in no pain whatsoever at any time during her entire last half-hour intercourse with Tony and that the dude had given her the best fuck, she ever had her entire life. What if Tony was the one lover who made a much deeper connection with her than I ever could, encompassing her sexual, physical, and spiritual beings?

When I thought I saw everything I needed to see about a woman being transformed into a zombie-like entity, sexually speaking, I was dead wrong. Teressa, after having orgasm on top of orgasm and that Tony, still under the influence of some enhancing performance drugs, had yet to show any signs of slowing down, let alone climaxed, Teressa began to turn numbed and unresponsive to Tony's banging. That was when he decided to pull out of her, his still fully erect penis, and rolled over on the side floor next to her, completely exhausted.

Miami, Florida: A Sunshine State's Unauthorized And Unredacted
Journey

However, what happened next was beyond me, and was the last drop spilling the mud when Teressa, the cool, calm, collected, sophisticated, and well-composed lady that I once met at my bank, got on her knees to kiss Tony's feet like a submissive sex slave worshiping her master for making her see the light of life.

The secular mind in me, always seeking answers to human action and behavior, assumed that her odd, servile act toward Tony was perhaps a temporary shock and awe response, which could easily be blamed on the massive release of oxytocin during her elongated sex act's multiple orgasms. This chemical component, when released inside the female body, was believed by many sex experts to be the culprit behind instilling strong connection bonding with a male lover following orgasm. Tony's kissing feet incident, besides inflating the man's hurt ego from Cindy's earlier performance, also showed a real character flow in Tony and Teressa.

Something was irreversibly broken. I could sense it. It felt as if Teressa was irreparably compromised in my eyes coming out of that fivesome orgy experiment. I could never again look at her the way I used to before that Saturday evening orgy. Even Teressa herself had a tough time looking at me in the eyes, perhaps out of the empress' guilty feeling of having been unveiled by Tony the beast and finding herself with no clothes on. She was so sore, and she had a really hard time walking straight to my car when the time came for me to drop her off at the apartment where she was staying.

153

I was worried sick that she could suffer some internal vaginal injury or bleeding from Tony's rough sex act. When I dropped her off at home that night, she barely looked me in the eyes while thanking me for the ride. There was no goodbye kiss either between us. We looked and behaved as if we were perfect strangers. That was the last time I saw Teressa, the perfect likeness to the two ladies from my teenage fantasy years. She did not want to even be friends with me anymore, as she was not returning any of my calls and the number of messages left by me on her answering machine. I wanted to get to the bottom of what really happened that night, and only she could tell the truth.

I could not help feeling guilty if she were hurt that night by Tony, as I introduced her to the gang. Now that she was avoiding me, I started to lean increasingly on the possibility that harm might have been done to her, or else why she would insist upon not seeing me or having anything to do with me suddenly. I even thought of the possibility that Tony might have put something into Teressa's drink to make her act so submissive, completely out of character. I knew the man was a freeloader, a cheater, but not a criminal, so I quickly dismissed that thought. Either way, why was I being blamed by her for an orgy experiment going rogue in the last thirty minutes of it? I would never have answers to several of my inquiring questions, for the drop-dead gorgeous Teressa with the most beautiful pair of light green eyes to be seen on a black ebony skin woman vanished in thin air overnight.

## Miami, Florida: A Sunshine State's Unauthorized And Unredacted Journey

After a week of not hearing from her, I even had the gall to drive my car all the way to where she was staying, but I was told by her landlord, a middle-aged gentleman, that she had left Miami for good and had no plan to return anytime soon. She flew back home to Chicago three days ago, according to him, and she did not leave any phone number or any address where she could be reached.

The atmosphere in Cindy and Tony's Sabal Palm apartment where the fivesome orgy took place was anything but smooth either, in the aftermath of the orgy experiment. Elsie was forced out of the apartment and Tony was, after his mean-spirited performance, was given a week to move out of Cindy's condo, as she could barely stand him anymore and could no longer go on pretending that she was happy in her relationship with him.

What the fivesome experiment had done was to tear down the veils where everyone was hiding behind. A month later, a huge promotion was offered to Cindy at a Marriott's West Coast Resort that she could not possibly pass. After another failed attempt at convincing me to move with her to California, she invited me to come to spend her last remaining night in Miami with her at the Marriott's executive suite, where she has been staying since turning over her Sabal Palm apartment a week ago. We made love the entire night till the wee morning hours. That was also for the memoir record the last time I saw dirty blond Cindy. She was one hell of an interesting woman that I had loved in my own right, though not enough to throw off my cherished bachelor's lifestyle in exchange for spending the rest of my remaining days with her.

# PART II

Lyonel Gerdes

# Could Africa's Decolonization Be Haiti and America's Last Hope?

Fast forwarding to 2023, I always maintained through my past essay writings what both Haiti and the US had in common, despite their seemingly huge differences. Aside from the fact that they had been in many similar historical pathways in their lifespan dealing with European colonialism and slavery, both nations, to this day, had yet to set themselves free from the international financial banking cartel. Since their inception, both had been financially captured, controlled and manipulated by the spider web of the Global Money Empire. However, their respective captivities had served different purposes.

Haiti's nasty poverty plight, only a stone's throw from the richest country on earth, was to send a permanent, dissuasive message to any country from the Global South not to follow Haiti's historical attempt at taking its political freedom and financial independence into its own hands. In America's case, the global banking cartel had a different approach. They financed the US' war economy and afforded it its rising empire status, in line with its preassigned global mission to defend and protect the cartel's worldwide financial hegemony. We are now beginning to see how America is being thrown under the bus by the cartel when their 500-year-old global financial control began to slip through their fingers, thanks to recent pertinent challenges from the BRICS nations.

America's middle classes, last time I checked, had been on life support for decades, its industrial base gone, and its overall infrastructures in desperate need of repair. We could never speak of US sovereignty for as long as America's elite class was not permitted to print its own money, and when they were allowed to make important, critical decisions, they had always gone against the interest of most Americans. A case in point is to look at America's current proxy war in Ukraine against Russia, demanded by the Global Money Empire. Where is the general American and European population security concern by provoking a nuclear-armed Russia? The prevalent belief among many is that the psychopathic globalists leading the pack in the Collective West were both genocidal and suicidal, thus, the classic in real time cliché that the lunatics have really taken over the asylum! For them, it's all or nothing; it's their way or the highway, meaning total enslavement of everyone or nuclear self-annihilation for all living things on earth if they could not fulfill their self-appointed millennium dream to financially impoverish the entire globe. Or else, why would they allow their Americans minions to encircle and provoke Russia, a country that possesses a nuclear arsenal large enough to incinerate America's fifty states with all its European vassals' states, including England, under a pile high of nuclear ashes? Yet the white Collective West population, in their zombie-like march toward oblivion, seemed to be completely oblivious to such perilous life-ending eventuality.

The proxy war in Ukraine, fully financed and armed by NATO to counter Russia's Special Operation, is the setting stage for the final showdown opposing the forces of good and evil. A showdown between the world's known colonialists and esclavagists versus their proverbial nemesis, Moscow. Russia had always been the one true exceptional nation, always finding itself in the way of the earth's masters' predatory appetite to swallow up most of the planet's resources. This Centuries-old affair could be traced several years before the Napoleonic Wars, and in several subsequent wars all aimed to balkanize Russia and steal its vast minerals, gas and oil riches. The same usual suspects, meaning the International Central Banking banksters, were at their old bloody game during the last two World Wars, where they financed all the parties involved, even the Nazi's awesome military war machine, with the hidden goal to considerably weaken and dismantle Russia.

It was no accident that in the aftermath of the decisive, historic battle of Stalingrad, when the mighty German Army's back was irreversibly broken by the Red Army, one Russian General sadly noted that the Western alliance, supposedly an allied of his country against Hitler's genocidal war, would never forgive Russia for its Stalingrad's victory. His comment could not be any more accurate as Hitler's war against Russia was, in its time, the first global proxy war of its kind orchestrated, manipulated and financed by both the City of London and Wall Street, aiming at solving once and for all the Russian dilemma, meaning its complete dismantling, followed by its subsequent balkanization.

The same tragic proxy war scenario is being repeated today some three-quarter-century later by Zelenskyy's Ukraine, again backed entirely by the collective West, the same usual suspects. And if we were to believe some Independent War reports coming from Ukraine's battlefield, Russian forces, just like their ancestral peers, were gaining the upper hand in their special operation to force and impose a permanent security buffer zone against NATO's proxy war in Ukraine to establish a strategic nuclear primacy over Russia. This proxy war in Ukraine is a desperate act for NATO's abysmal failure to build hypersonic weapons, or any counter-responses to them, with the hope to place enough of their nukes on Ukraine's border with Russia, just a 3-minute flight to Moscow. All in accordance with a US scheme of a preemptive nuclear first strike to decapitate the Russian State and neutralize any possible retaliatory response.

Historically, the colonial powers of Europe had been quite successful in their inter-capitalist wars of World War 1 and 2 to get most of the global south, Africa included, on their side. Consequently, several African nations, which had been struggling for centuries to liberate themselves from centuries-old clutches of French, British and US Imperialism, were offered independence in exchange for their war supplies, raw materials and cannon fodders. But History showed us what happened in the aftermath of the last World War. Many of the so-called independent African countries were free on paper only, as their economies and their abilities to print their own monies were still in the hands of their former white European masters.

The Soviet Union back then was the only country that had tried to help the African continent to truly liberate itself from its long struggle for political and economic freedom from Europe, while the neocolonialist West, through the French DGSE, British MI6 and the CIA, went on a bloody war path to subvert Africa's decolonization struggles, denying all the promises made by the major Allied countries. Several authentic African nationalist leaders, the likes of Patrice Lumumba of Congo, Thomas Sankara of Burkina Faso, and Eduardo Mondlane of Mozambique, to name just a few, who refused to compromise or negotiate down their countries' independence, were simply assassinated.

Now with the current momentum build of a growing multipolar world, Africa had a real chance to make their long overdue dreams of independence and sovereignty become a reality, especially with the help of both Russia and China. For the first time in a long time, the French were being shown the doors in many of their prized African possessions with the help of Russia's mercenary Wagner Group. Wasn't it the late French president Charles de

Gaulle himself, who once stated that France would not have been France without Africa. Jacques Chirac went even further in the following quote, attributed to him, "We bled Africa for four and a half centuries. We looted their raw materials, then we told lies that Africans are good for nothing". In 2008, he made an even more somber remark about France's huge economic co-dependency on Africa's vast mineral reserves when he said, "Without Africa, France will slide down into the rank of a third-world power."

In 2023 with the unstoppable decolonization trend of the African continent, it's becoming clearer that the lights in Paris' Champs Elysée will soon be looking dimmer and eventually plagued by periodic blackouts like in Niger. In addition, Western powers' declining influence could be seen in their failure to rally Africa and many nations from the global South to side with them in their unilateral sanctions against Russia. Instead, many chose to remain neutral, while some brazenly supported Russia, and over 40 of them expressed their dying wishes to join BRICS' effective economic development plans and alternative to Western's World Bank and IMF development scheme of indebtedness, underdevelopment, starvation, wars and genocide. The irony behind the ugly face of neo-colonial, imperialist exploitation of Africa was there for anyone to see in the current situation in Niger, where the nation's iridium had been looted by France for decades to maintain Paris' city of lights eternal image. Meanwhile, many cities in Niger were still living in the dark at night or live in systemic blackout.

The collective white West, using the same old racist cliché in their cynical, heartless exploitation of the resources-rich black continent, was arrogantly blaming the entire region for its dismal poverty as if Africa alone is at fault for impoverishing itself without ever mentioning the Global North's centuries-old rapacious exploitation and plunder of its riches. The resourceless West never had the luxury of Russia's vast natural wealth to even think of engaging in any conceivable win-win economic exchange with the Global South. Instead, they had ensured that the imposed win-lose economic scheme between the North and the South remained unchanged at all costs to guarantee the West's economic survival.

International Mainstream Media, a mouthpiece of Western propaganda and disinformation, had lately been in a desperate frenzy, warning Africa and the rest of the Global South countries against Russia and China's alleged predatory capitalism by urging them not to join China's Road and Belt Initiative. Speaking of historical and psychological projections, there's not one shred of historical trace of Chinese and Russian colonialism on the Global scale of Spain, Belgium, France, Italy, Germany, Portugal, the Netherlands, America and the chief among them, England.

Panic obviously reigned supreme following the latest BRICS historic gathering in South Africa, where six additional countries,

Miami, Florida: A Sunshine State's Unauthorized And Unredacted
Journey

Saudi Arabia, Iran, Argentina, Egypt, Ethiopia and the UAE, officially became new members. Saudi Arabia's membership alone might, in the long run, undermine the Petrodollars' worldwide dominance, which had given the US a long and unfair economic advantage over any near-peer competitors. Added to that was US' unilateral use of economic sanctions and indiscriminate extra-jurisdictional decisions taken against any country not in lockstep with their worldwide economic warfare agenda. Thus, BRICS' top goal is to find a long overdue alternative to the US petrodollars imperial scheme sooner rather than later.

The advent of the internet and the proliferation of free and independent media would one day be credited for the rising current global awareness of who the world's true owners and masters are, as George Orwell's 1984 dystopian Ministry of Truth's three main slogans: "War is Peace, Freedom is Slavery, and Ignorance is Strength" seemed to have lost some of its perfidious charms and appeals over the world's credulous masses. Since an increasing number of people from both the Global North and the Global South have been getting some eye-opening informations on the handful of people who made life-and-death decisions in their names every day. Here at home, millions of truth seekers Americans were now in the loop that the three main branches of the US government, the Executive, the Legislative, and the Judicial, were corrupt, compromised institutions bought and paid for by big money and, hence, would not answer to the tax paying public, responsible for their paychecks, but to the shadowy Deep State, unelected government who owned them. They also understood that their votes had been inconsequential. For regardless of how and for whom they voted, their votes had yet to make any fundamental changes in Washington or stop the downward spiral the country had been fallen into. No candidates seemed to be capable of delivering on any of their campaign promises. And to add insult to injury, there were many critical economic decisions with disastrous, criminal consequences to the welfare of the general American public taken by the elites with no fear of any repercussion from voters' backlash or getting indicted, prosecuted and thrown in prison if found guilty.

The notable widespread political apathy from millions of well-informed Americans came from them knowing that their so-called Democracy and well-propagandized freedom were everything but a big nothing burger, as US voters had no recollection when NAFTA [The North American Free Trade Agreement] was ever put on a ballot for them to vote on it. They also had no recollection either that they were ever asked by their representatives for their consenting votes to send over untold numbers of billions of their tax money to finance NATO's losing proxy war in Ukraine.

Accountability is the least concern of the US financial and ruling elite, as they had morphed into full-fledged corporate fascism on steroids since the 70s when they froze the wages of American workers and shifted the entire tax burden away from US Corporations to America's working class. Unaccountability at the Pentagon is a joke in their contemptuous price gouging on everything and the billion-dollar fiasco of their high-tech weaponry like the high-maintenance F-35 planes, which have yet to show how battle-ready and mission-capable they are. Big banks, oils and Big Pharma's entrenched corporate fascism had been around for decades, but during and after the fake pandemic instigated by them, they literally went berserk. Thanks to America's Corporate fascism going rogue with no checks and balances, the US is looking more and more like a big banana republic with a pile high of accumulated debt and fallen infrastructures. Its once powerful military which has frightened many non-compliant nations to submit to America's reinforcement of the international financial hegemon as the World's Police seemed to have lost its big stick effect. Just the actual continuing showdown in the Red Sea water opposing the Houthi rebels in Yemen and the mighty American fleet is a case in point.

The latest report card coming from Ukraine's war front had not shown the Pentagon's highly over-priced military arsenal in any state-of-the-art performance over that of its Russian counterparts. Instead, the emperor once again was shown to have no clothes on. It may be a good thing that America's own 'comprador' elite, like Haiti's, are both nervously bracing for a time of serious awakening where they will have to finally answer and pay for their crimes of complicity, corruption and misappropriation of their nations' finances, treasury and the countless suffering imposed on their respective population. It's also a critical time for a peaceful transition to avoid a full-scale nuclear annihilation with no winners. A multipolar world with its enlightened message and promise to lift and free every nation on earth from the Global Money Empire's long neocolonialist, imperialist and fascist wars against humanity, which in no doubt will benefit Haiti and America's poor.

Fast rewinding to where I left off, it had taken me a while before I could see my day-to-day life back at its regular routine space following Teressa and Tony's epic ordeal. I spent lots of quality time with my past old friends, especially with Nènè and Rosy, old childhood buddies that I grew up with in Martissant. Through them, I was put in contact with Rosy's younger brother, Maurice Junior Manigat, a.k.a. Toutou. I have not seen or heard of him for nearly twelve years, and it was refreshing to renew ties with my old childhood friend over the phone. He was still living in Los Angeles and had a wife and three children. I always wanted to visit L.A., so I scheduled a trip to go spend a week there.

Toutou, to my greatest amazement, picked me up from the Los Angeles International Airport in his 1930s convertible Mercedes-Benz that he himself had built from scratch. He was the nephew of one of Haiti's greatest intellectuals, scholars and geopolitologues, Professor Leslie F. Manigat. He never came close to having his uncle's gift. Instead, he had a technical brain, a penchant for handy works and mechanical stuff. So, I was the least skeptical when he proudly told me, upon leaving the L.A. terminal on the way to his house, that this beauty that I was riding on was his own creation. My visit with Toutou was beyond incredible. We reminisced a tone on several of our early teenage adventures, like the time when we rented a small canoe, trying to paddle our way to the islet across his family home without our parents knowing. We talked about Ciné Senegal's awesome matinee showing and the Sunday morning gathering on the outside stairs of St. Bernadette's Catholic Church, with the main intent to impress the neighborhood's girls attending masses. We could not reminisce about Martissant's beautiful girls at the time without mentioning the prettiest of them all, the most charming one: our Carole.

For those readers who have not read my second book memoir, Carole was the girl who lived next to Toutou's house and with whom I experienced the puppy love of the decade. I was somewhat unhinged with Carole's memory, even though I managed as much as I could over the years to keep it well concealed in my memory's remote oubliette. I nevertheless relived the devastating heartbreak I struggled with for months when her family relocated to Paco, putting an abrupt end to what I believed back then was true love. I was even more devastated when, two years later, I learned through the grapevine that she had married her first husband, a

Columbian, whom she met on a visit to New York.

I received some fresh updated news about her. First, she divorced some years later her first husband after giving birth to two little girls. Then, she remarried another Colombian with whom she had her third child, a little boy. The most surprising of all the updates on Carole was when he told me that she, with her new Columbian husband and their three children, was living somewhere in North Miami Beach.

My friend Toutou took an entire week off from work to take me to as many breathtaking places while I was in L.A. visiting. We went to Malibu and Santa Monica's fabulous beaches, to Downtown Los Angeles, the Arts District and to Hollywood Boulevard's Walk of Fame, where I was in awe with the most people-watching crowd ever. I could not help feeling like a celebrity myself while riding in Toutou's 1930s vintage Mercedes Benz. He also took me to the closest road below the famous hillside to take a picture of the huge HOLLYWOOD sign perched on it. Then we drove around into the upscale residential areas of West Hollywood and Beverly Hills, where all the celebrities lived in their multi-million-dollar mansions. We hit Hollywood's well-known and unmatched nightlife anywhere in the States, bar hoping to some of its trendy hotspots. But I was not as lucky as others did, spotting any celebs known to come down to party their hearts out in Hollywood's bar scenes.

## Miami, Florida: A Sunshine State's Unauthorized And Unredacted Journey

The best treat I had during my week stay in LA was when I purchased the last two remaining tickets for Toutou and me to attend a show with the legendary Herb Alpert's reuniting concert with its Tijuana Brass Musical band at the historic LA Greek Theater. What a treat for me that was to be in LA for that one-in-a-lifetime concert venue. I was an all-time fan of Herb Albert's various musical genres and his towering collection of hit albums! I arrived at the Greek Theater just in time for a delicious heart-stopping moment when the celeb American trumpeter opened the evening show with his one-of-a-kind instrumental piece, 'The Lonely Bull'. The heavenly-like sound coming out of his trumpet sent a shiver of excitement and delight down my spine. And it was just the start of a startling performance of Herb Alpert and the Tijuana Brass' towering repertoire of hit tunes throughout the evening at L.A.'s open-air Greek Theater.

There could not have been a much spectacular way to end my weeklong visit to Los Angeles. My return flight to Miami was scheduled for the next day. I promised myself not to make it my last trip to the city of flowers, also nicknamed The Entertainment Capital of the World. One major US city's name scratched off my list and many more big ones to follow, as I began to develop a keen taste for traveling within the States for now and later abroad.

I learned recently from a phone call with my dad, living in Waukegan, that my younger sister Marie Marcelle, who had joined the US Army a year earlier, had been transferred to Frankfurt, Germany. I remember how profoundly disturbed and upset I was when my brother Willy told me that our sister, Marcelle, had joined the US Army. I was profoundly disturbed by that news. My sister, in my mind, has just put herself on Uncle Sam's disposable list of cannon fodders for his raging, nonstop planetarian war of hegemony. The news of my sweet, darling sister Marcelle joining the US military was the worst one that I received in a long time. The idea of my sister being used by the American Empire as a mere disposable body to feed off the US war machine was beyond me. Especially considering the geopolitical knowledge I have now about America's involvement in hot, cold and proxy wars for the greater part of its 200 years of history. Many of those wars could have been avoided, as they had no real security concerns for America, a nation protected by two major oceans, the Atlantic and the Pacific.

Besides, the bulk of America's hot, cold and proxy wars occurred thousands of miles away from its territorial borders and waters, logistically forcing America to pay a heavier toll in blood, logistics, and treasure. In the end, the only winners in all our misguided wars were the merchants of death and the banksters behind them, financing the US forever war machine. In the long run, America found itself in 30-plus trillions of dollars in debt for generations of Americans to repay later.

Hence, in my antiwar philosophy, joining the Army, in my

sister's case, was a non-starter when I first learned about her decision. Due to Marcelle's exceptional intelligence and her Ivy League educational background, soldiering should not have even been contemplated by her, to begin with, let alone as an optional choice for her. I knew from my brother Willy's own insider account that Marcelle never got along too well with my dad's second wife, Ronnie. They fought and argued constantly with each other. Could joining the US Military was for Marcelle a much lesser evil choice than living with her dad's second wife, Ronnie? Because of her multi-language ability to speak four languages and started to learn German, my sister, a go getter, chose an open opportunity to serve abroad in Frankfurt, Germany. Her vertiginous rise in upward mobility within the rank and file was nothing less than spectacular. In less than two years since she transferred to Frankfurt, my sister was able to move out of her military barracks' living conditions to an enviable chic suburban apartment. That was the time I reached out to her, and together, we arranged a trip to visit her at her suburban Frankfurt home. She also planned to take a few days off from work and booked in advance a ten-day Tour package that would take us to Austria, Switzerland, Lloret de Mar – A charming coastal town in Spain near Barcelona - and finally Paris, France. I was looking forward to my first Transatlantic crossing trip to Frankfurt, Germany. I have not seen my little adorable sis for quite a few years now since she and Willy were the first two of the siblings to join my dad in Waukegan, Illinois, one month before I migrated to Miami. So, I had many reasons to get excited by such prospects to visit four European cities, including Paris, besides spending quality time with my sister. Marcelle and I were very close and had a special sibling bond.

I flew off Miami International Airport for a seven to eight-hour flight to Frankfurt's International Airport, where I was picked up by my sister. I could not believe my eyes when the tiny little sis I remember not too long ago showed up to pick me up at the terminal. She was much taller and leanly muscled, and wearing her medals military uniform did not ease much my confusion. She was a highly decorated Sergeant at the time. She made a stop at the Military Base where she worked to get some documents. I was very impressed to notice the many salutes she was getting from lower-ranked soldiers on her way to her office. One thing was for sure: the little sis image I remember of her was way outgrown by her new assertive sergeant image of a careered military person.

We later drove to her place, a fifteen-minute ride on the Autobahn high-speed freeway to arrive at Marcelle's residential apartment. It was a newly built complex, chic and charming, and I had to admit that she was undeniably living in style and doing way better than any of her other siblings, including me. Part of Marcelle's brilliance was her keen knowledge of how to access and use many of the Army's elusive perks, services and benefits. Her kind was not made to vegetate at the bottom of any hierarchical structure, be it at the Army or anywhere else for that matter. Her joining the US Army was not as horrible as I previously thought, despite my early biased reaction to the idea. She seemed to find her niche there and looked happy and fulfilled.

I was particularly relieved and happy when she told me that my mother was going to start receiving a $400 Army check starting next month as part of her family's perk. Document papers were submitted for her to receive her residential green card. I welcome wholeheartedly Marcelle's financial maneuvering to help the rest of the family still left behind in Haiti. In my case, I could not find any papers for any member of my family until I became a US citizen myself. But with Marcelle's military status, she was able to bypass this civilian five-year wait time imposed by the US Immigration rule. For sure, the monthly Army remittance going to my family back home was quite a relief of sorts for me, as I was the only reliable source of income to them since my father only sent them money sporadically.

Two days later Marcelle and I were comfortably sitting in our assigned coach's seats to start off our 10-day long tour. I would never in my entire life forget that early morning rise when we arrived at Salsburg's countryside. It was so breathtakingly beautiful that I had to pinch myself to make sure that I was not dreaming of any of what I was seeing. On one side of the coach, perched on a luxurious hill, was a stand-alone Castle. On the other side of the coach's high and wide windows was a string of several cute little country homes that seemed to mysteriously appear from behind the fading early morning brume. It was one surreal panoramic country scene that normally belonged in movies, paintings or books.

What an unforgettable introduction to Austria's breathtaking landscapes, which was just the start of several more spectacular sightseeing, appearing and disappearing one after the other throughout our coach ride. Each new panoramic scene is more magical and unreal than the last. We spent one and a half days in Austria and moved next to Switzerland. The latter was equally blessed by mother nature, like Austria next door, with the same vast greenish, luxurious landscapes sprinkled with lakes, rivers, prairies, mounts and valleys. The sceneries of all types of various fields of purple, blue, pink, and red roses and flowers were simply beyond contemplation. Large sun flowers' fields were everywhere in endless display for the eyes of the riding visitors to be startled with. That unique, incredible love affair between nature, the lands, and its inhabitants was on spectacular display in the countryside of both Austria and Switzerland, for the eyes to see and admire. Coming from Haiti, a country which had over the years turned into a godforsaken place, battered by both humans and natural disasters such as floods, droughts, hurricanes, and earthquakes, I could not help reflecting on how fundamentally unfair Dame nature could be,

and that grace, charm, and beauty were not evenly distributed among
all living things.

Marcelle was a little tense at the beginning of the trip, but
with the passing hours, she began to let her hair down a bit. She did
not have to worry about the rigid military protocol, as she was miles
away from the military base, where she was constantly interacting
with superior officers and lower-status soldiers. She appeared that
she really needed this break to recharge her depleted batteries. I had
no doubt that she was under lots of pressure to perform, not simply
as a woman but also as a black Haitian woman. The Army was no
place for a fainthearted person.

After spending two days in Switzerland, we made it to
Barcelona by mid-day, and because it would take another one and a
half hours to arrive at Lloret de Mar, our next destination, Helen,
our German tour guide, decided to give us one unscheduled hour to
shop and have lunch on our own. Barcelona was a booming
international city with one of Europe's largest ports full of people
from all over the planet. Its miles-long pedestrian Street, known as
The Ramblas, began in the vicinity of the port area to stretch all the
way to Plaza Catalogne.

There at La Ramblas, one of Europe's longest pedestrian
streets, was a sea of humanity where all the converging actions were.
Street performers, clowns, and musicians were everywhere along

the strip doing their daily tricks. Marcelle and I were not hungry and were in no shopping mood either, so we decided that the best way to spend the hour was to chill and relax by hanging out right here amid that huge crowd of tourists and locals. We had never laughed so hard at the various entertainers who were teasing many unsuspected visitors and passersby by playing all kinds of jokes and innuendos around and behind their back. It was very hard for Marcelle and me to leave the pedestrian Street to return to the Barcelona port where our meeting rendezvous was.

Our tour guide, Helen, was already there waiting near the bus entrance, doing the passengers' headcount, making sure that everyone was accounted for. Apparently, four people from our group were still missing and running behind. They were the usual suspects, always making the whole thirty-five of us wait for them. They finally made it to the coach with everyone inside the bus clapping as they entered. It was a cool way to make them feel embarrassed for being late. They seemed to enjoy the attention they were getting from being fashionably late most of the time. Helen was happy that they were late for only ten minutes this time, as opposed to the last time when the group had to wait for nearly twenty minutes for them to return. Our driver, Maurice, was an interesting, excellent, driver with a German accent when speaking English to us with a great sense of humor. He started the bus's huge horsepower engine, and off we were once again on the road and on our way to

Lloret de Mar, where we were scheduled to stay for two nights.

We arrived there on a late Monday afternoon, at what appeared to be the peak of the tourist season, and what a scene that was for a Monday! This old Medieval coastal town not too far from Barcelona was a zoo packed with thousands and thousands of young vacationers from all over Europe and elsewhere. We checked into our hotel, where the group would be staying for two nights. From my hotel room window, I had quite a wide view of the Mediterranean Sea and Lloret de Mar's overcrowded beaches, with a multitude of sun worshippers' bodies spreading for miles on its beautiful white sands. To my left on the east side, there was the famed medieval Castle of Saint Joan built on a hilltop.

After we were done settling down all our belongings, Marcelle and I went looking for a place to eat, and that was when we finally realized that we were amid the number one party town in the whole of Spain, if not in the entire Western World. I was convinced that my sister had chosen this tour package without knowing that Lloret de Mar at this time of the year was a modern-day version of Sodom and Gomorrah where an untold number of boys and girls came to this town with three things in mind, get wasted, laid, and party to no end. A mostly young teenage crowd and with over one hundred bars, restaurants, clubs and discotheques open 24/7, it was not the ideal spot for some relaxing vacation days at the beach and in the sun.

179

I thought I was a fierce party animal with my routine weekend nightlife partying at the Grove until I arrived here. This place, where thousands of people partied all day and all night, made me feel so amateurish. Before going to bed early the first night, as we had a load of activities and places to visit the next day, we went for a brief bar hopping to check out Lloret de Mar's wild nightlife party scene. Every club we visited was jam-packed with wild, drunken young partyers doing many crazy, outrageous things that would make our American Spring breakers at their Orlando or Acapulco bars' beach parties look dull in comparison. Our first night's sleep was anything but restful, as it was being interrupted several times by rowdy, drunken kids on the beach and in the streets around our hotel. It was our brutal introduction to Lloret de Mar, the party town known for its sleeplessness. The following morning, on our way to our group breakfast, there were still a few ongoing beach parties filled with patrons who would not quit until they dropped. Hence reinforcing once more the international image of Lloret de Mar as "the holiday destination that never sleeps."

Our tour guide, Helen, took us to the medieval hilltop Castle, where I had an amazing aerial view of the place. Next, she took us on a tour of the charming central Iglesia de Sant Romà Church and the Santa Clotilde Gardens, which offered another pleasant view of Costa Brava's gorgeous Mediterranean beaches, as the latter was built on a cliff at the edge of the sea. I could never seem to have enough of the drop-dead gorgeous-looking crowd gracing the narrow, cobblestone streets of Lloret de Mar. I could easily see myself making this place de facto my next adopted town, like several Americans, Danes, and Russians had done just that when they first landed here. From the brief exchanges I had with some residents' expats who relived the impact this place had made on them when they first arrived here some years back. According to some, Lloret de Mar had such a transformational effect on them that they never once considered returning to their homeland. If only I had the courage to walk away from everything the way they did, to never look back. But absent of such courage, I promised myself to return one day to this breathtaking coastal town in the Catalonia region for a longer stay to explore its charm, beauty and vibrant culture.

The sole consolation I had while waving adieu to Lloret de Mar while sitting in my comfortable coach's seat, was that Paris, the final city to visit in our 10-day tour package, was next. And I knew for certain that there was not one person on earth who had read, seen movies, and pictures about the city of lights who would not have wished to be in my lucky shoes. Millions of people the world over had entertained the desire to one day make their dream voyage to Paris an exciting reality. I was no exception to such anticipatory excitement, as I was only a few hours away from the city of lights.

After a few bathroom stops and a group lunch on the road,

we finally made it to Paris in the late afternoon. Our tour guide, Helen, checked everyone in for our expected three-night hotel stay. We had quite a busy schedule ahead of us and many must-see landmark places to visit in Paris, such as the Arc of Triumph on Champs-Élysées, the Louvre Museum, a Seine River Cruise, the Eiffel Tower and the Versailles Palace. We started our first bus tour ride to the center of Paris' unique, majestic architectural buildings. We drove along the famed Seine River and by many historical buildings and landmarks within the city-center while Helen, our knowledgeable tour guide, was giving us much needed information and the history behind each site.

We made our first group stop at the Arc of Triumph and after touring it, we were given an hour to explore one of the world's most famous avenues stretching to nearly one and a quarter mile from the Arc to the Place de la Concorde. The latter was the largest square in the French capital, which was once the site of bloody public executions during the 1789 French Revolution. It was briefly renamed Place de la Révolution for having been the location during France's Reign of Terror, to witness many notable heads going under the guillotine blade, including those of King Louis XVI, Marie Antoinette, and Robespierre. Saying that I was impressed by "La Ville-Lumière" [The City of Light] could be one major understatement. From the moment I first saw Paris, my fascination with the city's vibe, charms, and beauties was immediate and beyond the realm of my wildest imagination.

My sister Marcelle, who had visited Paris on two occasions before since her transfer to Frankfurt, was still impressed by the city, though not at the goo-goo gaga state that I found myself in. We strolled leisurely on Champs-Élysée's broad and endless sidewalks on both sides of the avenue for a magnificent "Bain de Foule", and exciting crowd's shower. It was, indeed, the most fashionable, vibrant and attractive crowd of shoppers, visitors and locals for the ultimate people watch.

Here were numerous outdoor cafes, bars, restaurants, and high-end stores and chic boutiques all along the miles-long stretch. Sis and I sat at one of the outdoor cafés for some French wine and to toast to the occasion. Leaving the café where we were sitting to go back to the assigned meeting spot with our tour guide, was an even bigger struggle this time. Now I completely understood why our famous two couples always late on their way back to the bus. So many things to see and to do, and in so little time. Helen advised the group to go to bed early, as we had a full day of activities to cover the following day.

We started off early the next day, soon after breakfast. We went first to the famed Louvre Museum, where the Italian painter Leonardo da Vinci's original Mona Lisa portrait was exposed. We had an excellent guide, a middle-aged lady who showed us around the Denon, Richelieu, and Sully wings. When we finally made it to room 6 in the Denon section, da Vinci's famous portrait had everyone falling under the spell of her mystic smile. However, being a student of history, I was not only impressed with thousands of Artworks and pieces of sculptures on display within the Louvre Museum's walls but I was also captivated by the long history behind what was originally built as a fortress in the 12$^{th}$ Century. It became later a Royal Residence for several of the French kings, all the way to Louis XIII. If only the Museum's walls could speak, they would have talked about many stories of betrayals and plots of all sorts.

Alexandre Dumas, whose father, Thomas Alexandre Dumas, born in Saint Domingue [Modern day Haiti], as the son of a French nobleman and an enslaved Haitian black woman, had written and published several historical fiction novels to give us some historical insights on what was really going on behind the Royal Court of France's palaces. He wrote extensively on political machinations and intrigues and the shadowy power behind the throne in the palaces, including The Louvre. In his three most popular novels, The Three Musketeers, Count of Monte Cristo and Queen Margot, the gifted novelist revealed a frightening portrait of what France was like during the late 16$^{th}$ Century.

Again, I wondered what if the Louvre Museum's walls could suddenly speak, what more could they have revealed to us about the sham, arranged marriage of Henry de Navarre with the

nymphomaniac Princess Margot. What other unknown secrets that
Dumas might have not been aware of about Margot's wild,
rampaged acts of adultery, incest and sexual promiscuities with
various sex partners, including her own blood brothers? What would
they have added about the murderous conspiracy being plotted
within those walls preceding the bloody day of St. Barthelemy's
infamous massacre in Paris late 16th Century's religious civil war
opposing Catholics and Protestants?

We moved on to our next scheduled stop at the iconic Eiffel
Tower. The line was discouragingly long, but we saved some
precious time as our tickets were reserved by Helen ahead of time.
We, at once, made it to the narrow platform at the top of the massive
iron structure to have one astonishing view of Paris' Champs de
Mars and beyond. The Eiffel Tower, built by Gustave Eiffel of the
same name, was not his only chef-d'oeuvre. He was also the
architect behind the metallic structure of the Statue of Liberty in
New York's Liberty Island, reportedly a gift from the people of
France to the Americans.

The early afternoon found us near the Seine River lining up
for our most anticipated boat ride, where we had another panoramic,
spectacular view of Paris' Musée d'Orsay, the Notre Dame Church,
the Louvre and the massive, metallic Tower while cruising on one
of the most famously known bodies of water in the world. After our
boat tour, we were given the rest of the evening to explore more of

Paris on our own. A young American couple from our group tour joined me and Marcelle for our evening exploration of the city of love. We went to the Luxembourg Gardens, Paris' answer to NY's Central Park; then we headed toward the French Quarter located nearby for a bite to eat. On our way there, we briefly visited Sorbonne, Paris' most Ivy League university, where many known Haitian scholars obtained their doctoral degrees. Though we wanted to spend a little more time at the vibrant, exciting French Quarter, we had to keep on moving as we wanted to cover as many sites as possible during our brief stay. We then purchased subway tickets to make it to Montmartre's large hill located in Paris' 18th arrondissement. It was a place worth seeing for many reasons, first because of its high elevation, which afforded anyone an unforgettable aerial view of Paris. Next, Montmartre was famously known for its white-domed Basilica of the Sacred Heart Church and its vibrant nightlife, where numerous musicians and artists were displaying their trade. From our 130-meter-high elevation, we could easily observe why Paris earned Fair and Square its City of Lights nickname.

And what a surprising discovery when we finally made it all the way up to the plateau top. We ran into a cozy, romantic ambiance up there, a hidden, surreal atmosphere with many of its outdoor cafes, bars and restaurants full of people having dinners while being serenaded by a violinist on one side of the square and an accordionist on the other. The various fashion displays of patrons and performers, some even wearing Period clothing and costumes, appeared to have suddenly chosen to walk away from several of Pierre-August Renoir's impressionist paintings. We found the perfect sidewalk café conveniently located for a maximum people-watching treat. We immersed ourselves in that suave Montmartre's evening while slowly sipping our French wine. The following day was unfortunately, our last in Paris. The plan was to spend it at the magnificent Palace of Versailles.

Located about a dozen miles west of Paris, we arrived at the Golden Castle by midday, and it was already a zoo with hundreds of thousands of people gathering all over the vast outdoor space near and around the Golden Palace. I was again left dumbfounded by our tour of Versailles, by its vast, rich display of gold ornaments and sumptuous, elegant architecture. The incalculable amount of wealth being displayed inside and outside of Versailles was mind-boggling to the average person, myself included. Its well-manicured outdoor gardens spread as far as one could see were covered with various colors of tulips, roses and low flower beds. Nothing was spared by the outside Versailles' Garden handlers to startle the visitors' eyes from fountains to large lakes and small streams.

Versailles Palace, which was originally built by Louis XIII as a hunting pavilion, was later vastly extended by Louis XIV, and in so doing, he had turned his father's tiny, little castle into what it had become under his reign, a symbol of wealth, power, arts and culture in the most vaunted century of Enlightenment. And as someone rightly noted, "By the late 17ᵗʰ Century, Versailles' majestic architecture was inseparable from the memory of the Sun King, Louis XIV". It had since been the principal residence of all the French kings from Louis XIV to Louis XVI.

In fact, "it was at Versailles that on October 6, 1789, an angry mob came to carry off Louis XVI and Marie-Antoinette from the seat of power", observed a historian. My student-of-history wondering mind again ran into some hard-to-swallow issues amid all these extravagant displays of wealth, precious stones, gold ornaments and magnificent interior decorations! Knowing fully well that Louis XIV was an unapologetic racist and a diehard esclavagist. And that under his so-called reign of enlightenment, Goldberg, following his dictate, enacted the infamous Code Noir, legalizing the subhuman treatment of black African slaves throughout the French colonial empire. Louis XIV had established the legal justification for France's next generations of rulers' genocidal wars against any of their rebellious colonies, from Napoleon Bonaparte's extermination war in Haiti to Charles de Gaulle's war crimes in Algeria.

I could not help pondering in my mind on the river of blood, sweat and tears, the sufferings, and looted, stolen treasures extracted from my enslaved Haitian ancestor and of all the French colonies in

Miami, Florida: A Sunshine State's Unauthorized And Unredacted Journey

Africa by the Sun king to build his 17<sup>th</sup> Century Versailles Palace. It took me a while before I allowed this somber historical reality check to subside in me and resume my otherwise fabulous outing at the Versailles Golden Palace, undeniably one of the most memorable highlights for me the first time I visited and saw Paris. We returned to our hotel at the end of the day, all exhausted, and following our last dinner with the group, we went straight to bed. We were scheduled to hit the road in the early morning hours after breakfast for our long return ride to Frankfurt, Germany. I made it back home two days after returning to Frankfurt. This first European trip, if anything, had awakened in me that undying urge to travel the world, explore and visit as many countries as possible. I discovered a few years back by migrating to Florida that the center of the world was not Port-au-Prince, and now, after my recent tour of some marvelous places in Europe, I was also made aware that the center of the world was not the US either.

Realistically speaking, I did not have the courage of the expats I met in Lloret de Mar, as such a risqué option was simply beyond my range of action. I remember how challengingly painful my early years in Miami were. Now that I seemed to come a long way to start building a decent livelihood for myself here, I was not in such a hurry to begin a whole new life from scratch in another part of the world. I could still visit many of those places, while at the same time keeping Miami my base. That was exactly what I

189

intended to do in the future. Whenever the opportunity for me to travel and visit a new place, I would jump to the occasion and make it happen. For the moment I was just pleased to make it back home in Miami, as it was the longest time I had stayed away from home for this long. I sort of missed my unassuming, frugal bachelor's lifestyle, and I could not wait to resume it where I left off.

I came back at the perfect time to start a new course at FIU's Undergraduate Sociology program with Dr. Alex Stepick. He was a professor of Anthropology and Sociology there and was doing research study on the impact of immigration on Miami. I established quite a rapport with him. I was involved in one Dr. Stepick's comprehensive study of the economic impact of Little Haiti's newly emerging informal market on Miami's larger, formal economy.

I found myself walking the 54th Street stretch, in my old neighborhood where I lived once, to survey what was a rising trend of Haitian businesses, formal and informal. The 54th Street strip, starting from Northwest Second Avenue all the way to Northeast 5th Avenue, was where most of Little Haiti's economic activities were centered. And especially Little Haiti's informal trades' underground activities, which were, in essence, a similar replica of the homeland's old ways of exchanging goods and services. My survey was a lot easier, logistically speaking, as all the economic activities were occurring within the stretch. Besides getting a good grade for my survey field in Dr. Alex Stepick's project, my name was also published in the survey's publication for my contribution.

However, the best perk of working in the research study came unexpectedly when one of the class female students, Mariana, signed up to work with me on the Little Haiti survey project, too, for some extra bonus points. Mariana was undeniably the most attractive female student in the class.

She was a third-generation Cuban immigrant. Born here from a wealthy Cuban family, she looked more German-European than the typical expected Hispanic look. Her grandparents were part of the first wave of wealthy Cubans who fled Cuba on the eve of the Cuban Revolution. They brought with them their own money and enterprising knowledge to continue building wealth here. She was her parents' only daughter, turning her into the stereotypical Cuban princess. At first, I was a little standoffish when she proposed to join me in Little Haiti for my next on-site survey. It was a good thing that I accepted, as she was not a snub. We had some great work done at our first surveying field activity. I treated her afterwards to dinner at the very first Haitian sit-down restaurant which had just opened its door on the 54th Street stretch. I was impressed by how comfortable she acted while being there, even though the atmosphere was not as fancy for her kind. She adored the Haitian 'griyo' [fried pork] with its hot spicy pikliz, the fried plantains and the rice and beans. Following that, we became the best of friends.

191

She invited me to her Little Havana family home to study and work on our term papers together. That was when my early suspicion that she came from wealthy parents was confirmed, and the mansion estate where she lived spoke volumes in attesting to that. She introduced me to her parents, who were very engaging and friendly. Her Dad was a big-time Real Estate investor, where he undoubtedly made his money, while her mother was a socialite and a community activist, deeply involved in Miami's overheated Cuban politics. Mariana's last name would not be revealed here out of consideration for her privacy. We ended up in a sort of undeclared informal dating, for we always found an excuse to meet somewhere after class.

She was the one who took me to my first Le Glacier experience, a French restaurant off Coral Way in the Gables, which was a very fine and excellent place for dining. She also took me to my first Art Deco Weekend in the South Beach area, an Art Festival that started three years ago, showcasing not just art and crafts but also the beautiful Art Deco Historic District comprising of over 800 buildings and structures built from the early 1920s to the mid-40s. This yearly festival celebration was one of the early signs indicating what was in the making and the soon-to-come swift transformation of South Beach's old retirees' dull image into one of vibrant, youth-gathering, world-class holiday destination and entertainment that it had become in the late 1980s and early 90s.

# Miami, Florida: A Sunshine State's Unauthorized And Unredacted Journey

Following an evening out with her at an Art Deco Weekend event, we both ended up at my bachelor's pad. It was not her first time there, but nothing serious ever happened between us short of some light making out and timid kisses. She was the hesitating type, especially when things started heating up or were about to get out of control. I could sense that she wanted to go all the way, and yet, at the same time, something always held her back from crossing her own self-imposed redline. By principle, I was never one to push or force myself on any woman. In my book, when a girl says no, her no means no. And besides, what kind of lovemaking would that be anyway when the person you were with was not a willing participant? But this time, Mariana had never felt so comfortable and relaxed in my room compared to the last two times. As soon as she entered the sleeping quarter, she went to rest her nice, lovely lean figure on one of the two beds. I had some keen suspicion that she made up her mind that tonight was the night. Enough with all the forbidden, guilt-ridden, nonpermissive sexual taboos that had so far prevented her, twice in a row, from letting herself go all out for it on this very bed. She was so ready now that she could barely hide it. It was all over her smile, body language, and innuendoes. As always, I set up the usual romantic atmosphere to set the mood. I put Moody Blues' Nights in White Satin album on. And when that sweet, romantic song came up, Mariana wanted me to dance it with her, for the Nights in White Satin was her all-time favorite from the album. I excitedly complied with her demand. She was my height, and the passionate embrace of me initiated by her was anything but a confirmation of my earlier intuition that she was out for blood.

Our making out now was very different in comparison to the last two times, when Mariana panicked and abruptly stopped everything as I was just about to cross her Rubicon. This time around, she appeared to be much freer and much more in the mood to go all the way. When I was unzipping from the back her long, fashionable, vintage dress, revealing her lean figure, she did not stop me. I was captivated by her amazing svelte body. I helped free her nice medium-size pair of teats from their repressive bra, then sat her down on the edge of the bed and slowly removed her underwear. As things began to heat up very quickly, she again stopped everything in the middle of our steamy lovemaking, but this time not to put her clothes back but to reach out for a rubber condom from her Gucci bag. She handed it to me and, by so doing, was given me the green light to take her.

Then, I decided to slow down the pace a bit and not go immediately for the kill. I began to have her even more aroused by not rushing in too quickly into her inviting Latin treasure chess. I wanted to take her to such momentous hype that she would be the party, this time begging me to be had. I stuck to the plan by opting to give her oral sex while keeping her G spot heavenly stimulated with my devilish Haitian fingers. I slowly but precisely licked her steamy, marvelous bottom along with the rest of her hot Cubana body, whose white skin was as soft and as porcelain looking as that of dirty blonde Cindy's. My patient finally paid off when her flat belly began to display a succession of sneak-like motions. I doubled down with what I was doing on her, encouraged by the increasing moaning sounds coming out of her. She got so steamy that she could no longer wait anymore and was the one imploring me to get it on, cut through the foreplay and stick it through her already!

She was saying all that by using the two languages known to her, Spanish and English. That was certainly a new added excitement to my ears, as she was the first Hispanic woman, I ever made love to. Finally, I did the deed by entering her inviting wet treasure chess with the ultimate morning glory like erection that I could ever wake up with. I kept a steady pace by hitting her bottom part in a circular accelerated motion with my fully erected tool. She subsequently delved into a strange type of tongue-like monologue, a sort of linguistic parley where whatever she was saying was now being uttered in Spanish only. Her English seemed to temporarily be lost and frozen in time, especially when I started to increase the tempo and hitting her sideways within her vagina walls.

Watching Mariana's Latina body being devoured to its core by her vagina's involuntary contractions, a prelude of what was about to hit her, my fainted heart could not help but joining her, as we both violently climaxed together. She continued for a whole minute to scream into my ears the words "Papi Chulo" in a sobbing river of joyful tears. Yes, Mariana, the Cuban princess, was crying inconsolably in my arms. I did not know what to make of it. It was a first for me. Were they tears of joy, regret or pain, I pondered? I had seen from time to time some weird reactions from women after they orgasmed, but I never saw a girl crying so hard as if a dear friend of hers had died. I tried to console her, but she quickly reassured me that she was fine, and that was a rare behavior with her each time she reached both clitoral and vaginal climaxes simultaneously having sex with a male lover.

# The 1980s: A Transformational Decade for Everyone

Let's begin with one of Vladimir Ilyich Lenin's best historical quotes when he wrote, "There are decades where nothing happens, and there are weeks where decades happen."

I received a call from the operator telling me that there was a long-distance call placed to my phone coming from Karl-Henry Gerdes in Canada. Would I take it? I answered yes, and I recognized my brother's voice on the other line. I learned from our phone conversation that he was in Montreal, traveling with a Haitian Athletic team and that he was making a stop next week to Miami on his way back to Haiti. That was one emotional call for me. It had been several years now since I left home, and Karl-Henry, a.k.a. Carlos was eleven years old at the time. Now, he was making a stop in Miami to visit within a week. I wrote down all the information needed about his flight, and lo and behold, I picked up my little brother from the Airport on the afternoon of his arrival.

I did not recognize him at first, for he was slightly taller and bigger than me, not the short, small, skinny Carlos I had in my mind when I left home some years ago. I have not changed much in appearance, so Carlos had no difficulty pinpointing me from the group of people waiting for their friends, relatives and loved ones to exit the terminal. We greeted each other warmly. We did not have to go down into the luggage section, for he only had one carry-on luggage with him. On the way back home, I decided to make a stop at a popular Thai food restaurant on Biscayne Boulevard, a few blocks from my place, for a bite to eat with Carlos. It was my way to make him feel welcome before going back to Haiti. We spent a good hour at the restaurant reconnecting with each other after having been separated for so long. I needed to reevaluate my rapport with the now grown-up Carlos, as we were age-wise a generation apart and was no longer the little brother that I left behind.

Two shocking things happened during the time we spent at the Thai restaurant. First, Carlos told me bluntly that he, along with two others, had defected from the traveling Team in Canada, making him de facto an illegal, if not a fugitive alien in the eyes of the US Immigration. As if Carlos' latest bombshell revelation was not enough for an evening shocker, another one was about to hit me in the face when we left the restaurant. As we approached my parked old Chevy car, for I did not use my weekend's bourgeois Cadillac to pick him up at the airport, I noticed lots of broken pieces on the floor near the back driver door. I was in total panic, someone just smashed my back window, and Carlos' only luggage was gone. Not exactly what I had in mind for a welcoming celebration with Carlos. Amid all the excitement, I totally left my guard down by not securing Carlos' only belonging in my car's trunk.

It was an emergency that needed to be addressed

immediately. So, instead of going home after dinner, we went shopping to replace some of Carlos' stolen items. We made it home late that evening, and Willy, who lived across and who was expecting us to be back by now, was beginning to wonder what had happened to us! We told him about our misadventure, and despite the unpleasantness, we all agreed that things could have been much worse and that we should all be grateful that the three of us, brothers, were alive, safe, healthy and reunited. Anything else could be dealt with as long as we were in it together. I was still working at Harvey's Printing shop, and when I told him about my brother Carlos living with me, who had just arrived from Canada, Harvey's quick reply was that he had a job for him too.

I brought Carlos to my workplace the following day, and Harvey, upon seeing my brother, hired him on the spot. Carlos was very bright, smart, ambitious and, above all, a go-getter. In no time, he learned how to handle most of everything at Harvey's shop and was subsequently promoted to a responsible managerial position.

He was doing exceptionally well for a just-come. He had a nice job and a nice place where he was staying, as he was renting a nice efficiency room from my longtime friend Nènè who just purchased a 5-unit apartment building 3 blocks down from mine. Still, there was one major issue: he needed to get his legal document to avoid being deported on the spot if caught by an immigration officer. An arranged marriage was preventively suggested with

Yvonne, my friend Georges' ex and mother of his two children. Both were no longer living together, and Georges had a new woman in his life. Carlos and Yvonne got married with the understanding that it was just for one purpose only to obtain his legal paper. It was a relaxing break for Carlos, as he was worried sick about a possible encounter with an undercover Immigration agent either at the Printing Shop where he was now working or while out on the street.

Though I recently became a US citizen, I still could not by law legally file for any green card documents for my two sibling brothers, nor for my mother. Marcelle, my younger sister, who was a member of the US military, could file papers for my mother to become a US resident, but she could not file for our brothers either. The only option left to us was to work with my father to convince him to file legal documents for not only Carlos and Frantz but also for our other half-brother Gerald by using a new Immigration law. My father, who was still a bit paranoid about running into trouble with the US authorities for his own past immigration trouble, was not easily convinced by us to go ahead with our proposals. It took considerable pressure from Marcelle, Carlos and me before he could have the courage to follow through and do the right thing.

Hence, documents for legal US residency for my all three half-sibling brothers, Carlos, Frantz, and Gerald, were in less than a year filed in Miami. I knew a lady friend that I met at the Village Inn and who happened to work at a high level at the Immigration office in Miami, helped me considerably with the dos and don'ts for a quick and successful filing. Now, it was just a matter of wait and see, and above all, patience. Meanwhile, Carlos was having the time of his life. At work, he became Harvey's favorite 'adopted son'. The son that he wished he had. He could get away with practically anything with Harvey. The new studio apartment where he was staying on 28th Street off Biscayne Blvd was full of the latest electronic gadgets that were given to him by Harvey as perks for his hard work at the shop. Like I did when Willy first moved here to Miami, I introduced him to the Village Inn's Sunday afternoon Reggae ambiance. And like his two older brothers, Carlos had his own smooth ways with the ladies and had many successes.

I initially set him up for one delightful introductory with my on and off girlfriend Melodee, a Village Inn bombshell, professional belly dancer. She did not seem to mind at all the idea when I asked her for a threesome with my highly stressed younger brother, Carlos who had just arrived here. I remember taking him to Melodee's place one Saturday evening, and after spending some quality time with her first, I asked Carlos, who was watching TV in the Living Room, to come join us in the bedroom. How was that for a steamy welcoming to the Sunshine State!

Carlos, in those early days, was far from the hardcore, business-minded person he later became. He was reserved and had that charming country-like persona that made him a soft, puzzling

201

thing especially to the ladies. An example of such candid image of Carlos, was when we both were crossing US 1 at a red-light intersection; he spontaneously held my hand. I had a quick reaction to that, for Carlos was as tall as I was, and I did not want to give the wrong impression to anyone watching that we were a couple. I pulled my hand away so fast. For those who read my second book memoir, it was a routine thing when we lived in Martissant for me to take both Jean-Willy and Carlos to school every day by holding them both by their hands, especially when crossing a large busy intersection to making sure that no one got hit by a car.

What Carlos did by holding my hand that afternoon in the Grove was an involuntary regressive mental gesture of the five-year-old he once was when he held his big brother Ronald's hand to cross a busy, dangerous intersection. That was the Carlos I missed, as he was beginning to turn overnight into a different, unrecognizable creature by the unintended influence of his Jewish boss, Harvey Moldoff. My take on that was that my little brother, a light skin mulatto was so spoiled by Harvey that it had gone way over his head. The many gifts, promotions and privileges he received at the Printing shop had such nefarious effects as to disconnect him completely from who he was and where he came from. He ended up living in a bubble of petty self-aggrandizement. He started to identify himself too much with Harvey, his boss, by emulating his mannerisms and materialist/capitalist thinking. He wanted to be remade of Harvey's successful image. Not that I was against Carlos striving to be rich and successful, but not cold-bloodedly and at others' expense including his own family. He tried several times to open his own business ventures, to find out unfortunately how difficult it was for anyone and specially a Haitian to make it to the top like his white Jewish boss Harvey.

His arranged marriage with Yvonne fell apart within weeks. Being the attractive couple that they were, both might have mixed pleasure with business. Apparently, Yvonne might have wanted some sentimental perks out of the arranged marriage deal. But Carlos, who now had another option to get his green card documents through his dad, did not want to be trapped by Yvonne like his father was once by his wife, Ronnie. So, they both agreed amicably to end their marriage.

In the meantime, little brother Carlos, as part of his Jekyll and Hyde transformation, had gotten so bossy at the Printing shop that it was only a matter of time before I put him in his place by reminding him who got him there at the first place, and who had kept him fed and sheltered for all those trying years in Haiti. The spoiled, entitled ingrateful brother that he became, jumped on the first occasion he had to deny that the most needed monthly remittance checks that I was sacrificing myself to send to them in Haiti for many years did not really help much. That was one bloody redline that he crossed that day when he uttered such a snotty comment, placing him deep into my forever douchebag doo-doo list. With the passing of time, I learned how to forgive his immaturity, but his delirious hubris will never be forgotten.

The irony of little brother criticizing and mocking my frugal living came into full display when, pending approval for his green card, a $30,000 deposit in an account was required by the Immigration Bureau. When all three parties involved were in near panic, as the deadline was quickly approaching for the money to be deposited in a sponsor's account, I surprised everyone with the $30,000 needed. To this day, I'm still waiting for a vocal or written apology. Something of that sort: "Thanks to big brother, Lyonel, who led a frugal existence; he saved enough money in his bank to rescue and sponsor our green card approvals, long live to him".

The year 1980 was a significant one for my unauthorized and unredacted journey in Miami, as so much was happening all at once. Hundreds of thousands of people migrating from both Cuba and Haiti started to arrive on South Florida's shores. The long and inhumane US' economic boycott of Cuba was creating havoc on the island's economy, battered in addition by numerous reoccurring seasonal storms. Under such extremely volatile socio-economic pressures, the only alternative left to prevent the Cuban Revolution from imploding was for Castro's communist regime to open what became the infamous "Mariel boatlift" exodus gate, sending boatloads of Cuban refugees into Miami.

Simultaneously, the economic situation in Haiti, one of Cuba's closest neighbors, was getting worse and worse under Jean-Claude Duvalier and Michèle Bennett's corrupt and brutal dictatorial rules. What started in 1972 when the 52-foot wooden sailboat with 65 Haitian made it to Pompano Beach exploded by the late 70s and early 80s to an estimated 70,000 Haitian refugees living now in Miami who needed help and services.

It was in this context that I received a phone call from none other than Pierre Mendez Alcindor a.k.a Dada telling me that Florida's Health and Rehabilitative Services [HRS] was looking to employ qualified Haitians with a bachelor's degree minimum to help with the surge of Haitian refugees in Miami who needed assistance. The timing could not have been any more perfect as I just completed all my undergraduate courses in Sociology at FIU, qualifying me for the job. I was hired for the position by the Cuban supervisor in charge of the program, the minute I mentioned Pierre Mendez Alcindor's name, who was already on his way to become the radio personality that he became in Miami's early Haitian diaspora days.

I transitioned overnight from a string of low-paid blue-collar jobs like restaurant, hotel, janitorial, factories and shops to a more respectable, better-paid white-collar job with added perks and fringe benefits. I was so glad to quit my old Printing job at Harvey, as the atmosphere there had considerably changed. All the 'premis' people when I started working there left one by one, and so did Michael Jarvis, a.k.a. Jacques, now a known fiction writer. If anything, I would not be missing my little brother Carlos' growing bossy attitude at the workplace.

My take on the convenient timing of leaving Harvey's Printing shop was as if I were on a mission to open a pathway for all three of my half-sibling brothers. In fact, Frantz, my youngest brother, who was the last one to migrate to Miami from Port-au-Prince, went straight off the plane to go work for Harvey. He made a long career working there until he retired from the Printing shop several years later. It was his very first and only job.

In short, it was no accidental hazard that I came to work at Harvey's in the first place. Now that my work was done, it was past time for me to move into much greener pastures more to my speed. I remained in touch with my old boss Harvey throughout the years, as I had quite an excellent rapport with him. Even though we both had conflicting political and economic philosophies, we always at the end agreed to disagree in many of our heated, controversial discussions. I met with him occasionally for lunch up until meeting with him became a logistic nightmare, as I moved further away to the North from the South Miami area where he lived.

Miami, Florida: A Sunshine State's Unauthorized And Unredacted Journey

# Brutal Government Crackdown of Haiti's Independent Press

Since Carter's 1976 election, the newly elected American president committed to his Christian values embarked on his faith-inspired campaign to promote human rights not just at home but also abroad. It was in this politically charged context that by the late 70s and early 80s, many outspoken religious leaders, the likes of Sylvio Claude, Pastor Luc Nérée, emboldened by President Carter's inaugural speech, joined the long, perilous struggle for human rights in Haiti. Gerard Gourgue, a lawyer, an opposition activist, and President of Haiti's Human Rights League Association, presented legal arguments demonstrating how incompatible the archaic concept of Jean-Claude's President-for-Life was with the very concept of Democracy. Grégoire Eugène, president of Haiti's Christian Social Party and the director of a highly vocal opposition magazine named 'Fraternité', kept the regime's rulers awake for many nights. On the other end of the spectrum were the pioneered champions of Press Freedom still being represented by the usual suspects like Marcus Garcia and Elsie Etheart from Radio Metropole. Radio Haiti Inter, run by the indefatigable defender of press freedom and civil liberty, Jean Dominique, a.k.a. JanDo, his wife Michelle Montas, Richard Brisson and the iconic, sensational duos Konpè Filo and Liliane Pierre Paul were all in lockstep for the fight for freedom and democracy.

The written Independent Press with Fardin's 'Le Petit Samedi Soir', which had been a leading voice since my late teenage years, as a young journalist, continued with its 70s mission of speaking truth to power. From the original team of young writers/journalists, only Jean-Robert Herard and Pierre André Clitandre were left. The latter became the magazine's Chief Redactor. The new LPSS team of journalists became more combative and militant specially following Gasner Raymond's shocking murder by the regime in 1976.

By the late '70s and early '80s, Jean Claude's regime was cornered from various angles and forced against the ropes by the well-orchestrated attacks from an outspoken local opposition, encouraged by Carter's non-supportive foreign policies toward tyrants and dictatorial rulers like Baby Doc. As it had been historically and amply demonstrated, Haiti was once again targeted by the Globalists to be a model example of Washington's zero tolerance for tyrants everywhere. All the various sectors of Haiti's internal opposition, using Carter's new stand against global poverty, were brazenly criticizing and holding Jean Claude's regime as the sole entity responsible for the Nation's direst economic crisis. They blamed his dictatorial rules and the rampant corruption within his regime for provoking the massive exodus of thousands of Haitians out of the country. Political repression and the prospect of starvation, they argued, drove into despair large sections of the impoverished population to put their lives in great peril on rickety boats with the hope of making it to the Bahamas and to Miami.

In short, they condemned the regime in place for the scandalous, humiliating 1980s wave of the Haitian boat people phenomena on the shores of Miami. The natural impulse from the regime's old dinosaurs was to go all out against that threatening opposition, but cooler heads recommended waiting for a more favorable political climate in the US, as they feared Washington's swift economic retributions. The US, being the largest single contributor to Haiti's annual budget besides Canada, France, West Germany, Israel, and Taiwan, placed Washington in the imperial posture to dictate to the regime all the terms and conditions under which the Collective West's financial contribution would be given, making a servile lackey out of the recipient nation of Haiti. All that would change with Ronald Reagan's classic electoral coup d'état over Carter's reelection bid for a second term in November of 1980. Champagne celebration was said to have taken place at the national palace following the highly suspected Reagan's electoral landslide, which made Papa Doc's toasting celebration of JFK's assassination look blemish in comparison. Hardcore elements from the regime were firing in the air their automatic weapons as a celebratory gesture of what was about to happen to the out-of-control Haitian opposition. A day of reckoning for the local opposition was coming, as the regime's foes had it with the daily broadcasting of voices in popular radio shows, which have turned into mouthpieces for syndicalists, opposition political parties and leftist-oriented groups, according to accusations leveled by the government to justify its long overdue political crackdown.

In all, they had it with Sylvio Claude, Gerard Gourgue, Gregoire Eugene, and the Luc Néré of the world. The gangs at LPSS, Radio Metropole, and Radio Haiti Inter crews were also on top of the undesirable list of personae non grata. They would not even wait for the coming Ronald Reagan's January 1981 inaugural installation. They wanted to avenge, once and for all, the abject humiliations they had suffered in the last four years from the opposition's mounting criticism and accusations of economic mismanagement which was a euphemism for theft and corruption. On November 28, 1980, Jean Claude Duvalier's massive political machine turned against members of Haiti's Independent Media. Journalists from both the written and spoken Press, syndicalists, political party affiliates, Human Rights activists and religious leaders who had embraced Gustavo Gutierrez's Liberation Theology messages were targeted for arrest and political expulsion. They lined up truckloads of their political opponents to face the regime's three stooges: Col. Pierre Albert, a.k.a Ti Boule, Jean Benoît Valmé and Emmanuel Orcel.

Here is one harrowing account of my old journalist friend,

## Miami, Florida: A Sunshine State's Unauthorized And Unredacted Journey

Pierre Andre Clitandre, Redactor in chief of the weekly magazine of "Le Petit Samedi Soir" [LPSS], still traumatized by that decades-old nightmarish incident and yet so fresh in his memory: Upon learning that Duvalier's sbires were on their way to Jean Robert Herard' home, a colleague journalist of his, to arrest him, instead of running in the other direction, Clitandre brazenly ran headlong to his friend's place, hoping to stop the arresting agents. The journalist-paint-artist that I knew Clitandre to be was under the illusion that his mere presence as a distinguished member of Haiti's Independent Press could have dissuaded the plainclothes arresting agents from following through with their arrest mission.

That did not go well for Clitandre, especially after he demanded to see an arrest warrant from a judge. When he was asked by the visibly annoyed agent in charge who the hell he was, and after stating his name, he was immediately taken into custody, as the head agent realized that his name was next on their list, saving them a trip to his house in nearby Carrefour Feuilles. It was just the beginning of Clitandre's nightmare, as they started beating and punching him even before he was taken for questioning. When he finally made it to the interrogation home, he was asked many questions by Colonel Jean Benoît Valmé, sitting in the middle of the two other interrogators, Colonel Albert Pierre, a.k.a Ti Boulé and Colonel Emmanuel Orcel. Behind Clitandre were two huge male executioners waiting for Valmé's pen signals to hit the person in front of him who was being interrogated. He did just that when he noticed that Clitandre was still insisting on his civil rights being violated and his right to an attorney. Clitandre, who was a judo and karate expert, sensing that something was about to hit him from behind, quickly lowered his head by reflex to see the big dude behind him almost lost his balance when the 'Kalòt' [slap] aiming at his head missed its intended target. Now, he had really gotten under their last nerves, he was not only confrontational and argumentative, but he was also avoiding getting hit. In their mind, Clitandre needed a quick reality check. What happened next to my endearing friend, was a total disgrace to the dignity of a popular member of the Haitian Independent Press. They tied him up like a petty common thief and placed a long stick across his legs to restrain all possible movements from him. Then they began to beat him silly with their 'Koko Makak' [Big sticks].

Meanwhile, the news of multiple arrests of regime's opponents spread like wildfire through "Radyo Dyòl" [Word-of-mouth news], a century-old way of passing the news known to our culture. 'Radyo Dyòl' was the only way of knowing what was really going on behind the scenes, as the two most vocal radio stations, Radio Metropole and Radio Haiti Inter, were silenced overnight by the regime's sbires, and no pro regime radio stations still in the air would have dared say a word about the ongoing crackdown. It was reported that when Valmé's agents arrived at Jean Dominique's

Radio station, besides arresting everyone on sight, they also vandalized and destroyed every piece of radio equipment inside the building. Michèle Montas, JanDo's wife, Richard Brisson, along with Konpè Filo and Liliane Pierre-Paul, were taken into custody like common criminals. Marcus Garcia and Elsie Etheart would be arrested in the following, ensuing days.

Jean Dominique, who was not at the radio station during the uproar, perhaps sensing that something was up while driving into the unusually quiet streets of Port-au-Prince, fled into a secured hiding place and then to the nearest Venezuelan Embassy for his own protection. A brief controversy of sorts surfaced on how JanDo, the leader of the pack, ran fast into hiding to save his own skin on the slightest sign of trouble without sending a warning signal call to his own wife, Michèle Montas, let alone the others, to immediately vacate the radio station. But according to JanDo's own defense, he honestly thought if there was any act of government reprisal, they would only be coming for him, as the radio's owner, but not for his employees. He also emphasized that he could not possibly place any call to anyone from where he temporarily took refuge without jeopardizing the safety of his prominent government protector. A sign that not everyone in the ruling elite agreed with the current political crackdown. It was reported that Colonel Valmé himself was highly suspicious of the regime he served, in the sense that he felt that he was being used to do all their dirty work and then thrown under the bus as the fall guy. Indeed, he was later forced into early retirement few weeks following the November 28th. Crackdown.

From Marcus Garcia's own personal account to me in a recent interview for the purpose of this writing, it so happened by some mere coincidence that he was sick from malaria-like symptoms when he was bitten by mosquitoes while scuba diving at a Montrouis Resort and was recovering at home from the illness. He had not been seen or heard of during the first 72 hours of the government crackdown, which triggered some suspicions from many that Marcus was perhaps in the know. But Valmé's agents knew exactly where he was, as everyone had been under tight surveillance by the regime's spies and informants two to three weeks before the crackdown. Marcus, upon learning what was happening, suspected that the power that be was playing a game of chicken with him, like they did with his former boss and colleague, JanDo. They wanted him to panic and run into the nearest embassy, but Marcus, who would not rush into the trap of voluntary exile, which would have given the regime plausible deniability that Marcus Garcia went into exile of his own volition. When they realized that he would not blink, they finally came for him while he was still recovering from his malaria-like sickness. He confessed that he benefitted from some special treatments while in prison: first, he was not beaten or tortured like some of his unfortunate colleagues before and after him; second, when the prison's guards knew that he was very sick with malaria, though they could not provide him with an extra warm cover which was against prison regulations to prevent suicide from prisoners, they, nevertheless, brought him a light mattress so he could put on top of him to keep himself warm. Baby Doc was, after all, one of Marcus Garcia's biggest fans and might have ensured that he was not in harm's way.

My poet friend, actor and journalist Richard Brisson, who could easily be labeled as the friend of the common street folks in testimony of how down to earth the man was, received no such special treatment. He was no better off than his LPSS friend and colleague Clitandre, nor was he as lucky as JanDo, who got away at the eleventh hour, for Brisson was savagely beaten by his jailers, and who would ever know what other things might have been done to him while under custody.

Raped female and sodomized male prisoners at Fort Dimanche, the National Penitentiary, or Casernes Dessalines Military Barracks' prisons were known to be stubbornly silent after such despicable acts were committed against them. Apparently, it was common knowledge how angry the president's wife, Michèle Bennett, was with Richard Brisson when the poet-actor had the temerity to substitute Brigitte Bardot's name for hers in one of his staging acts where he aimed his toes at her two eyes in such disdained, contemptuous way – a vitriolic animosity known to Richard Brisson toward the rich and the powerful Haitian elite. So, many believed that the near torture treatment that he received during his time spent behind bars had a lot to do with an old settling of scores with the President's wife.

Anthony Pascal, a.k.a. Konpè Filo, with whom I had the pleasure to grow up during my mid-teenage years in Martissant, received an equally ferocious beating while in custody for two reasons. The first for being the only Creole news hour program, using his iconic 9 pm radio emission with Liliane Pierre-Paul to mock and ridicule the regime in place. Konpè Filo and Lili, his partner in crimes, were able to set an unprecedented record in the history of Radio listening audience rating in the country. Millions of listeners would turn on their radios at the 9 pm rendezvous hour, from the slums of Cité Soleil's dilapidated neighborhoods to the wealthy suburban mansions on the Port-au-Prince's hills to listen to both. Our two legendary Creole broadcasters were able to take the entire country in a sort of listening hostage through their fighting spirit, journalistic courage and bravery. But not everyone from the power elite was enjoying the party, and many were waiting for the order to come down and put an end to all that.

The second reason why Konpè Filo had it that bad while in jail was when, at the height of his fame, he disappeared without letting anyone know where he was. JanDo, in a panic mode, made an urgent radio announcement about Konpè Filo not showing up to the studio, and no one knew of his whereabouts. In less than an hour after JanDo's S.O.S call, thousands of concerned fans showed up at Radio Haiti Inter in solidarity and on the street in front of the station to protest the possible arrest of the beloved broadcaster. Though, there remained to this day many unanswered questions about Filo's disappearing incident, the 9 pm radio star came out from wherever he was to resume his work behind the microphone. However, it was rumored that some people in power did not digest well the mobilization protest of his many fans, demanding his immediate release. Valmé, himself, the regime's chief security police, privately admitted that he could not wait to put his hands on both Filo and Lili, believing that it was long past time to put them in their place.

Elsie Etheart, Michèle Montas, and Liliane Pierre Paul, a.k.a. Lilli, all three iconic female figures of Haiti's Independent Press, had not gotten any special red-carpet treatments either from the regime in place. They were when arrested verbally insulted and humiliated by their prison's guards and were forced to cross the large detention courtyard totally nude for their early morning showers while sick onlooker soldiers were shamelessly making disgruntling, sexual remarks about their female body parts.

Words were out that Liliane Pierre Paul might have even suffered more than just verbal abuses and disgusting sexist remarks from her prison's guards if we were to believe many of the insiders' stories. She was not only physically assaulted but was allegedly gang raped by her jail cell's tormentors. There was even some talk

217

that she might have gotten pregnant by one of her sexual abusers. Later in some rare interviews about her horrific time in detention, Lili herself would confess to having been abused and physically assaulted during her stay in prison but stopped short of addressing or denying the gang rape allegations' stories she suffered in the hands of her 'bourreaux' [executioners] while in the tank.

The obvious separate treatment received by Lili, who was not a mulatto and a well-connected journalist like her two celebrity jailed colleagues, Elsie Etheart and Michèle Montas, had once again raised the old stubborn issue of colorism in the Haitian society, which would not go away despite the bourgeois Haitian elites' denials of it. In the minds of many, Louis XIV's Black Code's legacy establishing the color hierarchy throughout all his French colonies, especially in Saint Domingue, present day Haiti, was alive and well despite the belief that the color issue in Haiti has been solved. Many argued against the deniers of colorism in Haiti that power, wealth, social status, and, yes, even punishments were still being distributed and rewarded in Haiti based on skin color in line with the old dicta of the Sun King of France, despite several unsuccessful attempts at eradicating it by past Noirist administration like Dumarsais Estimé and later under Papa Doc's autocratic rule.

Black Code's guidelines, continued the argument, had been followed to the letter by colonialists, neo-colonialists and imperialists alike, as it was based on the fundamental concept of 'divide et impera' [divide and conquer]. It was followed by Napoleon Bonaparte in his vicious, divisive war to bring back slavery in Haiti and reestablish control over France's richest colony by playing high-ranking black Haitian generals and officers against their mulattoes' counterparts. The neo-colonialist Germans used the same divisive footprint in their near-complete takeover of Haiti's economy from the late 19th to early 20th Century. And so was the imperialist Yankee Occupation of Haiti from July 28, 1915, to August 1, 1934, which remained in and of itself an astonishing case study of America's deep-rooted, loathing racism vis-à-vis Haiti. US' Occupation forces quickly delved into the nation's color prejudice legacy by pinning blacks versus mulattoes to weaken any resistance against its imperial rule.

The overnight silencing of the two major Independent Press Radios, Metropole and Haiti Inter, along with their independent printing Press colleague at LPSS, sent a cold chill down the spine of Haiti's growing internal opposition. A level of fear never seen since the harrowing, brutal days of Papa Doc's autocratic rules, seemed to have taken hold on large sections of the opposition. Though the atmosphere on the streets remained strangely calm all throughout the clampdown, the international reactions to the government's brutal silencing of Haiti's Independent Press were swift and loud. Street demonstrations erupted throughout the Haitian Diasporas in New York, Montreal, Miami, and Paris in support of the beaten, tortured exiled journalists, as Richard Brisson would shamelessly drop his pants down to his knees, exposing to the International Press the severed beating, wounds and bruises received on his rear end. Opposition members in the Diaspora were enraged and, in their anger, put all the blame on the US Government's shoulder for their implicit support for the anti-democratic regime of Baby Doc.

Put under such tremendous pressure by the number of outcries from the Congressional Black Caucus and by various international organizations championing Democracy, press freedom and Civil Rights in Haiti, the US State Department was forced into a face-saving response by canceling the visit of high-level Washington officials who were due to meet with the Haitian Government to address their latest financial aid package request for the coming yearly budget. Washington, in this context, was quite annoyed by the regime crackdown's unwise timing, as the crackdown came on the eve of difficult renewed negotiations with big donor countries. The US State Department issued a virulent condemnation of Jean Claude's ruthless suppression of Haiti's Independent Press, and the civil rights violation of all the journalists and members of the opposition. Washington asked for the immediate release of over 200 people picked up by police since that forsaken day of November 28.

Thanks, perhaps, to the power of the purse exercised by Haiti's top donors, many of my colleague journalists' lives might

have been spared and were instead sent into exile to appease the
Washington's make-believe democratic dystopia. In the case of
Konpè Filo and Lili, our iconic duos might have owed their lives to
the brave and courageous interference of Colonel Paul Rosny
Casimir alias 'Interieur'. He was in the area when he suspiciously
noticed that the group who was about to take both to jail was a
known ruthless death squad on a mission to carry out some
extrajudicial killings on the two loudest voices on the radio against
the current regime.

Casimir, who was a fan of both icons, sensed that if he failed
to take both journalists under his own custody to the Casernes
Dessalines' precinct, it would have been the last time he would have
seen them alive. Despite the group's persistence to take the famous
pair to jail themselves, Casimir overruled them. Both legends
following that close call with death would later admit in private and
in public that they had no doubt in their mind that Colonel Rosny
Casimir, a.k.a. 'Interieur' saved their lives that day.

The power elite in Haiti wanted to shut for good two of most
daring, popular voices crying out every night against the injustices,
the corruption and the dire economic deterioration of the everyday,
average Haitian, and this despite the tremendous boom in Haiti's
factories, in the tourist industry and in the fivefold increase in
international aid packages. Haiti's bottom classes had yet to
experience any slightest improvement in their extreme low standard

of living, viewed as the poorest and the lowest in the entire Western Hemisphere. The heartbreaking economic reality was that the bulk of Haiti's economic activities and the international investment funds were invested in projects benefitting only the rich, first and foremost Wall Street's economic hit men, The City of London Corporation through Canada, along with Haiti's vassalized comprador class embodied by a handful Haitian oligarch families.

A huge part of the investment profits allocated to Haiti went straight up into the rich Haitian families' deep pockets and never trickled down to Haiti's bottom classes. The reported 1980s weekly average salary of $13.20 was never intended in the first place to keep up with the mounting rise of inflation, as most Haitian workers saw their purchasing power drop by more than 46% just right around the time Miami was dealing with the 'infamous' Haitian boat people's daily invasion. Consequently, Haiti's dire economic deterioration along with its repressive autocratic rules had amply contributed to sending untold numbers of desperate Haitians to risk their lives on the high seas, hoping to avoid both political repression and hunger at home.

Notice that I had not even mentioned the general state of the endemic corruption intrinsic to the Duvalier-Bennet family's exploding financial holdings, estimated into millions of dollars hidden in various offshores' accounts. In fact, many keen observers and historians saw in the May 27, 1980, marriage of Jean Claude

Duvalier with his childhood sweetheart crush, Michèle Bennett, a wealthy Haitian mulatto herself, the beginning of the end of the nearly three-decades-old Duvalier Pax Haitiana Dynasty rule that I wrote so much about in my second memoir. She was the one wearing the pants and would be seen sitting in every ministerial cabinet meeting, remarked an insider. Her heartless, extravagant US$ 2 million wedding à la Marie Antoinette of Versailles, France, alone flew in the face of millions of starving, poor Haitian children going hungry to bed every night. With the display of her opulent lifestyle at the presidential palace, only a stone's throw away from the nation's worst slums, the President's wife could easily reply to her critics about starving Haitian children under her reign, "To just let them all eat cake".

Most of the expelled journalists, syndicalists and political activists ended up in New York, Montreal and Miami. Jean Dominique joined his wife, Michèle Montas, who arrived in New York a few days before him. Jean Robert Herard and Pierre André Clitandre were also living their early exiled days in New York. Marcus Garcia and Elsie Etheart, after staying at the Big Apple for a brief period, made Miami their exiled place of choice. Richard Brisson followed them soon after.

In the meantime, the official Little Haiti neighborhood had since known an influx of Black Baptist ministers, Catholic priests and Haitian exile activists coming from New York and elsewhere to help their fellow black Haitian brothers who arrived here illegally and were detained in Krome. The former provided food, shelter, and financial support to many of the released refugees, while the latter offered legal assistance to hundreds of Haitians still being held at the Krome Detention Center. Two interesting characters stood out among this group: First, the Rev. Gerard Jean-Juste, a Catholic Priest who had been getting lots of Press coverage for his many spontaneous street protests on the 54th Street block where his office stood. The goal of his street mobilization protests was to advocate and demand legal status for hundreds of Haitians sitting in Krome awaiting deportation back to Haiti, a place they had risked their lives fleeing away from.

Next was Roger Biambi, who, fresh from New York, as a young, dedicated community activist, hit the ground running in his social, political and economic advocacies to improve the plight of the growing numbers of Haitians living in my old neighborhood. Both Rev. Gerard Jean Juste and Roger Biambi formed an informal partnership in their herculean struggle to seek justice for the vast majority of the "Haitian Boat People" either stuck at the Krome Detention Center or living in dilapidated, badly kept apartment building in Little Haiti. Both were often seen making the Miami Herald's front page newspaper or on Channel 10's Evening News, advocating and speaking on behalf of thousands of voiceless Haitians. Haitian refugees, several children among them, were not getting the red-carpet royal treatment like that of their Cuban counterparts, who, upon stepping onto US soil, were de facto qualified for legal refugee status with all the goodies and perks that came with such status.

However, with the famed lawyer-activist Ira J. Kurzban now joining forces with Father Jean Juste and Roger Biambi, it was a real game changer in the routine double standard mistreatments of Haitians by Miami's Immigration Office. Kurzban successfully argued two breakthrough cases at the US Supreme Court, which ended up releasing all the Haitian refugees who were detained at Krome. His two landmark wins at the Court contributed enormously to the striving, growing Haitian community in Miami. And thanks to his relentless legalistic victories backed up by the politics in the PR Department cultivated by both Father Jean Juste and Roger Biambi, the "Little Haiti" community in the early 1980s became a fait accompli.

Against the backdrop of all this happening, suddenly surged Bernard Sansaricq, an obscured, little-known character said to own a gas station business in the Fort Lauderdale area. He came out of nowhere to claim the title of the uncontested opposition leader in the Haitian Diaspora. He had an effective, well-funded enlistment program to recruit as many volunteered male combatants within the Haitian Community along with possible financial sponsors. Sansaricq, to give credit where credit was due, had two undeniable

225

things going for him at the time: first, his huge charismatic personality and second, his rare cunning ability to sell sand to Arabs living in the desert. Added to the above two qualities, he also found a vulnerable Haitian Diaspora that really had it with the brutal, corrupt Duvalier dynasty and was blindly responsive to any armed invasion aiming at ending Jean Claude-Bennett's dictatorial rules.

That was the prevalent volatile political atmosphere in Miami where the charismatic militant leader Sansaricq had convinced himself first, then the rest of the community, that this time it was for real and that the repressive, undemocratic regime of Baby Doc was simply living on borrowed time. Following the elaborate, convincing narrative by Sansaricq, of support from several militant networks within and outside of Haiti, he was able to win the support of important members in the Miami Community, like Roger Biambi, to join his campaign.

Biambi, who became the director of HACAD, found time to utilize his own independent community network to back Sansaricq up to such an extent that he became Bernard's right-arm man and his sole representative spoke person at the movement's headquarters in Miami. He helped him raise lots of money all throughout the Haitian Diaspora and even from some unhappy Haitian oligarchs like Antoine Izméry, a wealthy Haitian businessman and a pro-democracy activist. The latter contributed a purported $80,000 to finance what was being sold as the unprecedented preparation for the mother of all invasions ever against the Duvaliers' Macoute regime. Here, I found myself once again in the middle of all that political meme in Miami's Haitian Diaspora at the time. One could not be exempted from the constant beating of the drums of war on the weekly radio programming hours or in the hallways' antechamber of political gatherings, routinely staged to flare up patriotic fervor for the coming invasion and for more financial support and contributions. I participated in many of Father Jean Juste's protests against US's racist immigration policies toward Haitians in Miami and elsewhere in the Diaspora. I made modest contributions that I could afford to make for the cause, as I was not about to enlist myself in the training exercises, which were being kept on a remote training field for those brave young Haitians in Miami who wanted to be part of the armed invasion. I simply did not have the combatant stomach in me. I was and still am more of a lover, a poet, than a warrior. The closer I came to using something remotely close to a weapon was a pen to attack in catimini the corrupt regime of the Duvalier when I was Director of Djakout, a school paper, and as a journalist at LPSS.

I also had, aside from my strong non-violent inclination against war, some serious reservations about the entire Sansaricq's broadcasting invasion of Haiti, as I believed that the real thing would not be advertised or televised on any evening news. Besides, everything about Sansaricq's planned invasion was in direct clash with Sun Tzu's "The Art of War" classic recommendations.

However, due to my latest involvement in the volatile political atmosphere in Miami of the 1980s, I reconnected with many old familiar faces from my old days of hanging out at Radio Haiti. It was refreshing to see Marcus Garcia, Elsie Etheart, Richard Brisson, Konpè Filo to name just a few, though I wished it were under different, less traumatizing circumstances. I obtained contact numbers for Pierre Andre Clitandre, whom I called immediately, and within days, I was on my second visit to New York and meeting with the old crew of "Le Petit Samedi Soir". Dany Laferrière, who migrated to Montreal in 1976 in the aftermath of Gasner Raymond's assassination, joined us for the occasion. In all, Clitandre, Jean Robert Herard, Dany and I gathered at the house where Clitandre was temporarily staying.

Our first meeting was nothing less than a surrealistic moment of tremendous epiphany for all four of us to reunite once again, at last, after so many years of separation. Late Gasner Raymond was the only one missing, but we felt as if he were with us in spirit. Dany, who had made photocopies of some of my published essay articles and poetry from the LPSS archives brought them to me in New York. That was one unbelievable act of true friendship and camaraderie, as this whole period in my writing career would have been forgotten. We immediately started working on Clitandre's new magazine project entitled "Haiti Demain," like in the good old newsroom days when we all used to gather either at my place on Titus Street or at the magazine's Redaction Headquarters in Fontamara.

It was at one of these emotional gatherings that the larger-than-life Jean Dominique, a.k.a. JanDo, graced us with an unannounced afternoon visit. That was one memorable evening for all of us who looked up to Jean Dominique a.k.a. JanDo, as the ultimate mega-celebrity in Haiti's radio broadcasting history, in the same vein as a Mike Jagger was to his Rock and Roll fan base. JanDo, the indefatigable, lifelong human rights activist appeared somewhat somber despite his charming, charismatic smile. He had his signature smoking pipe in his mouth and was wearing his militant hat à la Che Guevarra. His wife, Michèle Montas, could not accompany him, but she had sent all her love and support to the LPSS team, now in exile, working hard to put in place an opposition magazine abroad to combat the anti-Democratic regime in Haiti. A week later, Marcus Garcia and Elsie Etheart would offer their collaboration with "Haiti Demain", already considered to be the number one exile Newspaper in New York. "Haiti Observateur", the Brooklyn, New York-based weekly paper founded in 1971, was bracing for some serious competition. I returned home to Miami but continued to send articles and poems to be published in the magazine until due to lack of funds, it discontinued its publication.

One afternoon, Pierre Mendez Alcindor a.k.a. Dada called

me on my phone to tell me that he was with Richard Brisson, and both were on their way to my place. Within a few minutes-time, they were at my bachelor's pad. Poor Richard Brisson, he was still traumatized by the brutal event of November 28th. He brought me a complimentary copy of his latest disk of poems that he autographed. I still hold dearly that thoughtful, generous gift from Richard in my old collection of vinyl records. We had a few exchanges about the day's hottest topic of conversation related to the Sansaricq's planned invasion of Haiti. Both tried to entice me to join the campaign, but again, I let them know that all I could do was make a financial contribution to the cause.

I even went against my usual instinct of not spoiling anyone's dream to warn both Dada and Brisson to pay attention to details from Sansaricq's overall invasion plan, as the devil was always in them. I specifically warned both not to allow themselves to be used as disposable cannon fodders in anyone's cynical, Machiavellian invasion chess game. Unfortunately, they had already been sold and had long drunk Bernard Sansaricq's Kool-Aid, and nothing I could say or do would have them reconsider their commitment to the planned invasion of Haiti. In Richard's case, his deep-rooted depression would not subside until the current repressive regime in Haiti was overthrown. For Dada, he was left behind, as he was way too sick to embark on Sansaricq's flagship.

When, in January of 1982, the news hit the airwave that

Sansaricq's invasion miserably failed, it was no big surprise for many of us in the community. The usual excuses given for the long list of foiled, armed insurgents' invasion of Haiti such as: not enough supplies of arms and munitions, weapons' malfunction, no show of expected more armed insurgents, plus a whole laundry list of other excuses. The leader of the invasion, accused the US of interference when 25 of them, including Sansaricq and my late friend Limoné Joseph, were rescued from their leaking 40-foot 'flagship' and brought back to Miami.

The entire thing could have been seen as one laughable subject for a comic strip template if it were not for the unfortunate tragic end of our beloved friend, poet-journalist and actor extraordinaire, Richard Brisson, along with two others, Robert Mathurin and Louis Celestin. The regime lied that Richard Brisson and his two companions died following serious wounds taken in combat. However, a conflicting reliable report confirmed that all three were captured alive and transferred immediately to Port-au-Prince, where they were summarily executed by the regime. Years later, in 1994, Bernard Sansaricq, who had turned into a politician and was subsequently elected president of Haiti's Senate from a dubious voting arrangement, would finally come clean and reveal in an interview that he had had high-level contact with Washington all along his planned failed invasion. Thus, an admission by Sansaricq that he was a CIA asset throughout his failed attempts to overthrow the Duvalier regime. It sounded like "Déjà Vu" all over again. Whenever Washington's Deep State was unhappy with the direction Haiti's internal politics were heading, they staged bogus invasion plots to pressure the unruly, lackey Haitian government, running off script, to get straight back in line.

From the classic CIA book, the way it all played out was: First, you create a problem or provoke a crisis, then when the party reacting to it was too overwhelmed by the crisis' escalation, cried out for help, then you came out from nowhere as the ultimate savior to offer a readymade, way out solution which always worked to the interest and advantage of Washington's secret agenda in the first place. This clever, cynical Machiavellian strategy known as "problem-reaction-solution" had been used countless times on nations' head-of-states and on the general population, creating what would be later called by Robert Malone "Mass Formation Psychosis".

Papa Doc, despite his vocal sovereign stand in public against his DC masters, was forced to go on his knees in many an occasion begging to be saved by his Washington's handlers. Baby Doc who was not as politically stubborn and hot-headed as his dad, Papa Doc, benefitted from a near decade-long invasion-free during his political reign. But all has changed when he went disastrously off script in his government's brutal crackdown on religious leaders, political parties affiliates, syndicalists and journalists. Going against the neoliberal global narrative and agenda would set the stage six years later when Washington's Deep State would help provoke Haiti's first modern day color revolution in 1986, years before the name was even coined in the geopolitical lexicon.

Richard Brisson's unnecessary, violent, and brutal death in Haiti by firing squad, if we were to believe some reliable sources, had not achieved anything. Yes, he had rejoined other martyrs the likes of Jacques Stephen Alexis and Gasner Raymond, but besides that, all it had accomplished was to leave many of us who were close to him a sense of profound guilt. The guilt of not having done enough to help him cope with that deep sense of loss and emptiness. I remember, in my own limited way, trying to distract him a bit from all those bad vibes by taking him once to Coconut Grove's distracting nightlife and outdoor cafes. Sure, he enjoyed the ambiance there, but I could tell that something deep inside him was irreversibly broken, his zest for life. Upon learning about his tragic end, many among us could not help feeling that we had failed him for not having been there more for him in this difficult transition period of his forced exile. We could have done more to convince our poet friend that the Sansaricq option was simply a no-brainer to start with and that he was, in all probability, setting himself up as a facile, disposable cannon fodder. Marcus Garcia also felt bad for failing to dissuade him from making this fatal voyage when he met him at one of the gatherings before the planned invasion.

He recalled pulling Richard's arm on the side of the hallway to tell him point-blank that the whole Sansaricq thing was a big nothing burger and that it was not too late for him to make a volte-face, and back out. But he also recalled that Brisson was resolutely stubborn in his arrested, fatal decision to go!

# The Lady Who Thought Me There Was More to Love Than Sex

My life at Izidor's bachelor pad, as the French would have put it, continued, "Son petit bonhomme de chemin" [Gone its merry way] despite the latest earth-shattering kaboom occurring in my old homeland of Haiti and here in Miami's Little Haiti. I continued to sign up for the required number of courses toward my master's in international studies at FIU's Tamiami Campus. My new HRS job assisting newly released Haitians from the Krome Detention Center with financial help, food stamps and health care has given me a unique life-learning exposure to the US welfare system for the poor. It is also the closest I have ever come to a section of the Haitian population fleeing from poverty and political repression called the infamous 'boat people'. The administrative office looked like an old unused hangar remodeled into a makeshift emergency Center to deliver the well-needed services to the Cuban Marielitoes and the Haitian refugees.

In the office section where I worked, I was the only Haitian social worker there, and I cannot to this day comprehend how unfriendly and unwelcome my Hispanic co-workers were toward me. I felt that I was completely made invisible by them. There was not one black Cuban social worker among them that I could at least interact with. I felt so lonesome in my new job environment during the first three weeks, except for a significant unexpected distraction when I showed up for work on my fourth week. Right across my desk, a few meters away, was stationed one very young attractive social worker in her early 20s. That was one heck of a consolation prize to my lonely-starving brown eyes, as most of my female colleagues were in their middle age bracket. After sizing her up from across and making some compelling eye contact with her, I knew instantly that I would never again be in solitude for as long as that picture-perfect creature was stationed on that office floor just meters away from my desk.

She was another girl from a third generation Cuban American with more of a Caucasian stock than many of her other Hispanic colleagues. Because of her curvy built, her light pale skin, blue eyes and blonde hair, she was quickly put on the highest pedestal by all the social workers on our office floor. A testimony that her type was, to most of them, the ultimate in their psyche of whiteness' racial purity, and superiority. It was a staunch white supremacist view held by a majority of Cubans living in Miami. Traffic was nonstop around her desk as everyone came forward to greet and welcome her. I wished I had had such a welcome when I first started work there. Being the youngest among the staff, she appeared to be a lot less conservative than the rest, though she was carefully savvy not to display any sign of friendliness toward me to preserve her high status in lockstep with the prevailing conservative attitude around the office.

She would not smile at me and had even avoid making direct eye contact with me since the first initial exchange we had in the beginning. I was convinced that I was an object of curiosity and intrigue to her despite her apparent distant attitude. The incorrigible lady's man in me simply could not help sending out my usual flirtatious vibe to her, as she was the only glittering sight making those long, working hours a lot less boring. With each passing day of working right across her station desk, a sort of wordless amorous affair started to develop between us. Was it possible that the feel-good charm given to me once by Margie was again doing its magic on her? I caught her several times looking at me in ways that could have landed her in so much trouble with her co-workers enslaved by the poison of colorism.

She was the forbidden fruit for me in the same vein that I was for her in accordance with the unspoken general rule of the grand racial divide. And most of her older conservative colleagues were more racist than the Ku Klux Klan's Imperial Wizard himself in maintaining the racial boundary and purity of the white race. However, I believe there was a part of her that was repulsed against all the racial taboos coming from her old-school Hispanic co-workers. Consequently, her discreet, but distant platonic affair with me was her own courageous way to soften up the way I was being treated. Knowing who I was and where I came from, I never once

Lyonel Gerdes

allowed such unproductive vibe to impact, let alone disturb me. I continued to help and assist several of my Haitian compatriots who desperately needed food stamps, financial support and health coverage, all the while enjoying her distant supportive vibe.

I had absolute certainty that had I met her under a different set of circumstances like at a Coconut Grove's club, a Jamaican or Haitian Beach Resort, it would have been game over as in a neutral territory no oppressive societal rules would have kept her away from me! The real sensuous chemistry traveling back and forth from her desk to mine was so conspicuous that some of her own co-workers began to suspect that something was up, though they could never figure out the exact nature of it. She would not talk to me, but everything else she did was to encourage me to desire her more. She started coming to work wearing risqué low cleavage tops displaying how well-endowed she was chest-wise. Her collection of hot tops and jeans were so tightly fit on her that I wished to be a fly on her bedroom's wall to watch how she managed to fit into them her voluptuous insane curves, let alone her exceptional Latina behind.

Our HRS office moved from its South Tamiami makeshift location to a more office like building in Coral Gables. I was a little concerned that the relocation would signal the end of whatever I had going with the still nameless lady across, but to my big surprise, her desk was again placed right across mine like in the old setting at the hangar. I was under the impression, judging by the discernible smile

238

on her face on the official day that we all moved into the new office building, that she was equally delighted with the unchanged desk setting arrangement with mine still facing hers. We were a lot closer to each other in the much smaller office space, augmenting the already tremendous body chemistry existing between us. With the passing of time, our amorous situation had evolved into a love affair that would never dare speak its name! I remember how blemished my days were when she took off from work. A Haitian lady friend of mine working on the same floor and who knew about my business with her told me that she looked very depressed on the days I did not show up for work.

Many changes have occurred at our new office location. I was no longer the only Haitian working at the program. They hired four other Haitian social workers to help with the increasing number of newly released Haitian refugees from the Krome Avenue detention camp. My longtime friend Philippe Carrie was working next door to me at a federal office connected with HRS to help with the transitioning process of all the refugees on US soil. Marcus Garcia himself, the unsung hero of Haiti's Independent Press, came briefly to work in the new building, as an advisor of sorts. The director of the program, who was aware of Marcus Garcia's high-profile status in Haiti and in the Haitian community in Miami and beyond, gave him a celebrity red-carpet treatment, which by extension, rubbed off on me. I began to become less invisible, as there was strength in numbers, and Marcus and the newly hired Haitians would come often to visit me at my office floor. Our group brought a whole new positive vibration to that office floor, for we were quite an impressive, competent, handsome-looking bunch of well-dressed professionals with commanding respect. Added to the fact that two among us spoke Spanish fluently. Marcus' last name, Garcia, might have also played some role in the relaxing office atmosphere, perhaps many of my Cuban co-workers mistakenly believed that he was one of them. Regardless, the cool Haitian vibe was so overwhelming that even the director's own gorgeous daughter defected from her routine, dulled Hispanic group at lunch time to join ours. She was having a fun, pleasant time with us.

Being a third generation of young, liberated Cubans, she was a lot more accepting of blacks and non-Cuban groups than the older generations of exiled Cubans who came before her. She shared some cool common experiences with at least two of us in the group, for she was a frequent partyer at the Coconut Grove's busy night life. She and I had a friendly blast talking about the insane clubs and bars' scenes meme there.

The warm camaraderie being displayed toward me by Marcus, and the director's daughter was a definite game changer in the way I was being treated before. I was so snubbed that I could never get an opportunity to introduce myself and get to know the names of any of my colleagues including my enigmatic, distant,

amorous lover. But now, following the ice-breaking element
brought by the new Haitian crew, my co-workers began to smile
freer at me and make eye contact.

Consequently, the changing mood at the office had made
possible some daring moves from the still-nameless bombshell
beauty across. She recently made a routine habit of coming near my
desk to chat with another colleague friend of hers without paying
one iota attention to me. At one of her afternoon chats, she leaned
her majestic figure on the tip of my desk on the day that she wore
her all-time steamy pair of white jeans, raising to high heaven my
already fragile body temperature. But, in one lucky afternoon, she
finally broke with her endless, torturing, silencing tease by
addressing me directly for the first time after months of that ongoing
nonverbal, flirtatious platonic thing between us. I first struggled
with my breathing in disbelief, for I had a hard time keeping my
composure, as I long resigned myself that she would never speak to
me or make any attempt at becoming friends at the very least.

I regained my composure to answer her back but still
tremendously mesmerized by the deep, fatalistic expression coming
from the blueness of her eyes. They were not just sky blue pretty but
were also captivating and enchanting. Now, I fully understood why
I fell so quickly under the distant projecting spell of her eyes from
day one. She told me in our brief conversation that her first name
was Lara, which I quickly referenced as Lara Antipova, the main

female heroine in Dr. Zhivago's dramatic movie. She resembled the famed British actress, Julie Christie, whose timeless portrayal of Lara's impossible love for Yuri made her immortal. She smiled and was flattered by the comparison. Upon learning that my first name was Lyonel, she returned the favor by saying, "As in Richie," which brought a relaxing smile to my face, as I heard such reference before.

I would later learn through the grapevine, that she was unhappily married to a wealthy, jealous Cubano husband who was abusive to her. He was very insecure and constantly accused her of cheating. Besides being abusive to her, he paid no attention to fulfilling her emotional needs. I was taken aback by the latest revelations. Who in his right mind, I asked myself, would make such a stunning-looking creature like Lara suffer as a 'Mal-Aimée', unless this guy was utterly insane and not well!

Her marriage crisis, as she was still in love with her abusive husband despite his emotional abuses, fitted this old Haitian proverb, "Kote ki gen chenn pa gen kou" [Where there's a neck, there's no chain]. Understanding that an untold number of men, including me, would line up the street to be in Lara's husband's lucky shoes! Now, considering the latest infos, the ongoing platonic thing between me and Lara made a lot more sense. I was known to be cursed with a rare gift of absorbing people's pain, hence affording them instant comfort and relief from their grief while in my company. A sort of a messianic savior complex toward people, and it was no different when I saw Lara for the first time. Though she was picture perfect from her outer shell, there was something blurry around her aura interfering with her true natural shine. I could sense that she was vulnerable and craving love. Her craving was such that she settled for that feel-good energy offered to her by me from across her desk station. We both embarked on that voyage, which needed no physical contact or no verbal gimmick to fill her with unconditional emotional love.

The office was celebrating Lara's birthday. It was going to be a surprised event. Contributions and gifts were being accepted by a committee without her knowing. I was not one good at finding the right, appropriate birthday gifts for friends, acquaintances and lovers alike, but in Lara's case, I wanted to outdo myself by finding the ultimate gift that would convey to her how much I felt emotionally connected to her. So, I went shopping at Grove's Mayfair looking for Lara's gift when I found in one of the high-end boutiques there, the perfect present for her. It was the cutest vintage musical box ever, and for some happy coincidence, it happened to play Lara's main musical theme in Dr. Zhivago's film: "Somewhere My Love". I purchased it on the spot and did not care about the cost. They wrapped it very nicely, and I wrote on the card: "From Lyonel to Lara with love". I delivered it the following day to the head committee person in charge of the event scheduled for the following day, which was a Friday. I was so excited, as I could not wait to see on her beautiful, femme fatale visage the impact of my gift on it, which was essentially a disguised love declaration for her. The birthday celebration on the next day went just fine. I even earned an unexpected, sweet hug from her, thanking me wholeheartedly for my thoughtful gift.

That Friday afternoon event was the last time I saw Lara at the office; like in the Dr. Zhivago's film, my own Lara vanished in thin air to never be seen again at the desk across. I waited until the following week, and the next week after, hoping that one day she would reappear in the same way she vanished. I found out through office gossip that our flirtatious platonic affair had finally reached her husband's jealous ears, and his jealousy had had the best of him. He had a serious fight with her over our innocent flirting at work. I saw him twice visiting her at the office to size me up and check me out, but he did not make any scenes with me. I remember slowing down the pace of my flirting with her after learning that she was married with a jealous husband. I knew plenty about Hispanic males' possessiveness and their deranged, insane jealousy, where they would not hesitate to murder their own wives when caught them cheating. They were often in the evening news for killing their wives or girlfriends, a classic case of "if they could not have them, no one else would". They were notorious for starting a fight over someone looking with lusty eyes at their ladies' posteriors. So, being aware of all that, I was extremely cautious not to make channel 10's

Miami, Florida: A Sunshine State's Unauthorized And Unredacted Journey

Evening News murder story about a Haitian male, an HRS employee, who had just been murdered by a husband over the suspicion that his wife was having an illicit affair with him.

I later had a greater scoop of what really happened to Lara from the Director's daughter's own account when she revealed to me that I was the sole culprit behind that huge fight between her and her husband that Friday of her birthday when she brought home all her gifts. My musical box caught her jealous husband's eyes, and especially the note written on it. That was all the proof her husband needed to confirm that she was cheating on him with me. And that she was a whore, a 'nigger' lover, followed by a plethora of denigrating epithets that he could find in the Cuban language's filthy lexicon. She was also physically assaulted and received numerous facial injuries and bruises, keeping her away from work in the two weeks following the incident. Meanwhile, under duress from her jealous husband, she made an urgent request to be transferred to another HRS office to avoid any possible contact with me. According to the same source, Lara never called the Police on her wife-beating husband to report the physical assault incident.

I have never felt so guilty in my entire life for having directly or indirectly caused so much trouble in Lara's marriage. Some two years later, I accidentally crossed her path at the popular Coconut Grove Art Festival, graciously pushing a baby stroller with her gorgeous newborn infant child in it. Our eyes instantly crossed in a brief, but soothing gaze, revealing that she never really left me, and vice versa. She smiled. I smiled back. And we both went our merry ways without uttering a single word, for there was never a need for words in our genuine love chemistry.

The fundamental lesson I learned from that distant, nonphysical love connection with Lara, was the realization that there was more to love than sex. I sincerely hoped that whatever happened between us in the realm of our transcendental spiritual love affair, that something decisively transformational occurred to positively impact and redeem her once dysfunctional marriage into a more functional one.

# The Day Reggae Music Died at The Grove

Stating that I was a busy man would be an understatement. I was a full-time HRS State employee, a full-time student at FIU's Graduate program in International Studies, and a party animal at Coconut Grove's clubs scene. How I managed the pace in between those three time-consuming lifestyles was beyond me. I displayed a completely different persona in each one of the three. I tended to be very serious and professional at the workplace, following the wise old recommendation to never defecate where you eat. At the bar scene, there was a whole other persona on display, while at FIU, the studious, scholarly persona took precedence.

Every once-in-a-while, I would take a short break from the long research hours at the school's library to chill out around a glass of draft beer or at the Campus cafeteria checking out the ins and outs parade of the ladies. At one of those afternoon breaks, I saw coming into the cafeteria's large doors' entrance the mother of all bombshells blonde beauties. Here we go again, story of my life! She was about my height, and taller in high heel shoes; her all-around figure was a bit on the voluptuous side, which was never an issue for the Haitian in me. She wore thick bouncy blonde hair cut at shoulder lengths. Her flawless, waspy pale skin could be grasped from afar by my voracious, piercing brown eyes. Aside from her formidable curves, she was the owner of one incredible derrière that would make several well-endowed black sisters themselves fear such heated competitive pressure coming from her! Yet, the absolute coup de grace for me came in her provocative catwalk way of walking and parading all that majestic body ensemble of hers. The sick, incorrigible lady's man in me went into full mobilization mode. I wanted what I saw that afternoon so badly, that I wanted it the day before yesterday.

The following day, as if I was being guided by some invisible entity, I chose to go on my afternoon break to the popular school's pub for a beer and guess who I just saw was at the bar's counter with some friends having fun drinking time? The yesterday afternoon bombshell blonde I saw at the cafeteria. Sensing that the hand of manifest destiny was in the making, I went to sit on the opposite side of the bar to face her directly. By so doing, I was having a real good look at her with a desperate wishful hope to perhaps catch her fancy. After repeated failed attempts at engaging her in an eye-to-eye flirtatious dance, I finally succeeded in getting her attention. She smiled at me, and I smiled back at her. I raised my glass to her, and she returned the favor. I was very encouraged by how spontaneously friendly and responsive she was toward me. I frankly did not expect that of her. The likelihood for a girl of such imposing bearing to be snubby with a big-time attitude was extremely high on the supply and demand scale, as she was, by a country mile, the ultimate American dream girl. She was that type of white girl most white

boys wanted to take home to their mammy as the perfect ideal
spouse in the next procreation cycle for the ultimate continuity of
the white Aryan 'master race'.

I had to quickly exit the pub as I was running a bit late to my
next class thanks to the immense distraction coming from her side
of the bar, as we both were flirtatiously eying one another. The
following day, which was a Wednesday, I returned to the pub hoping
to see her again, but to my chagrin, the bombshell beauty was not
there. Same thing the next day. Finally, she showed up at the pub on
Friday, but with an even larger group of friends, making it
practically impossible for me to try to engage her in any meaningful
way. She was the first one to acknowledge my presence by holding
up her glass at me followed by her ravishing, confident, imperial
smile. From where I was sitting, I could tell that competition among
the white boys for her attention was voracious and approaching her
in such a competitive, volatile atmosphere was immediately ruled
out for my own personal safety to avoid getting into a fight. She
appeared not to be in a relationship, for I had not seen her cozying
up much with anyone of the guys around her. It was a good,
encouraging sign for me. But time was not on my side, and if I
wanted to make my dream come true of having her, I had to be
resolute by acting fast and by outsmarting all the males'
competitors, encircling her like dogs for her sexual favors.

I referred myself back to an old tactical strategy that I often used at the Village Inn to pick up girls. It consisted of waiting in the narrow walkway near the lady's room, where the targeted girl would have to pay a visit soon or later at one point. When that happened, I would jump at the opportunity for a fast pickup line, landing me 90% of the time on the dance floor with the girl.

But the situation at FIU's pub was quite different; it was not the Coconut Grove's Village Inn, not the dominant, charming mixed crowd, no dancing floor and no Roots Uprising. Regardless, I had a much simpler, old-school plan; it was for me to patiently wait when she was due for a visit to the lady's room, to position myself in such a way to give her a brief written note asking her to come meet me for a talk at the 6 o'clock hour behind the school's library. It was bold and daring. The sort of unconventional approach that would intrigue a girl like her. Minutes after I was done with writing my note, I saw her heading toward the lady's home, as if she read my mind and wanted to play along with my scheme. I discreetly followed her and positioned myself in that one strategic spot where she had to pass me on her way back to the bar. Lo and behold, I saw her coming out of the restroom with her hot, sexy, swinging walk. I gently approached her with my most confident smile and handed her the note by saying, "It's a message for you from me, my lady".

She looked at me, kind of shocked, all the while taking the note out of my hand. She quickly read it and with her large signature smile uttered those words, "See you there." She appeared to be both dazzled and amused by the unconventional means I employed to reach out to her. I immediately left the bar to go do some more research at the library while hoping that she would follow through with her promise. I was so nervous about the potential outcome of such a suspenseful situation that I helped create for myself. Trouble always found me. I had no doubt that she had by now figured me inside out; my flirtatious smile and the desiring look from my ensorcelling brown eyes were obvious signs to her that I was one heck of her diehard admirer, and that despite all the odds against me I found a desperate chivalric way to express my romantic interest toward her. Another thing in her mind was that I wanted her more than anyone of the male competitors around her on Campus.

I left the school's library ten minutes before six to go straight to the east side of the building and sat on that long, low-level wall, waiting for her to show up while holding my fingers crossed. I kept checking my watch anxiously. The last time I checked, it was seven minutes past six, not a good omen sign at all. As I was about to leave the meeting site full of heartbreak and disappointment, came rushing toward me, America's favorite dream girl, apologizing for being late. Not only did she show up to meet with me as requested by my note, but she was genuinely apologetic for not being on time. I reassured her that everything was fine and that her sole presence here with me absolved her from any lateness. After greeting her and formally introducing ourselves, I invited her to sit by me and talk for nearly a whole hour.

Her name was Beatrice. She was from Auckland, California and was of Jewish descent. She was a newcomer on Campus in her first semester and had just signed up for the International Relations undergraduate studies. I had a common academic connection with her, which helped break the ice between us. She was a world traveler and had been to many of the European cities I recently visited with my sister Marcelle. We talked about our common experiences and how we felt about the places we visited, like Barcelona, Paris, Austria and Switzerland. Knowing that I was from Haiti and spoke French, she joked about how unfortunate we did not meet beforehand, I would have prepared her better with her broken French when she was in Paris recently. She apparently came from a well-to-do banker family from Auckland, as her folks were paying for all her undergraduate courses in the program plus her FIU's off-campus' dormitory suite she lived in. Beatrice was so down-to-earth and comfortable within her skin that it took me a while to digest the nature of what was happening in our ongoing real-life interaction on that side wall of the school's library. I was slightly embarrassed by all the pre-conceived ideas I had about her type. First, I thought she would be a snob on roller skates, and second, a dumb blonde by judging her solely on her awesome physical appearance and attributes. So, I was quite touché to learn that she preferred dating black brothers over her own kind since her first teenage date at an

Auckland's ivy league high school was a black brother from one of the Antillean islands of Saint Martin. She joked and proudly blamed the unusually extended buttocks, to be seen on a white girl, for all the unwanted attention she got from black brothers who tirelessly hit on her. She has been confronted, she added jokingly, by many black sisters asking her to return the derrière she borrowed from the Black race and to stop stealing their black males. I was simply beside myself to see how frank and open she was with me, a person she barely knew. I remember asking her if she was married or seeing anyone at this time to be on the safe side, especially after my last volatile platonic affair with Lara.

To both of my inquiries, she answered no, making me feel more relaxed in her company. At one point, the conversation between her and I got so cozy up when she had teary eyes talking about her family's disastrous divorce. I spontaneously passed my arm around her shoulder and gently held her soft hand within mine in a loving gesture. Her sweaty palm was an indicating clue of her spontaneous physical attraction to me. She moved much closer to me, laid her head on my shoulder. Then, lightning struck, setting both of us in a fiery, passionate French kiss. I did not see that one coming as we began making out right on the naked wall behind the library, taking advantage of its hidden darkness.

The speed through which things were developing between Beatrice and me was hypersonic for my still slow, conservative

Haitian mind. My petty bourgeois reflexes from my Cayes' childhood upbringing were still holding me prisoner of the ideal image of a girl; a good woman tended to give herself up slowly and by well-protected, defended walls. Even though I was extremely flattered and astonished to have such a woman like Beatrice in my arms, I could not help pondering if that were not simply too good to be true. It was a mind-boggling situation where the reality of what was happening in real time was stranger than fiction. I began to suspect that what started as me pursuing her might have gone into a turn-and-twist scenario where the predator had become the pray and vice versa.

The jury, as far as I was concerned, was still out to this day on Lyonel and Beatrice's fast-developing sexual escapade. Regardless of who trapped or manipulated who, I did not seem to care much to find out, as I was way too busy enjoying every second of my making out with the mother of all blonde bombshells that was Beatrice in my eyes! She was hungry and proposed to leave the Campus grounds and drive to a nearby restaurant to eat. At this point, I was so intoxicated with everything about her that had she asked me to follow her to hell, I would have followed her, trusting she meant heaven! We ended up at a sushi restaurant, which was highly frequented by students from the university across. There, we resumed our cozying-up session, which began behind the University's library wall, while waiting for our food to arrive. I was not much into public display of affection as a part of my Haitian upbringing, but, emboldened by Beatrice, I found myself violating all those privacy rules. Her wish was my ultimate command, and I could not ask for a better place to be between her spoon-feeding me and her caresses. I followed her to her place after our sushi treats.

The plan was for me to sneak inside her dormitory suite in violation of the dormitory rules. As soon as we were both safe inside behind her apartment's door, she literally attacked me with such sexual voracity that I struggled to match her up. Beatrice was a sexual beast, a man-eater in the true literal sense of the term. For the first time in a long list of wild sexual encounters with ladies of her kind, I was really worried about the possibility for me not to make it back out from her dorm's bed unscathed. We did not even have the chance to advance anywhere near her bedroom, as we ended up both rolling on her Living Room's carpeted floor. She tore off her own gorgeous vintage dress in her eagerness to free that 6-foot-long incredible body of hers.

Her porcelain baby skin which first caught my eyes the afternoon when I saw her entering the school's cafeteria, was now fully exposed in full display on that Living Room floor of hers for my mesmerizing, stunning brown eyes to contemplate all its flawlessness. By now, I had seen quite a few white female naked bodies, but hers was in a class of its own. Her soft, light, pale skin, in comparison to my own naked brown skin, made mine appear so much darker next to hers. I could not help reflecting that it was just last week when the prospect of making love to her was such an unreachable feast that could only be accomplished in my wet dreams! But in a magical turn of events, against many insurmountable odds, Beatrice was now laying on that carpet floor, all drenched and embarrassingly wet, waiting for me to fuck her!

When it became apparent that we were way past the warm-up stage and on par for the main event, I put on the rubber condom she gave me. Concerned about being a big, nothing burger in her eyes, I told her to get on top for our first intercourse round of what would become a long, sleepless evening of sex. Judging by how fully ripened Beatrice was sexually, and how devilishly erected I was, the bottom bunker position was, for me, the safest way to outlast her. As she was pleasuring herself to no end on top of my tool, I could not help being part of that entire sexual euphoria, especially when I felt the bottom part of her voluptuous body, rapaciously grasping every inch of my hard sizable cock into her mighty infernal. The sensitive lover that I was known to be was seriously struggling during that first round of intercourse with her, as she appeared to be quite a pro at it.

Realizing that she was not anywhere near climaxing, despite all the tricks I used on her, like clitoris stimulation, French and nipples kissing, I found myself on the rope and had only a few seconds left before being disgracefully TKO by her. But then, as a last desperate move to save face, I began stimulating her anus ring with my finger, a sex region known to be an extremely sensitive pleasure point for lots of women. I was just hoping for a dignifying draw, meaning to have her orgasm at the same time with me in a spectacular, respectable fashion for a first good impression on her. Lucky I, it so happened that I hit one of her most vulnerable spots with my insinuating fingering around her anal ring. Beatrice's moaning screams were getting louder and louder in my ears. Her vaginal muscles' strong contractions grasping the whole of my penis were also an encouraging sign that she was well on her way to the promised land. Minutes after, the two of us convulsively climaxed together on the soft carpet floor of her apartment's suite. Her magnificent figure was still quivering in my arms while she was profusely thanking me for my patience and endurance in holding back long enough to make that happen for her.

She confessed that because of her lucky, fantastic build, most men, black brothers included among them, tended to come much too quick, while making love to her, sometimes before penile penetration was even in the mix. She continued with the critical issue of pre-mature ejaculation from her past sexual partners who failed her despite being in the second and third rounds of intercourse with her. Little did she know that I was in as much difficulty as the men she had been with before, who were obviously way too mesmerized by her near-perfect body to withstand the overwhelming sexual euphoria of coming, even before entering her kingdom's gate. Little did she know that when I was on the rope on the edge of failing her miserably like the ones before me, I just got a lucky break, saved by my last-minute stimulation of her anal ring.

We finally made it to her bedroom for a much more comfortable outercourse in her bed, preparing for another more momentous second round of sex. She was not finished with me yet; the night was still way too young for her, as she grabbed my hand to follow her into her bedroom just in case I had any intent to run away from her. While following her from behind, I had a full view of her formidable, extended buttocks. They were so well rounded, fleshy and bouncy and were made more lethal by her hot, sexy walk. I now completely understood why black brothers felt that she was one of ours, despite her waspy porcelain skin, blue eyes and blonde hair. She herself confessed her natural sexual attraction for black males as opposed to her own kind. She did not mind the constant attention she was getting from many of her black male pursuers. Or else, there was no way in hell I would have been here in her bed, period!

When I thought I had heard it all from the many chit-chats we had been having since she began to confide in me several of her sexual fantasies, it was only the start. Beatrice suffered from a mild case of hypersexuality, addicted to the pleasure of the flesh and orgasm. She admitted that there was no substitute for having her fix with a male lover, but in the absence of that, she had a whole set of toys as substitutes, which in many ways, according to her, performed way much better than her average male lovers. However, the most stunning revelation made to me during our evening confession was when she candidly told me that though she enjoyed different types of intercourse, anal was by far her favorite one. She argued that anal sex allowed her to reach the highest orgasmic peak ever. I was taken aback by her candid admission, as I understood that she was indirectly suggesting that I engaged in plain anal intercourse with her. I had never done that before with anyone of my past sexual partners, and I was not about to engage in that rabbit hole type of sex act, not even with a hot girl like Beatrice, who I assumed had one of the best buttocks in the whole white world. Besides, I had many religious and cultural inhibitions about the whole anal intercourse business. Even though I was not homophobic, as most Haitians were in general, I found the very act of 'sodomizing' Beatrice a deviant sex act, and simply too close for comfort. And I could not help falling in line with my old religious Catholic upbringing, which looked upon male-female anal intercourse let alone the male to male one as an 'a sin against nature'. Aside from that, there were the health and hygiene issues added to the mix.

I was in a dilemma with Beatrice insisting in her sweet way to do it to her the Greek way and made it the highlight of her night. I was torn on one hand between pleasing her by responding to her 'devious' desire and, on the other hand, ignore her request altogether. She did not make her anal sex demand an ultimatum or else, as we continued fondling one another in her pleasant, comfortable bed. Things started to heat up once more in her bedroom. When I came to a full erection, she got herself on all fours for me to mount her and penetrate her from behind. I was going and going fearlessly and relentlessly through my usual steady circular motion and deep sideway insertion through her vagina walls, which triggered some wild, deafening screams out of Beatrice.

At one point, amid what she would later admit as one of her most ravaging fucks ever, my eight-inch erected cock came out of her accidentally, but she quickly grabbed it with her hand, and instead of putting it back into her vagina, she either by mistake or by design, inserted the whole of it into her anal ring. I felt that something was a little bit different this time, as if her vagina got so tight so suddenly around my tool, making me feel as if I was having sex with a just born-again virgin. I did not make much of an issue about it thinking that perhaps she was about to reach another plateau, and that was a normal vaginal's reaction to tighten up and flex its muscles around the penis' head. So, I kept at it, though at a much slower pace than earlier.

However, what followed was anything but pure adulterated mayhem as I continued to stick it to her, not really knowing that I was in her God-forsaken rectum. The moaning screams coming out of her this time was so loud and alarming that at one point, I asked her if she wanted me to stop, but she quickly replied, "Heck no, please don't stop. Keep at it, baby…" all the while appearing to be gasping for air. She then begged me to spank her decadent extended buttocks for being a spoiled, bad-ass rich bitch. I did, but not hard enough to her pleasing. She insisted that I slapped both sides of her rear end harder, arguing that a stiff, genuine spanking always brought her faster to the hedge. I obeyed her order, and lo and behold, Beatrice was having a sexual epiphany event landing her in one momentous orgasm.

I saw her at one point when her entire snowlike bombshell body, still in orgasmic convulsions, chewing nervously hard her pillow and bedsheet cover. I was safe mounting her from behind instead of being under her. For I had no doubt that those bites and the chewing I saw her doing could have been done on me, the man-eater that she was.

She was haggardly worn down and appeared disoriented by that last round of sex with me. She was not even aware until later that I did not climax together with her like earlier, a testimony of how far gone she was in her orgasmic trance. She compensated me plenty by giving me one royal oral sex worthy of a king. And the ultimate cherry on my cake came when she did not let my juice go to waste by swallowing the entire load when I came into her mouth's deep throat.

Lyonel Gerdes

Later in our continuing chit-chatting pillow talk, she came clean by confessing that the last few minutes of our last sex act were not vaginal but anal. She felt that I was too hesitating to try it with her. So, she took it upon herself to introduce me to it without me knowing, as she cooked up a mendacious sex scheme. All she had to do, after applying enough lubricant oil around and inside her anal ring and rectum during a convenient, break at her restroom, was to wait when I was too intoxicated with sexual pleasure to purposely yank out my penis from her vagina. That was exactly what she did, pretending to insert my penis back, only this time not where I thought, as it was inserted into her well-oiled rectum canal walls. The puzzle of Beatrice tightened vagina walls was solved by her candid admission. She did not metamorphose herself into a virgin Marie from one minute to the next. I was simply tricked by her into having anal intercourse without me knowing and against my will.

Though I felt somewhat betrayed by her, but when looking at the sheer amount of pleasure she had had in a few minutes of anal sex, I forgave her. I was duped into doing it, but one thing was for sure: I came to realize that anal sex was not really my thing. Yes, the joy of full-spectrum dominance I had over Beatrice's both body and mind while I was taking her the Greek way, though flattering to my male's ego, was not worth the gamble.

I shall also come clean by admitting that in my growing sexcapade list of seduced Uncle's daughters, -- to sweetly avenge

262

centuries-old of sexual abuses committed by white men against my enslaved black women ancestors -- Beatrice, the blonde bombshell, topped the list. There was no sweeter revenge for me to watch white folks' jaw-dropping moments watching me making out with her in public. As she could easily be the white innocent girl next door, a sister, a cousin, an aunt, a wife, or a mother. Beatrice's conquest had considerably helped consolidate my already robust image of the lady's man.

Beatrice would not let me leave her dormitory suite that night. When I woke up late the next morning, she was already fully awake and still holding me tight against her. I was not the only rising creature in her bed, as I woke up with what they proverbially called the morning glory. She apparently had her own nocturnal clitoral arousal herself. Regardless, she interpreted my morning wood erection as a provocation that needed a swift, immediate response by her. So, she rolled over and quickly placed a rubber condom over my tool and began a whole new session of mounting me once again with the same voraciousness seen the night before, resuming, so to speak, our sexual odyssey right where we left off when we both felt asleep from exhaustion last night.

After we had our morning fixes, we started making plans to go down to my place first and later hit Coconut Grove's Nightlife party scene. She loved dancing, dining out, and the whole ambiance down at the Grove. It was a pity, she lamented, that she lived so far away from the scene. The final plan we arrived at, was for her to follow me in her bourgeois Mercedes Benz car to my humble bachelor pad off Biscayne Blvd and spend the weekend there with me. She packed a few clothing and essentials for her stay, and off we went on the 45-minute highway drive to Isidor's. We safely made it to my place. She loved the coziness of my pad and my music collection. I planned to treat her to an evening diner at Senior Frog, for she was craving Mexican food. And after dinner, the plan was to go for a barhopping experience. I put her on notice for an afternoon Reggae extravaganza the following day at the Village Inn. She could not wait for the latter, as she was a huge fan of Reggae music.

We had so many things in common that it was getting seriously too scarry for words. She adored people-watching with its marvelous see-and-be-seen buzz. She was a provocateur extraordinaire in her own right, as she loved to make out in public with me, knowing fully well the high level of voyeuristic attention that we both were getting, especially when she was doing it with a black man. However, she quickly made an interesting differentiation between me and my black American brothers on many grounds, such as ethnicity, cultural, language, history, education and upbringing. In her mind, she was not dating just any black man. She was with a well-educated, presentable and well-mannered black Haitian man. Thus, absolving her from the 'nigger lover' epithet.

Back then, my hair was long and braided à la Milli Vanilli's hairdo look of the late 80s, years before the iconic duos made it popular the world over. It was the very first attempt by me to dramatically change that old 'just come' nerdy image of mine. When wearing the right attire, with my imposing 6-foot height presence, I was often confused by many for one of the Hollywood celebrities hanging out in Cognito. Men as well as women would approach me wanting to know if I was so and so, Rick James, or a member of the legendary R&B group Earth, Wind & Fire. It was, of course, that celebrity image perception that had considerably helped me in my somewhat successful conquests with several of Uncle Sam's darling white daughters, including Beatrice. She told me that I caught her attention the first week of her arrival on Campus from Aukland because of my long hair look, my height and my elegant clothing, making me look special. She also candidly admitted that the moment that I sat across the bar, she was even more taken by my distinguished mustache, the charming smile, and the gravitational pull coming from my light brown eyes.

She had told me that she might have spotted me way before I noticed her myself. She put it bluntly, "I was just the type of black male that she was attracted to and under the right circumstances, she would screw me in a heartbeat". Then, I concluded that she was all along a willing accomplice of what had been since in the making between us. As the wise old saying had reiterated over and over, "It takes two to tangle". It was no accident when she was equally flirtatious with me at the bar in the same way I was with her, for she simply could not help it.

I was her dream black man as much she was my dream blonde, and when I made that move to pass her that note by the lady's home, she made up her mind quick to go meet with me behind the library. She would not let such an opportunity go to waste. That was why she was so nervous when she was 15 minutes late at the rendezvous fearing that I might have left. She was so glad, continued Beatrice in her long narrative, that I waited for her. I knew then that I was going to do just fine by her if I played my cards well, or else why was she rushing to meet with a total stranger that she had just met, followed by her sincere apologies for being late.

Back in my bachelor's pad, Beatrice had made herself so at home that, at one point, she came back in her birthday suit following a visit to the restroom. It seemed to be a reoccurring pattern with the ladies at my bachelor's pad. They would not keep their clothes on! She insisted that I stripped my clothes off to join her in the bathtub that she had just filled with soapy water. In no time, we both were laying down and cozying up in the warm tub's water. We could barely keep our hands off from each other even when we were fully clothed, let alone when we were both naked and, in such proximity, to one another. Beatrice changed her posture and was now laying her lengthy, curvy figure on top of me. From the bottom position where I was, with her full back frame on top of me, I had another awakening view of the magnificent build of that killer body of hers.

In this instant, I could not help pondering why on earth was such a near-perfect creature like Beatrice doing here with me totally nude in this bathtub! What were the gods or the devils up to by placing her in my path. Unbeknownst of higher intelligent beings concocting a plot or not, I was enjoying every second of it until such unbelievable tale lasted. Ergo, my fingers had been exploring the soft underbelly of her curvaceous figure and her awesome, rounded pair of big boobs floating and bouncing amid the soapy water.

From one caressing touch to the next, as it had been the case with her since last night, one thing led to another until we transitioned into one fiery fucking episode in the cozying space of the bathtub. It was the first and the only time for the record I had had sex with a woman in it. It was Beatrice's animalistic, female way to mark my place with her body scent warning any competing bitches to keep away. She was not doing anything different than any of the other women who had been here before and after her.

We rested for a good long hour recovering from our last sex act in the tub. We later began to get ourselves ready for our dinner reservation at Senior Frog. Beatrice, like a Hollywood starlet, looked utterly glamorous and stunning in her long, dark, sexy attire, clashing with her spotless porcelain skin. Her evening dress espoused all the curvaceous lines of her incredible figure, especially her historic rear end, emphasis added. I could see that between her low cleavage, silky long dress, revealing how extremely well endowed she was in the chest department, and her well-rounded extended derrière that she and I would take no prisoner tonight. I did not waste my breath telling her how ridiculously gorgeous and hot she was, for too many people had already done so, but she could read into my eyes that I was so heavenly pleased! Though she loved the attention she was getting from men lusting after her, she nevertheless was a dignifying lady and would not make a fool out of me flirting openly with other men while being with me.

She gave me her Mercedes Benz car key to drive, as she was not too familiar with the area where I lived. We arrived on time at Senior Frog. I valet parked for the occasion and entered the restaurant with Beatrice affectionately passing her left arm under my right arm leaning her head on my shoulder. We were escorted to a table centrally located for the maximum see-and-be-seen dining experience. After our copious dinner, I took her on a bar-hopping experience at the Grove party scenes. We danced our hearts out at Hungry Sailors, the Village Inn and at Taurus. I could never appreciate enough how comfortable she was in her skin while being with me. I was by a country mile, the one feeling a little awkward and self-conscious being with her than she was being with me. She was an excellent dancing partner with some unbelievable, provocative moves on the dance floor.

## Miami, Florida: A Sunshine State's Unauthorized And Unredacted Journey

We French kissed and made out on and off the dance floors. We were both stunned and tipsy, and the provocateur extraordinaire that Beatrice was, maliciously enjoyed showing off her hot, sexy body while dancing passionately and provocatively with a black man. It was in effect, the sort of provoking sexual display act that would have earned me a noose around my black Haitian neck under Jim Crow's deep South era. Beatrice surprised me with some cool dancing moves for a white girl, to be frank. She would lower the full length of her curvaceous, voluptuous body all the way down to the cement floor like a tantalizing moving sneak, fully aware that she was being watched by voyeuristic white males with lusty eyes who would have done anything to be in my 'nigger' shoes. I began to suspect that the hot sexual energy she had been sending throughout the evening had boomeranged on her big time when her sexual antennas were flashing all their red lights. I sensed that if she could, she would have me taken her right there in the dark, restricted VIP section of the club where we were and to hell with the rules of civilized society and decency. To avoid being thrown out of the club for being indecent or worse, getting in a fight with some white racist dudes saying something stupid and derogatory to us, I came up with a hasty suggestion to go back to my place and finish off the evening with a much bigger bang. She agreed, and as soon as we got inside my bachelor's pad, she threw the gloves off. She did not want to waste time taking off her high heel shoes; instead, she hastily pulled her long silky dress up to her waist, got rid of her J-string underwear and positioned her formidable bottom right on top of my kitchenette's counter sink. She then spread both of her legs placing them on each side of my shoulders, allowing me the deepest, penetration to take the whole of her and ravish it to oblivion. I did just that while she was feverishly begging me to go for the kill and leave not one inch of her untouched. She acted as if she had an uncontrollable sexual compulsion, a sort of sexual craving comparable if not more pressing than the physical urge one has for peeing and pooping.

Our extravagant dirty dancing and subsequent making out in the clubs throughout the night were like public, outside off-bed foreplays. So, by the time we made it back to my place, we both were so ripe, moist, wet and ready for showtime. Due to the lifting angle eased by her two legs over both of my shoulders, I was able to penetrate so deep inside her vagina that her entrenched cervix, another added source of sexual pleasure for her, was at the receiving end of my relentless banging. She directed me not to thrust in and out that fast, instead to stay fully inside of her while moving slowly in a circle and to gently rub the head of my penis on her hypersensitive cervix area while at the same time using the base of my penis to pressure, rub it against her clitoris and the rest of it against her inside vagina G-spot. The result of her directive led to an all-time orgasmic explosion which was long overdue, finishing our crazy night out with an unexpected volley of fireworks. It was one heck of a wild sexual finale, with Beatrice's shaking legs and feet still in their high heels crossing over both of my shoulders.

We hit the sac early that night because we were both exhausted but also out of concern about not being in tip top shape the following day for our scheduled Reggae Satsang down at the Village Inn. I did my best to describe to Beatrice the unbelievable, magical atmosphere she would be encountered there, the awesome looking mixed crowd, and the excellent Reggae music being played by Roots Uprisings. She could not wait to check it out. We briefly made a stop there last night in our bar-hopping rampage, and she seemed to like the energy inside the place. But I made it clear to her that the afternoon Reggae was an entirely different animal.

After waking up late and well-rested, we greeted each other with another round of love making, as we simply could not keep our hands off from one another. We then showered together, an entire scene all by itself, and went for lunch at the Omni International Mall. Following lunch, we walked around the stores and boutiques at the mall and headed home to get ready for the weekend's main event.

Contrary to my last night's look when I wore my long-braided hair in a subdued ponytail, but today, for a much wilder look, I raised the bar a notch by letting my hair down on my shoulder to keep up with Beatrice's wild set of attire. I wore a stylish light blue denim, baggy pair of pants with their legs inserted inside my tall leather black boots. And with my white puffy pirate shirt, I was dandily ready for battle with that renaissance look of mine. Beatrice was quite impressed with me by exclaiming, "My tall, dark and handsome Haitian lover". But, if one thought I was ready for battle at the Village Inn war theater, Beatrice was even readier for battle and was in no mood to let herself overshadowed by me!

She had a killer set of attire consisting of a braless top that barely covered her formidable nipples while at the same time revealing a significant portion of her sizable pair of melons. Her top, besides failing to cover her entire back, revealing the smooth squaring of her feminine shoulders, came to a stop right on top of her cute belly bottom, exposing her flat, sexy belly. Her bottom sexy shorts were so short that whenever she bent down, a significant portion of her G-string underwear, along with the two fleshy parts of her buttocks were displayed, offering quite a sight to the voyeuristic eyes. Her shorts, besides accentuating her already phenomenal rear end, also put in the forefront her tall pair of hot legs, aided and abetted by her high heels. Her entire outfit was so skimpy that it left very little to the imagination, and the color of it, to top it all off, was an off-white color so pale that it disturbingly blended with her porcelain skin. From any respectable distance, most people would fall for that optical, visual confusion that Beatrice was out in plain daylight in her birthday suit.

# Miami, Florida: A Sunshine State's Unauthorized And Unredacted Journey

The conservative Haitian in me again was freaking out by her over the top risqué outfit to the extent that I had to take one more puff from the reefer joint I was sharing with her. I knew then that there was no way I could, with a bold straight face, introduce Beatrice to my folks as my fiancée and future wife. Not in a million years by the way she was dressing now, regardless of how blonde, pretty, and rich she was. For as much I enjoyed having sex with her, I would have to come to terms one day with some serious reality check that Beatrice was simply too hot and too high-end for me to handle. For one thing, my still meager HRS' salary could barely afford the high cost of just dating her.

Besides, I was struggling to reconcile the split personality in her. The image of the down-to-earth, clever student who dressed decently in school with the party girl who at the clubs dressed like a high-paid escort. But wait a second, wasn't I way ahead of myself! We were only on our third day of dating, and the ultimate wisdom call was for me to relax, get over her shocking skimpy outfit and enjoy the mind-boggling roller coaster ride I was having with her.

We left my bachelor's pad a little earlier so we could get the best table inside the Village Inn in anticipation of the usual overcrowded house. When we arrived there, people were beginning to arrive. We managed to secure a cool spot near the stage. Roots Uprisings' musicians were on stage tuning in their instruments. By now I have earned Roots Uprisings' #1 fan trophy, and all the

273

musicians were waving at us from the stage. The group's main singer came to personally say hi to us, introducing himself to Beatrice, and reaffirmed to her that I was the band's top 10 supporters. The usual suspects, meaning my Haitian buddies, in their relentless pursuit of the uncle's daughters, were all at the routine Sunday matinee rendezvous. Patrick Duperval, like the others, came by to say hi, though I suspected that they came more to check out Beatrice, that hot date of mine than to really greet me. Handsome-looking Patrick, a court-certified lady's man upon realizing that I just hit the 'freakin' jackpot with Beatrice, lowered himself down to make a comment in my ear, "Ki kote w bare ak kokenn chenn fanm blond ak cheve pit sa a?" [Where on earth, have I found such a knockout blonde babe with that sisal like hair?] "Cheve pit" [Sisal Hair] was the Haitian Creole way of labeling European and North American blonde hair color. I did not encourage anyone of my old pals to stick around long around my table; knowing them for the pigs that they were, they would have started hitting on her right under my nose and not making a big deal of it. Knowing their old tactical scheme, they would patiently wait in one of the bar's dark corners for me to make a trip to the john to shamelessly run to my table and ask her for a dance. The little I knew of her from the 3 days I dated her, I would not have been shocked upon returning from the toilet to find the suave-looking Patrick rubbing his cock on my date Beatrice. Of course, none of those embarrassing scenarios ever happened. I was just imagining such a potential worst-case scenario if I were not vigilant and careful at surveilling and protecting my turf. The Village Inn was a jungle where I saw many unsuspected white dudes come with their first hot dates to later leave the club without them.

Roots Uprisings that afternoon opened the matinee show's first round with Dennis Brown's signature love song, "Should I". It so happened that this was one of my favorite songs but also Beatrice's. We both ended up on the dancing floor. To my big surprise, Beatrice's dancing Reggae moves were right on par with any skilled Jamaican Rasta sisters. And because of her glamorous look and sexy curvaceous figure, she made her well-choreographed steps, the only dancing act worth watching on that dance floor. She put so much energy into her dancing moves that they had become contagious, as I rose to the occasion to join into that dancing euphoria of hers. What a class act, Beatrice was as a Reggae dancer. We never returned to our table. We stayed on that dance floor song after song. Her thick short blonde hair and my braided long black hair became part of our dancing choreography. Funny that Beatrice's behavior at the Reggae scene, in comparison to last night's exhibitionist rampage amid the predominantly white crowd, was, in stark contrast, mild and quite subdued. The provocateur extraordinaire in her had taken a rain check on provoking any shock and awe amid the mixed crowd at the Village Inn as if she felt so completely at home and in a familiar landscape, so, no need for her to have a temper tantrum like last night.

The unusual and unnatural self-restraint displayed by her throughout her time spent at the Village Inn exploded when we got to my bachelor pad that night. She wanted nothing to do with foreplay. She wanted to skip the appetizer part of the sex menu and go straight for a gargantuan main entrée. She was so wet down there and so darn ready for sex that she scared me. I just had seconds to place a condom over my member before she sat her entire bottom into it, using both of her arms to rotate herself in a rapid circular motion around both the base and axis of my tool. She let out a succession of moaning screams, all the while thrusting her formidable buttocks up and down and around my hard, erect cock with such intense voracity that I did not know she had all that gusto sexual appetite in her until that night. I helped drive her even more ballistic by simultaneously stimulating both her sensitive nipples and her clitoris, plunging her into the ultimate sexual arousal ever.

When we both were on our way to climax, she begged me to please sodomize her. How could I not acquiesce to her boiling desire, and deny such a hot, scorching creature like Beatrice, imploring me to please sodomize her buttocks? Besides I was way too immersed in having the wildest sex act ever with her to even think of denying her pressing request. I said to her, "Let's get it on, bitch". She sure brought the worst in me. That was not how my mamma raised me to talk to a lady in such an impolite, demeaning tone. In response to that, she swiftly changed her reverse cowgirl position on me to placing herself on all fours. She used her fingers to lubricate both her internal and external anal sphincters in preparation for a smooth, comfortable penetration of her anus. What followed in the next following minutes was a déjà vu all over again. And like the last time I had anal intercourse with her unknowingly, the moaning screams coming out of her grew in hyperbolic intensity and were so harrowingly loud and piercing that had I not known for sure that they were of pleasure and not of pain, I would have gone awry and panicky by stopping and calling 911.

Like Friday night, when I got conned by her to enter her anal canal's walls and subsequently witnessed Beatrice's rapid body metamorphosis into a trance, zombie-like state, I relived that ultimate sense of power, I felt I had over both her body and mind. It was once again that full-spectrum dominance scenario being replayed. Except for this time, without waiting to be asked by her to give her a sincere well-deserved spanking for being a badass Jewish blonde girl, I took it upon myself to whoop her two bouncy fleshy parts of her extended behind. While I was striking her rear end real hard and roughly pulling her Sisal-like hair, I also threw a few vexing insults at her for being rich, hot, conceded and spoiled rotten. For a few seconds, a strange mysterious entity seemed to come in possession of me, as if the spanking I was giving her, and the insults were for real in my mind and that I truly meant to give her a real whooping while demeaning her along the way. It was simply way too odd and scary for words!

Because I took charge of the entire sexual theater in the room and initiated on my own the harsh spanking, the rough pulling of her hair and my insulting words, all that appeared to have had a culminating climaxing effect on her psyche. During those moments of absolute euphoria, I became in real time her true domineering master, especially when backed by the in dept, complete insertion of my relentless hard cock through her lengthy rectum. Words could never describe enough the long, gasping, choking orgasms that seemed to have taken full hold of Beatrice's body. Her entire curvaceous white snow figure was now turning bloody red, caused by a succession of non-stop convulsions. I had seen earth-shaking orgasms of her during our last three days of sex, but this latest one she just had with me was in a class of its own, for the record. And subsequently joined her with my own blasting orgasm seconds after her. And, like last Friday when I got mercilessly conned by her to unknowingly enter her anal canal walls, the same exact scenario was again repeating itself as in an encore. Then, I subsequently saw all of Beatrice descending into that trance, zombie-like state, following her devouring climax. It was, by all accounts, a mind-boggling and scary scene displaying the impact, and the devastating power anal intercourse had on her whole being.

It was not easy when Monday morning came for us to split

from one another after such a momentous, memorable weekend full of non-stop actions. Looking back at that first weekend spent with Beatrice, we did so much in so little time, thus making it the longest, action-packed weekend, spent by me with anyone. We both wished that life was an ever-ending weekend of wild sex, good food, and dancing like the one we just had, but that was not the way life's paradigm was set. When we both woke up that Monday morning, we managed to create enough time for a short and sweet 'quickie' in the shower. I resumed my regular weekday schedule of reporting to my daily HRS office job and then attend my graduate night courses at FIU. Beatrice herself had to attend her afternoon and evening classes there, too. The only consolation we had would be our planned meeting on the wall behind the library during breaks or in between classes on Monday, Wednesday and Friday when I was on campus.

We arranged for us to spend alternate weekends at each other's respective apartments. This arrangement went on for nearly two months. But somewhere along the way, as it had happened many times with several of my female dates before, Beatrice appeared to want more from me than just sex. She just like the others before her wanted the missing emotional connection she rightly felt was sort of missing from my side. She began to reproach me for my lack of emotional attachment, and genuine loving attachment toward her. And despite the exceptional sex we both were having, something was not budging from my side, as I kept in place a thick, impenetrable walls all around me.

I started to suspect near the end that she was beginning to experience a sense of fatigue with me. I even had some keen suspicion that she might have started seeing other people behind my back. Every now and then, she would come up with some excuses not to meet. One Friday night, she called to tell me that she would not be meeting me that weekend as she would be visiting her folks in Auckland. I decided to investigate her, as I had reason to doubt that she was genuine. Saturday night, the day after she called, I drove to one of her favorite clubs in the West Kendall area. She took me twice to that club during two of the weekend's stay at her dorm.

I got to the club by the midnight hour and, lo and behold, guess who I saw was on that club's dance floor dirty dancing with a big black dude? It was the bombshell blonde Beatrice, the girl with the sisal-like color hair. Even though I was not in love with her, I had some good, genuine feelings for her. I had some significant sentimental/physical bond with her. Consequently, I could not help feeling hurt and devastated when I caught her lying and cheating on that dance floor with that big black dude. I was not the type that would walk to that dance floor and make a big scene of jealousy, so I decided to quietly exit the club without letting her see me. I had been faithful to Beatrice in the two months I dated her. I even stopped seeing Melodee, a white belly dancer, that I was seeing on

and off for the last two years. I took Beatrice's betrayal so hard, and
the heartbreak I suffered to watch her in the arms of another black
dude, was immense and devastating.

Another sentimental cost I had to endure for my stubborn
persistence at keeping any woman from breaking into my emotional
walls of vulnerability. Or my stubbornness at maintaining my
incorrigible bachelor's lifestyle, thus missing on some meaningful
opportunity with the ladies. For how much longer I intended to live
by that old motto of mine, "Falling in lust, yes, but falling in love,
no." If only I could learn how to make myself halfway available
emotionally with some of my past dates, I would have had a much
greater fulfilling experience, or at least a longer, more gratifying
time with them. I certainly knew how to best lay the traps to seduce
and conquer them, but as soon as the initial phase of conquest was
over, I became severely impaired and emotionally challenged to
keep the dazzling fireworks I started going past the initial blasting
days. Two of my recent past dates had the honesty to tell me the
reasons why they wanted out by blaming it all on my total emotional
unavailability to them. This deep emotional malfunction did not
come in a vacuum or from nowhere. It all stemmed from a difficult
childhood upbringing in Haiti, first in my adopted provincial city of
Les Cayes and next in the capital city of Port-au-Prince.

I was raised as a love-deprived adoptee by both of my parents.
My own biological mother had her own emotional walls erected

281

against me. I sort of inherited that from her. All I ever wanted as a child was to be wanted, accepted and loved by my mother. She was to me like in every boy's heart, the first female image of beauty, grace, and unconditional love, except that the door leading to her love was constantly slammed shut in my face. I grew up completely estranged from her and suffered from being unloved and emotionally rejected all throughout the years I lived with my mother until I migrated to Miami. I began to develop a confusing, mixed feeling toward women. On the one hand, I was attracted to much older women, desperately seeking the missing motherly love, and on the other hand, despite my constant craving for love and attention from girls, I simultaneously built considerable emotional walls to protect myself from being hurt and rejected by another woman like my mother had done my entire life.

I came up with the perfect formula to protect myself from ever being hurt by women despite my compulsive attraction to girls. The formula was for me to never allow both the physical and emotional bonding to coexist with one another. It was either a purely physical relationship with no intent to ever go emotional or indulge in a platonic emotional bonding with a girl but never muster the courage needed to take it to the next level.

I even had some suspicions that the devastating puppy love I had with a girl named Carole while living in Martissant might have triggered my resolve to never again leave myself that vulnerable and

open to love and emotion. I wrote extensively in my last published
trilogy memoirs about my mother's emotional rejection of me, and
my epic puppy love deception as the possible culprits behind my
deeply ingrained emotional unavailability to woman.

I could not forgive or forget Beatrice's lie and betrayal. I
stopped returning her calls or telling her why I did not want to have
anything to do with her anymore. I had reason to believe that I was
not her only black lover and that there were others besides me. I did
not feel safe continuing the sexual relationship I had with her despite
the unbelievable sex we had together. Having sex with Beatrice was
like playing Russian roulette with my life health wise, as the lethal,
highly contagious sexual disease of HIV and AIDS were on the rise.
Untold number of people around the world and here in the States
were contracting the disease and dying from it within days, as the
deadly HIV-AID infection had no effective cures back then.

When I thought that the fallout between me and Beatrice was
the end of the world, plunging me into a huge depressing mood, I
had an equally bigger if not a much more disastrous one hitting me,
when Roots Uprisings' contract with the Village Inn was cancelled.
The band that had been behind the creation of the most dazzling
matinee ambiance ever in the Grove would no longer be playing
there. Rumors had it that the owners were under tremendous
pressure to cancel their popular Sunday Reggae matinee.
Apparently, the 'good old white boys club' who controlled and

283

owned most of the Grove's properties and businesses in the highly lucrative tourist industry, had an issue with the increasing numbers of pot-smoking Rastafarian crowd image in the heart of the Coconut Grove's tourist and business hub every Sunday. To their white racist view, it was a big eyesore in an otherwise pristine and all-white affair at the Coconut Grove.

The abrupt cancellation of Roots Uprisings at the Village Inn, with their huge mixed fan base followers, signaled the tragic end and death of Reggae music there. With it also followed the unfortunate end of that all-inclusive, pacifying ambiance where many of Miami's various ethnic whites, mixed races, and ethnic blacks, whether it be Hispanics, Jews, Jamaicans, or Haitians could come to the Village Inn for one amazing transcendental gathering feast each Sunday afternoon.

Next on the 1980s' neoliberal/counterculture agenda would be to phase out the long-haired, colorful group of Coconut Grove's hippy subculture, representing the last remaining embodiment of a bygone 60s and 70s eras of free love and sex. The old Coconut Grove's groove reminiscing of New York Greenwich Village's 'Let's Make Love Not War' would forever be a thing of the past. With the beginning construction of Coco Walk, a huge open-air shopping mall, sounded the death knell of all the area's Mama shops which irreversibly altered the genuine chemistry of what the yesteryear Grooving community used to stand for, feel like, and be

Miami, Florida: A Sunshine State's Unauthorized And Unredacted Journey

like during the last two decades of the 1960s and 70s.

# PART III

## On The Black American Experience

Malcom X's best quote on the dystopian Orwellian world created by the white Western propaganda machine warned us, "If you're not careful, the newspapers will have you hating the people who are being oppressed, and loving the people who are doing the oppressing". Besides the cautionary tale above and my own personal conviction to always be on the side of the oppressed people's plights anywhere in the world, I never once bought into the plethora of clichés maliciously implanted in everyone's mind about black Americans, including black Americans themselves. Sure, as a young black Haitian male, coming from Port-au-Prince, Haiti, and being the product of a different culture, language and upbringing, I had to struggle hard to overcome the natural antagonistic, prejudicial barriers opposing me to my black American brothers and sisters. One of the usual stereotypical misunderstandings would have me believe that my black Haitian experience had somewhat of a historical advantage over that of the black Americans living in Miami's Overtown, Liberty City, and elsewhere in the State.

The malicious intent behind that comparison coming from the Haitian middle class and bourgeois elite was for us, the newly arrived immigrants here in the State, to feel somewhat better about ourselves on the sole historical ground that our Haitian ancestors had fought valiantly and successfully against their French enslavers and oppressors by chasing them off our shores. On the other hand, the black American enslaved population never had such grand historical moments of reckoning with their white Anglo-American oppressors and enslavers. Several of my Haitian countrymen felt for that facile trick of divide and conquer classic 101 brainwashing without ever taking in consideration the different historical contexts of both the black Haitian and American experiences.

First and foremost, in St. Domingue, now present-day Haiti, the embattled slaves were a much larger group, thus, had a more sustainable armed rebellion against the French Army sent by Napoleon to reestablish slavery. That French army, which was headed by General Leclerc, was being mercilessly decimated by the deadly yellow fever virus, making the latter a more formidable foe than the random, ragtag indigent troops they were fighting against. Whereas on the other end of the spectrum, the low percentage of enslaved blacks in America, mostly concentrated on the Southern plantations, despite their known historic and notable rebellions, could never attain Haiti's unique historical feast of being the only successful black slaves' uprising against their white Western masters and colonizers of the late 18$^{th}$ and early 19$^{th}$ Centuries.

Several plots occurred in antebellum America, such as the Gabriel's Rebellion in 1800 in Richmond, Virginia, the Louisiana uprising in 1811, the Denmark Vesey's plot, which was uncovered in 1822 in Charleston, South Carolina, and, of course, the most significant uprising and rebellion of them all: Nat Turner's slave revolt known as the Southampton insurrection where in 1831 an enslaved numbers of black Virginian led by Turner massacred over 65 white people in the Southampton County area of Virginia. Though his rebellion was crushed within days at Belmont Plantation on the morning of August 23, it was, nevertheless, the one that horrified white slave owners the most, not just in Virginia but throughout the slave-economy plantations in the South as well as in the North. Still, all four rebellions had one thing in common: they all failed to change the course of the institution of slavery. Instead, following each of these slave revolts, more repressive measures were taken against both the enslaved black American population as well as the free Blacks'.

The black American experience in its antebellum days of captivity, by the very historical facts of geography and the much smaller size of the enslaved black population in comparison to their white masters', was condemned to remain in its imposed historical state, that is a controlled, manipulated managed internal colored colony on the territory of the American Empire.

Even decades after the American Civil War and the ratification by Congress of the 13th Amendment abolishing slavery in the US, the South continued to use several deceptive means to bypass the so-called Emancipation Proclamation laws legislated by the winning North. In this context, Colbert's Black Codes provided

289

convenient legalistic justifications for all the Jim Crow legislation during the Reconstruction period designed to recapture in one form or another the former slave's cheap labor. Here is an observer's vivid comments on the situation in the postbellum South, "Under the Black Codes, many states required Black people to sign yearly labor contracts; if they refused, they risked being arrested, fined and forced into unpaid labor".

'The North, under Johnson's Reconstruction, with a non-interference policy leaning on states' rights, only asked the former Confederate states to 'acquiesce and uphold the abolition of slavery proclamation, swear loyalty to the Union and pay off their war debt'. Beyond those demands, continued the observer, "Southern white planters were given a relatively free hand in rebuilding the labor force through a system similar to the one that existed in the antebellum era". Jim Crow's laws were severely reinforced against vagrancy. Freed slaves were routinely arrested, beaten and ordered by a judge into unpaid labor for white planters. Black rural southerners were living during the Construction era under a violently repressive system where they had no voice and no political representation. Worse yet, they were being brutalized, killed and lynched with impunity by an all-white police and state militia forces recruited from the old Confederate Civil War's racist veterans.

The subsequent rise of white supremacist forces and the general spread of Jim Crow's racist containment laws all throughout the South from the late 19<sup>th</sup> to the first half of the 20<sup>th</sup> century would eventually provoke the State-wide civil rights movement of the 50s, 60s and 70s.

In the early-to-mid-20<sup>th</sup> century, during what was historically known as the Great Migration, an untold number of Black American families had moved from their rural Southern towns to the largely industrialized Northern cities in search of a more promising future for their loved ones. But it turned out that the North was not any more liberal than the South was when it came to the real advancement for the migrating Black population. They soon found themselves concentrated in many segregated slum sections in the Northern cities. A majority of them lived in dilapidated homes in the ghettos and lived off food stamps and financial assistance, as they could not find work. Besides the Black Americans' daily struggle to eke out a living in an equally unfriendly North, their kind had to deal constantly with both open and disguised systemic racism, police brutality and violence backed up by a biased judicial system built against them. To add insult to injuries, all the impoverished Black communities were being flooded by illegal drugs and weapons, provoking a disproportionate rise in drug addiction and gun violence among young Black males living in the slums. Blacks were disproportionally overrepresented in the Nation's jail system, as they were less than one-tenth of the general population, creating a state of affair that would later develop into the prison-industrial complex that we have today where hundreds of thousands of colored prisoners are used by major US corporations to produce many of their goods at a dismal zero labor cost.

However, in the background of all this, something big was in the making and would culminate in the great black American resistance movement in later years. It was brewing in several of the church meetings, masses and gatherings, in many of the sermons of Black preachers embracing an earlier version of what would later be called Black Theology of Liberation.

In the meantime, there was in the 30s and 40s, the back-to-Africa movement started by Marcus Garvey, a Jamaican political activist, a black nationalist and a Pan-Africanist. Garvey, being a keen observer of the internal colonial status of Black communities throughout America, came up with the idea known as Garveyism, consisting by urging black people to migrate back to Africa in great numbers. There, they should build a powerful black nation of their own that could not only rebuild the lost dignity of the Black race but also offer support and assistance to the myriad of colored folks scattered all throughout the World. W.E.B Du Bois had done much as a political activist, author and historian to advance the resistance struggle of black Americans in the first half of the last century. He helped create the historic National Association for the Advancement of Colored People (NAACP) in 1909 and used the Association's legal arm to first attack the general state of inequality in the US education system and second, launch an all-out legal assault against Jim Craw's segregation laws.

In the early 50s, Malcom X, who joined the Nation of Islam while in prison, became, following his parole, the organization's most vocal leader. He would join Marcus Garvey's campaign idea by advocating black empowerment and the separation of Black and White Americans. Malcom X would openly criticize Rev. Martin Luther King Jr. along with the mainstream civil rights movement for their advocacy on racial integration and non-violence. The Nation of Islam, under Malcom X's leadership, envisioned the establishment of a separate country for African Americans located somewhere in the southern or southwestern part of the United States. That would be the first comprehensive step before African Americans could finally embark on the final phase of returning to the motherland of Africa.

Malcom X came up with an idea that was new for its time when he also added in the mix that the "United States government owed reparations to Black people for the unpaid labor of their ancestors". He vociferously rejected also the "Civil Rights movement's strategy of non-violence, advocating instead that Black people should defend themselves. One major significant contribution Malcom X brought to the long struggle of the African American Resistance was when he left the Nation of Islam and announced his willingness to work with leaders of the civil rights

293

movement. He would do so pending some changes to the organization's policies. Malcom X believed that "Calling the movement a struggle for civil rights would keep the issue within the United States while changing the focus to human rights would make it an international concern. The movement could then bring its complaints before the United Nations", where Malcom X said that "The emerging nations of the world would add their support" he finally argued that "If the US government was unwilling or unable to protect Black people, Black people should protect and defend themselves from aggressors, and to secure freedom, justice and equality by whatever means necessary".

The Black Panther Party, created in 1966 by Huey Newton and Bobby Seale initially for Self-Defense against police brutality, had broadened the party's mission by including social activism and community assistance such as its free breakfast programs and the establishment of health clinics for lower-income African Americans. Both Newton and Seale, inspired by Malcom X's radical militantism, believed that violence might be necessary to create fundamental change, as nonviolent protests, they thought, could not truly liberate black Americans or empower them. Thus, both Black Panther Party founders adopted Malcom X's rallying cry, "Freedom by any means necessary". And like Malcom X, they came to realize that they were not alone in their struggle here at home against America's formidable imperial repressive machine. Their non-white

African and Southeast Asian brothers and sisters were also fighting against the same forces for their own political and economic freedom.

Angela Davis, who became the leader of the Communist Party in the 60s and had close ties and affinities with the Black Panther movement's Black nationalist and socialist ideologies, cut through the chase by holding US Capitalism as the sole and only culprit for the lamentable condition under which African Americans had been forced to live since their great migration to the industrialized, capitalistic North. She further argued that racism was an essential, inseparable part of Capitalism where she believed that "It will continue to exist as long as capitalism remains our secular religion". "The elephant in the room will always be capitalism…as it has been the driving force of so much when we talk about racism. Capitalism has always been racial capitalism," to paraphrase one of her famous quotes.

The diehard militant in her, will also advocate for the abolishment of prisons and the prison-industrial complex. Later in her long life of militantism, she would lament her regrettable omission of the gender issues from her earlier struggles, as she was fully aware of how challenging it was for women to be in any position of leadership in a male-dominated world, from her own personal experience as the US Communist Party's chairwoman and from others like her militant female colleague, Elaine Brown, when she became the Black Panther Party's sole female chairman. She found out the hard way how both had to toughen up quickly to assume their respective roles as chairwomen of both the Communist and the Black Panther Parties. In this context of gender domination not just by white males but also by our own black males, she candidly admitted, quoting her, "A part of me is glad that we didn't win the revolution we were fighting for back then because there would still be male supremacy. There would still be hetero patriarchy..." However, the diehard militant in Angela Davis would never waver, as she was quoted as saying, "I'm no longer accepting the things I cannot change. I'm changing the things I cannot accept."

Black Panthers Party's goal of total black emancipation from white supremacy was never achieved. By the mid-70s, the movement as we knew it had ceased all its community activities and fizzled out of existence.

Martin Luther King Jr., an American Baptist minister and political activist, stood out from the other civil rights leaders by a country mile. He was indeed the most prominent leader of the civil rights movement from the mid-50s until his brutal assassination on April 4, 1968, in Memphis. Thanks to his charismatic persona, oratorical gift, and his adoption of Mahatma Gandhi's nonviolent approach in his civil disobedience resistance against Jim Crow laws, he was able to mobilize untold numbers of people, as well as white liberals, in support of his civil rights struggle for freedom and racial equality in America. 1960 sit-in movement, 1961 Freedom Rides, and 1963 Birmingham campaign prepared the stage for Dr. Martin Luther King's iconic March on Washington, D.C., on August 28, 1963, where he delivered his "I Have a Dream" speech, heard by a quarter of a million people from across the nation. Considered the largest protest rally of its time, its success placed King's civil rights movement into the nation's historical archive. The marchers rallied that day at the National Mall near the Lincoln Memorial with a laundry list of demands.

They were protesting for "Jobs and Freedom, to demand an end to segregation, fair wages and economic justice, voting rights, education, and long overdue civil rights protections. By 1965, Dr. King had helped organize at least two of the three Selma to Montgomery historical marches. Those above historic marches were credited for helping to pass both the Civil Rights Act of 1964 and the Voting Rights Act of 1965.

The Reverand Martin Luther King, near his final years, had extended his political activism to register and manifest his appalling opposition against poverty in general, the Vietnam War and Capitalism. King knew by transitioning from his routine local civil rights protests to human rights, he, de facto, took his political militantism to a much larger, broader international dimension, thus, crossing an important red line set by the power that be. Especially in 1968 when he was planning days before he was murdered by the

297

US Deep States, a national occupation of Washington, D.C., to be called the Poor People's Campaign. This poverty protest was being sold to be the mother of all human rights protests, as it would be addressing the general state of poverty for all impoverished colored and white people alike. Then, the most prominent US civil rights leader of all time, was living off borrowed time for daring to keep his Wall Street foes awake for too many sleepless nights.

His fate was sealed, and it was only a matter of time, when and where, as his every move was being followed by his would-be-killers. Like several civil rights leaders before him who had been murdered by the US Deep States whenever they represented a vital threat to their bottom-line money interests, Dr. Martin Luther King Jr, on April 4, 1968, had been martyred like Malcom X before him. King's assassination did not put an end to the historic resistance of African Americans. As John Lewis put it, "By resisting, Black people have achieved triumphs, successes, and progress as seen in the end of chattel slavery, dismantling of Jim and Jane Crow segregation in the South." And finally, Lewis advised us "Not to get lost in a sea of despair. Be hopeful, be optimistic. Our struggle is not the struggle of a day, a week, a month, or a year; it is the struggle of a lifetime. Never, ever be afraid to make some noise and get in good trouble, necessary trouble."

# A Cozy Evening Recital with The Legendary Michel Legrand

I learned about a Michel Legrand's evening recital from Melodee, a white American lady that I met at the Coconut Grove's Village Inn. We had been seeing each other on an on-and-off basis. She was a federal court reporter by profession and a formidable belly dancer by trade. We became recreational lovers in the strangest possible way. To start with, I was not the type of black male she would want to have anything to do with, let alone sex, for she made up her mind about me way before we even met that I was not the faithful genre to woman. She had seen me on so many different dates, which led her to conclude that I was either a rare, addictive case of a womanizer or I was simply a man caught in a confused dilemma of love and hate for women.

However, one Sunday matinee at the Village Inn, all her prior impressions of me flew off instantly out of the window when we both started chatting with each other for the very first time. For some mysterious reason, the suspicious Melodee was taken by one of my simplest pickup lines or feigned to fall for it. I remember that before the evening was over that Sunday, she was sitting on top of my welcoming lap and making out with me like many others before her. "Allez comprendre les femmes!" [Would I ever understand women?] She would question herself afterwards in the facile way she had let herself be had by me despite all her prior unflattering reservations she had of me.

She was not too proud of herself to have become just another blonde on my growing conquest list. Melodee, though not the prettiest one among them, had her revenge in her explosive sex appeal. Besides her intriguing, sexy look, she had a six-foot-tall knock-out figure, which was on a par with the bombshell Jewish blonde Beatrice from Auckland. A perfect body built for the fabulous belly dancer that she was. What I enjoyed the most in what had become an on-and-off sexual relationship, was its unspoken non-attachment aspect of it. We both were free to see other people.

She knew from the get-go what she was getting herself into, and there was no need for me to tell her lies about the nature of our relationship. It was just sex for the good old sex's sake. Melodee was frankly the most adventurous of them all, and never shied away from trying new things. We tried everything there was to try. She said that there was something about me that sort of emboldened her to get funky and kinky. I remember the second wild, funky thing I talked her into doing, was a threesome with her best friend Sue, a much prettier, hotter-looking blonde than her.

Sue lived in the apartment next to her, and she had been joining us lately for some wine and reefer smoking whenever I was spending the weekend with Melodee. Sue knew instinctively by the way I could not help looking at her sensational rear end, especially when she wore those risqué short shorts, that I would not have minded her joining us at all one evening on her best friend's bed.

At first, she hesitated when Melodee, under my suggestion, mentioned the threesome idea to her. She was not sure about it on the ground that she had never remotely done anything that extreme before. Besides, she was concerned not to interfere or cause any unforeseen trouble. But Melodee quickly reassured her not to worry and that we had an open relationship. She even joked with her best friend Sue that not long ago, she had quite a steamy welcoming threesome with me and my younger brother Carlos, who had just arrived here in Miami. Sue, who grew up in a conservative all-white mid-western town in Maine before she moved to Miami, had never met any black man this close before, let alone dating one. Thus, she was kind of ungodly intrigued by the myth of the black male mighty stud image.

She candidly asked her friend Melodee what it was like to have sex with me. Melodee, who wanted to somewhat entice Sue's curiosity more, told her in a teasing manner to just join us one evening to find that out herself. Like Melodee, Sue was in an on-and-off long-distance relationship herself and was growing a little tired of spending weekends alone in her apartment. She finally consented to join us one evening, hoping to experience something exciting and dazzling for a change. I could not help feeling overly excited upon learning that Sue had agreed to join us in a threesome.

I had not one iota of complaints about having sex with Melodee. She was a remarkable lover, but there was something otherworldly to undress and make love to a woman the very first time that could never be substituted and replicated. There was that indescribable, emotional hype and dizzying sensation in every 'first time' that one had made love to a new woman. The bundle of joy, mystery, and excitement of the first time would gradually be lost in the second and third time of having her.

I seemed to fancy tremendously the wild threesome idea with the two bombshell blondes. I began to feel that I wickedly desired Sue even more than her friend Melodee for many reasons. First, she was prettier and had an equally hot, sexy body as well. Second, I was fuming in the mouth by the forbidden fruit syndrome provoked by her countrylike conservative upbringing, which had sheltered her away from any possible sexual encounter with a black dude. Which, in my mind, made her a de facto qualified white virgin who needed to be consensually deflowered by a black male. And I was more than flattered to be the one with such a golden opportunity.

It started like a normal ordinary evening at Melodee's apartment when Sue, as usual joined us for wines and some grass smoking in her Living Room. Except this time, all the parties knew what was about to be unleashed in the coming hours. Sue looked prettier and hotter that evening, and what she was wearing for the occasion was, if anything, a tacit indication that she was readier for the threesome encounter than the rest of us. She released her beautiful long blonde hair down to her waistline, making her appear hotter and more desirable. The killer instinct in me wanted to cut through the chase and go straight for the kill. But I also knew by experience not to confuse speed and precipitation and that the best possible outcome for such an exciting, promising evening could only come to total fruition when I slowed down the pace by going slow at it while making my top priority the maximum pleasure of the two ladies.

To break the ice, Melodee put on Gregory Isaacs' hit album Night Nurse. I seized the moment to begin dancing with her. To my surprise, Sue immediately joined in the action, and before I could recover from being dazzled, I was in the most enviable situation of being pressed tight and in a sandwich between these two beauties. One thing led to another. I had no recollection to this day of how we all three ended up butt naked on Melodee's extra-large bed. The momentum in her bedroom was going so fast that I had to take a deep breath to compose myself. It was a sublime bedroom scene with my contrasting dark brown body, entangling and crossing with the other two white female bodies. I started working on Melodee first, making sure that she was content and satisfied while saving her best friend, Sue, for last. The latter was no mere spectator; while I was giving oral sex to her friend, she was sizing me up through her mouth's deepthroat and was doing an excellent job at it.

I finally took Melodee to the point of no return, where there was no higher apex for her to climb than to climax. Then, it was her friend Sue's moment to shine in the sun. Oh Boy, if she had a body on her as I laid my face in between her thighs and, with my known devilish tongue and fingers, began with my historic mission to deflower her! Meaning that I was the first black man to ever get that close to that private, intimate part of her white Aryan body. She responded well to the stimulation coming from both my mouth and fingers as she let out several encouraging moaning cries, proving what I was doing on her was working fine. Meanwhile, Melodee was busy talking my pal Dick into getting himself up again and ready for her best friend Sue's first black fuck baptism.

Sue got so wet and steamy that with my now fully erect penis, I turned on my back after wearing a protective condom to have her mounting me in the reverse cowgirl position. Sue's dexterity with the bottom part of her body over my sizable black cock was beyond incredible and frankly surprising for a white virgin girl's first sexual encounter with a black male lover. She was just a natural, as she would use her formidable private part with adroit circular motion and thrust as to grasp the whole of my penis to its extremity. She was in charge and had total control of the situation being on top. I let her have it from my bottom position with some surprising, unexpected sideway hits and thrust moves of my own, provoking some wild moaning uproars out of her.

For the grand finale, I chose to deliver the deflowering coup de grace to Sue by taking her from behind, her favorite doggy-style position. At first, I went at it with a slow, rhythmic, and cadencing tempo, all the while thrusting the length of my penis within her vagina's walls all the way to her cervix. I purposely increased and decreased the pace of her pounding with the devilish intent to take her to where she was never taken before. It worked well, as her shaking body was overwhelmed by sexual convulsions, and the cursing words out of her mouth excited me even more. We both climaxed together as I could not help feeling overly delighted, like an avenged conqueror for having been in real-time her first black fuck ever. It was another surreal Maurice Sixto "J'ai Vengé la Race" [I Avenged my Race] moment!

Women handled their climaxing episode in different ways. Some cried, sang, and laughed hysterically, while others bite, hit and curse. But Sue hit the mark, as a big-time nonstop talker and curser alongside her wild moaning screams.

I was very pleased on the outcome of the threesome experience, as I helped perpetuate in some way the myth of the black male's stud image in Sue's eyes. I had no doubt in my mind that I left a deep, profound imprint on her psyche and that the sex act she had with me would forever stay with her. In fact, I learned from Melodee long after that threesome night that Sue had been dating black men exclusively, which again validated that old proverbial sexual myth that "Once you go black, you never go back".

Melodee, who had been a fan of Michel Legrand's large music repertoire, thanks in part to me introducing her to my wide French music collection, learned that the iconic film composer was giving an evening recital at a Fort Lauderdale Beach Resort Hotel. I had been a diehard fan of Legrand tracing back from my young teenage days, and I was not about to miss on such a golden opportunity to see my idol in a live performance. Three tickets were purchased for Sue, Melodee and me for the three of us to attend the evening show. When the day of the recital came, I showed up in glamorous style at that cozy, salon-style venue flanked by my two American blonde lovers on each side. The two ladies were impeccably sharp in their long, elegant evening dresses for the soiree recital. I was myself up on par with them by wearing my elegant long black coat à la Billie Dee Williams while putting my Milli/Vanelli long braided hair look in a distinguished ponytail.

I could have easily passed for any Hollywood or Motown black entertainer or celebrity. There were not, to my knowledge, too many black folks with the low-income HRS job that I had back then who could pull off such a stunt unless they were truly celebrities or were involved in some monkey business or being a pimp. Against the latter unflattering image, I was always a bit self-conscious being seen or looked down upon as a pimp due to my being seen often in the company of very attractive, hot-looking blondes. And having both Sue and Melodee with me did not help much with the negative pimp image portrayal. For this reason alone, you would never find me wearing, for the life of moi, a dandy hat under any circumstances. A French Renaissance beret, yes, but not a hat!

We three were placed on a VIP table near the stage where Michel Legrand would soon be opening his evening recital on that majestic nine-inch concert grand piano. It was a standing, welcoming ovation when the French icon stepped onto the stage to take his seat behind the piano. It was quite a performance all throughout the evening. The gifted musician, singer and composer extraordinaire played several hits from his extensive popular film themes, and from his jazz repertoire. He played some of the audience's favorite pieces like The Windmills of Your Mind and The Summer Knows. The atmosphere was intimately cozy. It was Michel Legrand at his best.

Michel Legrand, on his first break, came down into the crowd to mingle, greet and welcome several of his fans among the audience. When he finally made it to our table, I was just beside myself. Now, I experienced what some people really felt when being in the physical presence of their beloved idols. We introduced ourselves to Legrand, who was very jovial, engaging and relaxed.

307

He addressed me first by asking if I were a jazz musician with the hope if yes to invite him on stage later. But I told him no, much to my chagrin as I wish I were. I let him know how much of a fan I was of his towering musical discography and that The Umbrellas of Cherbourg was one of my all-time favorites. Sue and Melodee introduced themselves to the legend, and he had a brief, sweet exchange of words with both, especially with Sue.

He went around the room, greeting several of his fans. But what I did not expect to happen that evening was when Michel Legrand, the larger-than-life icon, came back and took a seat at our table. He spoke perfect English and was very engaging with all three of us. He was very touched by me being a diehard fan of his music. I could tell that he had eyes for the hot-looking Sue.

Michel Legrand went back on stage; this time, he was joined on the grand piano by his son. And the next astonishing thing of the evening came when he mentioned my name out loud to the entire audience as one of his all-time fans. Then he said that the next piece he was about to play, "The Umbrellas of Cherbourg," was dedicated to me. I never felt so lifted in my entire life. I was just stunned by such an unexpected dedication. I thanked him profusely when the recital was over for the honor and told him that moment would always be one of my most solemn memory ever.

The following day, both Sue and Melodee came down to

meet with me at the Village Inn. Sue, who was not a regular at the
Village Inn for she was not that much into Reggae, happened to
enjoy the ambiance. A Haitian oligarch fellow who had started to
befriend me lately came to our table to invite all three of us to a big
party that his family was given next Saturday in the West Kendall
area. Obviously, the invitation was intended more for the two blonde
babes that I was with than for me. I had to admit that he was quite a
cool, friendly dude and was part of that tiny percentage of white-
looking Haitians.

Despite his apparent charming mannerisms toward me, he
was still a product of an elitist mentality of white supremacy. In his
Haitian oligarch world, blonde chicks like Beatrice and Sue were
put on the highest pedestal of whiteness. He was simultaneously
dazzled and mystified by my entire persona, as I appeared not to be
phased much by such hierarchical distinction among the races. And
to add insult to injury, I seemed, in his eyes, to have been abundantly
lucky in the blonde girls' department! Last time he saw me with the
bombshell-looking Beatrice, he literally lost it. As he approached
me to tell me in Creole, "Kote w pran gwo pwen blond sa a, Pepe,
tanpri frèm banm adrès la?" [Where did you purchase that big
blonde spell Pepe, my brother, please give me the address]. I knew
exactly what he was going through in his Haitian elite mentality.

In Haiti, the age-old colorist legacy made it hard for average
Black Haitian guy like me to date an attractive dark or brown-

skinned girl, as most young girls were conditioned to better their stock by dating lighter-skinned guys. If dating an attractive colored girl from the middle class was not an easy task, thanks to colorism, imagine the near impossibility of dating a mulatto girl, let alone a White Haitian girl from the upper echelons of Haitian society. I lived through it all, however, here in the States, I found a magical twist and convenient loophole where I was able to use my dark skin color to my advantage. I had an enviable bachelor's lifestyle with several of Uncle Sam's daughters that all the Haitian oligarch's wealth and status could never afford.

My 'peculiar' taste for dating blonde girls was always dictated by a daring impulse to cross the racial boundaries, and take a huge bite at the forbidden fruit, but it was never with the intention to better my stock. While I could never say the same for the elitist bourgeois folks living in Haiti or in the Haitian diaspora who wanted nothing more than the whitening skin of their family's next generation of upsprings.

Both Sue and Melodee were all excited by the Haitian oligarch party invitation, and they made plans to attend it with me. I gave them a brief history of what to expect going to that party. I stressed the extreme conservative mentality of most of the people they were going to encounter there. How clannish they were and were not too engaging with anyone not born and raised in their close elitist circle. I told them, however, that because of their blondeness, they would roll out the red carpet for them.

As planned, the three of us showed up in style at the party. It was a multi-million-dollar mansion flanked by a mid-size Olympic pool in its backyard. It had all the sumptuous features that the oligarch ill-gotten money could afford. I immediately thought of how much of the money spent in the purchase of this property came from stolen wealth, drug money, and the blood and sweat of millions of overexploited Haitian workers. The crowd was pleasant looking, made up mostly of mulattos, whites, Hispanics and a handful of the black bourgeois Haitians with Middle Eastern features. The latter bunch was even fiercer in their color prejudice than their white/mulatto Haitian acolytes. A live band was playing around the pool area. The catering food was a mixed of Haitian traditional dishes and a various mix of other dishes. I bumped into some familiar faces at the party who were regulars at the Village Inn. We were having a really good time, enjoying the food, wine and the ambiance while mingling with some of the invited guests who were open and engaging.

Melodee and Sue, as anticipated, were being hit on big time by at least two to three middle-aged fellows who appeared to be quite loaded on both wealth and alcohol. They would come around often to ask the ladies to dance as if I wasn't even there or they were not with me. Their nonchalance was quite appalling. I remember someone once pointed out that Haiti's greatest misfortune lay in its economic, political, and intellectual elites' boyish womanizing impulses. As soon as they were away on the dance floor, according to the ladies, the guys would cut through the chase by propositioning them both as if they were high-class courtesans with a price tag on them. The ladies were not amused to find out that I was sadly right when I warned them ahead of time about such desperate, infantile sexual advances. In the collective psyche of those elitist fools, caught into the white woman stereotypical tourist image in Haiti that 'Tout fanm blanch se bouzen'' [loose woman], thought they had it made. It was a done deal. They seriously felt that if those two women could be with me, they were also fair game to them too!

The apparent owner of the mansion, whose name would not be disclosed, had the heart for Sue, and offered, right off the bat, to take great care of her for the rest of her remaining days on earth if she agreed to become one of his mistresses. He offered her to come live at one of his sumptuous Gingerbread properties on the highest suburban hill in Petion Ville. A full package deal with servants, gardeners and a chauffeured limousine. She could even fly on weekends to come shopping in Miami's luxury stores if she wanted to, as a bonus. The ladies were so rightly upset, as they felt insulted and disrespected by those erroneous offers that they wanted to leave the party right away. I did not know anything about those dance floor proposals until later when we were driving back to Melodee's home. After such an ending fiasco at the Haitian oligarch's mansion party, we ended up back at Melodee's Living Room space, where we started earlier when I picked both up for the 45 minutes ride to West Kendall. The only option left for the three of us was to erase this awful experience we just had with a much better one of our own, meaning another spontaneous threesome.

That was exactly what we set out to do with a vengeance for the remainder of the evening. This time around, it went even twice as smoother as the first time. Sue was much more relaxed, less tense, and much eager to engage in the threesome act when it was her turn. And because she was a bigtime talker and curser especially when she was about to come, she again started to spill the beans and cursing. Climaxing had a deteriorating effect on her, as I witnessed, once more, her transformation from the innocent-looking, soft-spoken Sue into a completely, different animal – mind you, that she was in her first year at the University of Miami's Graduate Law School. After our last threesome, it was unofficially a given that we were into a classic Ménage à trois, a typical French style of a sexual relationship between three people which, in our case, dared not speak its name. Sue had gotten herself so smitten by the whole arrangement that she broke up with her long-distance, traveling boyfriend. Hence, she did not have to deal with that strong sense of guilt she felt each time she was engaging in a threesome with us.

Our threesome affair had come to a critical point where the sexual chemistry between me and Sue was getting stronger and stronger each time we had sex. It was obvious to Melodee that her best friend Sue was slowly but surely stealing her man right in plain sight. I was beginning to worry that the whole threesome arrangement might fall apart, as Melodee could tell that even though I always started with her, I could not wait to jump all over her friend Sue and vice versa. Sue's loud, talkative mouth when climaxing also reaffirmed what her best friend Melodee was beginning to suspect all along that she was getting a raw deal with me, while Sue seemed to be getting the best fuck of her life each time I got to her. There was some truth to that. Though I always started with Melodee, I never climaxed with her. I always managed to save a great deal of my body stamina by holding back considerably from coming while I was having sex with her.

By doing so, I was genuinely saving a great deal of my energy for the anticipated grand finale with her best friend, Sue. We both routinely climaxed together in the few more threesome sex we had since we began this Ménage à trois affair. I would not have been surprised that climaxing together with Sue had, in effect, triggered that natural massive release of oxytocin and dopamine responsible for the developing bond between me and her at Melodee's expense, unfortunately. But body chemistry had a power of its own, and nothing the three of us could have done to tame that. I simply could not help getting overly excited and so much harder when having sex with Sue, which in turn seemed to drive her into a more tempestuous sexual euphoria than her friend had ever had with me.

Melodee and I had an honest, open sexual relationship for quite some time now. She did not want to know who I was with or see when I was not with her and vice versa. However, what was beginning to happen between me and Sue, was too much of a hard pill for her to swallow. It was not occurring behind her back or away from her; instead, it was out right in the open, right in front of her to see and witness it with her very own eyes. She could hear Sue's orgasmic, delirious monologue with her very own ears, candidly admitting under the euphoria of climaxing how she could never get enough of my jungle black fuck! In the end, my worst fear came true, as I ended up losing both women when Melodee did not want to continue with such a torturing threesome affair any longer.

I had plenty of opportunities to have Sue come down to my bachelor's pad without Melodee's knowledge to continue with that explosive sexual chemistry between us following that epic fallout, but I shied away from that on pure moral principle. I had some scruples, after all. She, as well as I, was devastated by the unexpected unraveling of the threesome affair, and she personally was not ready yet to let go of that newly found sexual awakening of hers. Understanding that, had I lived in a surreal universe with no moral compass and decency, Sue and I would have gone berserk over one another in an unrestrained 'three's a crowd' setting, as there would not have been any third-party interference. But, as much as I truly enjoyed sex with Sue, I, nevertheless, did not feel comfortable causing any fissure in their longtime friendship by sneaking behind Melodee's back to resume having sex with her best friend. The temptation was always there to go rogue at any time by meeting in catimini with the foxy-looking Sue. And I would have bet my last Haitian gourde that she would not have minded that at all based on the intense pleasure she had from our last two heated phone sex talks I recently had with her.

Then again, due to my petty-bourgeois upbringing, I insisted on doing just the expected right thing by upholding some basic moral principle of non-interference with the two ladies' endearing friendship. The same apparent philosophy I seemed to have not to cross certain moral and ethical redlines to acquire wealth and power at any cost was also being held and upheld by me for sex, too.

The student of Philosophy in me could not help, once again, reflect on the true nature of the human species and how, despite all the programming impacts of the nurture paradigm on the human psyche, it always came down to the domineering impulse of our true nature, i.e., the beast in us. At one point in our brief Ménage à trois experiment, it was not just Melodee who could no longer stomach sharing me with her best friend Sue, but Sue herself was beginning to display body language signs that she would rather have me all to herself if she could.

## Miami, Florida: A Sunshine State's Unauthorized And Unredacted Journey

Ever wonder how the utopian communal lifestyle of the 60s and early '70s, following the sexual revolution in the US, managed to navigate around the complexities of the beast in us? How did the communal hippy lifestyle keep the peace amid the natural tendency of our self-centeredness? Especially when all community members, in their free sex lifestyle of making love, not war, were sharing about everything, including wife-husband-partner-swapping. Ever wonder!

Lyonel Gerdes

# FIU's International Studies' Graduate Class Of 1984 with Dr. Mark Rosemberg

Dr. Mark Rosemberg's class was a must-take course for anyone to complete the Graduate International Studies program requirements at FIU. It was the most exciting evening hours, three days a week for an entire semester. There were several students in that class who stood out because of their unique personalities, attractiveness, charisma and their passion for the scholarly field of geopolitics. We had a perfect, natural chemistry with one another, as we were all investing countless hours in our studies and research. We were about 16 or more of us in the class. I was friendly with everyone; however, I had my favorites among that incredible bunch. Ted Schmith, Kevin, Jeanne De Quine, Joann Biondi, and Anna were the core group I hung out with the most.

Ted Schmitt was quite an interesting white fellow. He had a sharp, good look on him and was friendly and engaging with that pair of piercing blue eyes. He had an on-and-off job as a yacht captain. It was never confirmed either by Ted or Joann, but some in our group had reasons to believe that there was some amorous, discreet affair going on between Ted and the beautiful, red-haired, Italian-looking Joann. Ted was either divorced or separated and if there was any hanky pinky thing going on among them, it could have happened when he often crashed at her apartment on one of his

318

frequent boating assignments.

Next was Kervin, one of the coolest white dudes in the program and was the incorrigible party animal and the life of the party in the group. Aside from the academic assignments that we all had in common, we participated in numerous extracurricular activities off campus. That was how we developed a remarkable, long-lasting friendship which lasted for years.

My friendship with the fiery red hair Joann started years back when I began my Undergraduate studies at FIU's Sociology Department. We had an interesting platonic type of chemistry with each other, which could have perhaps turned physical had we met under a different set of circumstances. Still, we spent lots of time together at the school's cafeteria, where we often met to chitchat before classes began. Joann, who had gorgeous, naturally tanned skin, seemed to have been more interested by fairer-skinned white guys like Kervin and Ted. But she was diplomatic not to let her sexual preference and attraction be openly known. That was why, years later, I was shocked when she started dating none other than our dark-skinned musician artist Manno Charlemagne, the famed, beloved Haitian folksinger, songwriter and political activist.

I met with Manno Charlemagne when he came into exile in Miami for the first time as part of the 1980s contingent group of journalists, political activists and artist militants who were forced into exile by the Duvalier regime. But little did I ever anticipate that my friend Joann would have ended up having such a monumental romantic impact in the life of one of Haiti's most popular folksingers ever. The fearless, adventurous Joann had even brazenly moved briefly to Haiti's capital city to live with her newfound lover Manno Charlemagne around the time when he became the elected mayor of Port-au-Prince from 1995 to 1999. I met afterward with Manno on several occasions at Aux Palmistes, a Bar/Restaurant in Little Haiti, at Joann's house party and at South Beach Haitian restaurant TAP TAP, where he had a Friday evening gig.

Joann and Manno's endearing friendship for one another continued long after they were no longer lovers. In fact, when the iconic folksinger's health was quickly deteriorating after his lung cancer had metastasized to his brain, it was at Joann's place that he was being cared for. Manno Charlemagne's former lover, Joann, was reported to have been there at his deathbed that morning of December 10th when one of Haiti's most admired sons and beloved folksingers rendered his last earthly breath.

Jeanne De Quinne was the one lady in the class that I was also the closest to in terms of the spiritual love connection we had with one another from the onset. She lived in a super nice apartment in the heart of artsy Coconut Grove. How memorable were the parties she used to throw at her place with one of the coolest local crowds there? Jeanne was already a freelance journalist with Times

magazine, plus a couple of other news magazines. She and Michel
Montas, the wife of the late iconic Jean Dominique, became close
friends when both met at Columbia University's journalistic school
in the 70s. I was impressed by how much Jeanne knew about Haitian
history and culture, its ethnic food and its music. She startled me at
the first party she was given at her place when she played a popular
Tabou Combo song. She left me dumbfounded when I danced with
her the first time to realize that she had all the Haitian Compas
Direct's dance moves so down packed that I did not have to teach
her a thing. And if I were not up to par with her, she would have
thought me a thing or two.

She knew all the important movers and shakers in the Haitian
community and had written some stories about the Haitian refugees'
plights in Little Haiti. When I was writing a term paper about Haitian
literary giants who were still alive, Jeanne was the one who
introduced me to the larger-than-life playwright and poet Felix
Morisseau-Leroy, who was living in South Miami and was once a
Columbia University alumnus himself. I grew up being a bigtime
fan of Antigone's [Wa Kreyon] author for his literary courage to
dare use the then disparaged Haitian Creole as a linguistic tool to
write his poetry and plays at a time when no true respected Haitian
authors of Morisseau's stature would have gone through what was
considered as a suicidal literary move.

Furthermore, the student's paper 'Dyakout', which I was the

321

director at College Jean Price-Mars the year I migrated to Miami, was chosen in honor of Felix Morisseau-Leroy's pioneering literary works as a Creolophone's writer. I would have in the second tome of "Miami, Florida... A memoir", a more extensive narrative about the endearing mentor-friend relationship I had with the legendary playwright and poet Morisseau-Leroy until his unfortunate passing on 5 September 1998 in Miami.

Reverting to talking about my dear, beloved friend Jeanne, I would have to confess that she was as attractive as any of the other women I had ever been with. However, she was also a living example of what I was beginning to find out about myself, meaning that I could genuinely love a woman without ever attempting to go sexual and physical with her, even though we both were known to be the hottest dirty dancing couple at several of her evening house parties in the Grove.

In the eyes of many, there was an existing beautiful chemistry between us two, but such body chemistry had, for some evasive, unexplained reason, failed to transition into a sexual, physical plateau as many would have expected. Nevertheless, there were no such invisible, existing barriers between me and Suzanna, a drop-dead gorgeous Mexican journalist friend of Jeanne who was in Miami for the weekend working on a story. Indeed, Jeanne who apparently was driving around in the Biscayne Blvd. vicinity, made a stop at my bachelor's pad one Saturday afternoon with her. She was one hot Mexican woman! I could not keep my eyes off her the moment she came through my door, even long after Jeanne introduced her to me. Both ladies made themselves at home. It was not Jeanne's first time visiting me at my bachelor's pad.

I could see that her friend Suzanna was appreciating the entire setting atmosphere in the room. A cassette recording of the best collection of Haitian Compas Direct was playing in the background. After we started to mellow out following the consumption of some excellent Meiomi red Pinot Noir wine, Jeanne got in the mood to dance. She was my number one dancing partner, so we began our usual close-tight, sexually explicit Compas Direct moves. Her friend Suzanna's eyes and body language were all turned on by watching the two of us doing what would later be labeled as dirty dancing years before the film of the same name was released at the Cannes Film Festival on May 12, 1987.

Jeanne moved away from our tight embrace and took Suzanna's right hand, who was sitting on one of the beds watching us, to tell her, "Now is your turn; show us what you got". She answered Jeanne's advice by getting into the action and showed me quickly what she had in store hidden under her apparent reserved demeanor. She threw that hot, sexy Mexican body of hers at me in a much tighter embrace than Jeanne's. I was charmingly taken aback by her spontaneous assertiveness, and I was even more stunned by how quickly I found myself embarrassingly owning a hard-on, while 'dirty dancing' her in the true literal meaning of the term. For the record, with all the robbing dancing moves I had had with my dear beloved friend Jeanne, I never once reached such a level of arousal and excitement that could have been interpreted as fresh or at least not kind and appropriate.

Though in her friend Suzanna's case, far from being vexed or having an adverse pull away reaction to my hard tool robbing against her, she instead came down with her own below-the-waist moves by spreading both her legs allowing me an even more direct rubbing contact on her. That sort of dirty dancing made complete sense of the terms 'having a standing, vertical sex while dancing and fully clothed'. Suzanna was the owner of a beautiful light olive soft skin tone that sent an immediate turn-on effect down my spine. Besides her lustrous pitch-dark, long straight hair illustrating her refined facial features, she was luckily gifted with a small but curvaceous figure à la Salma Hayek, which explained why I found myself in a hot predicament dancing so tightly close to that lustrous, sassy figure of her. I felt like a man who had instantly been touched by grace to such an extent that I had to wisely step back away from her tight, strong embrace to avoid an embarrassing spilling incident that early in the game. Jeanne and Suzanna had to leave to follow up with an interview, but the Mexican beauty before leaving my place gave me an address and a phone number for me to call her. She was staying at a friend's apartment in the Grove. I could tell by the look

on her face after her goodbye hug to me, that I was in for a wild treat
tonight, especially when she insisted on seeing me later that evening,
for it was her last night in Miami and luckily for me, she wanted to
spend it with moi. The unexpected, sudden prospect of a night out
in Suzanna's company was beyond my wildest imagination.

I started to wonder why I seemed to always find myself in
the exciting pathways of a long collection line of 'femme fatale'! I
could name a number of those memorable female faces from my life
journey going as far back to my turbulent childhood upbringing days
in Les Cayes. It all started with Marie, the beautiful girl next door
who 'deflowered' me in that epic water basin scene at the tender age
of nine. Then, my two platonic grand fascinations with Marie
Marcelle, the gorgeous Haitian princess with the tall, lean figure,
and Yanick, the voluptuous girl on Gabion Street! In Port-au-Prince,
where my family had moved to avoid political persecution, I found
myself also entangled in another interesting web of beautiful femme
fatal. Starting with the immensely pretty Carole, my first puppy love
story, then came Fiyòtte, who taught me how to dance, French kiss
and making out with a girl by using herself as a live model for that
exciting sex education 101. Rosy, for as brief as the dancing incident
between us was had quite an impact on me. Ti Cam would continue
where Fiyòtte left off with my sexual education 102. And Aunt
Paulette, for whom I had another memorable crush on right before
migrating to the Sunshine State. Now, in Miami, the number of

femme fatal encounters by me had gone so exponentially high that I began to wonder why me! Unless there's an invisible magnetic pull influencing the ladies despite my somewhat average look and not possessing much in the way of wealth and power!

Back to where I left off, my partner in crime Jeanne, a femme fatale in her own right and who was not just a friend but also a confidante, reminded me right before leaving that her hot, sexy friend Suzanna happened to have one massive crush on me, and ordered me to make her last evening in Miami a marvelous one by sweetening it. Little did she know that Suzanna's spontaneous crush had also boomeranged big time on me. Jeanne was taken aback by the lightning speed at which the physical attraction between us occurred. She would later opine with much cynicism, as she knew of my life's turbulent journey, including my latest, romantic pursuit of blonde women, by saying, "What a pity that I was not bisexual, for I would have taken my historical, poetic justice straight to the white colonialists and Imperialists' male descendants' butts!"

I could not have been any more excited, as I was so turned on by my evening rendezvous with Suzanna, the Salma Hayek's look alike, that I canceled a prior uneventful date to give priority to the Mexican bombshell, Suzanna. The prospect that I would soon be undressing and making love to her for the very first time had sent the adrenaline rush in me to an incredible hype. Again, the first-time explosive thrill of having intimate, sexual intercourse with a near-total stranger I just met was the Archilles Hill of my now suspected undiagnosed sexual addiction of a peculiar type.

I arrived on time at the address given to me earlier by Suzanna. I was welcome to a nice Living Room when she opened the front door following my ringing of the entrance bell. I found her even foxier than when I saw her hours ago at my bachelor pad. The host where she was staying was out of town on assignment, according to her, suggesting that we had the entire place to ourselves. She was a jazz fan, and I was pleasantly surprised to hear Groover Washington's instrumental classic piece "Don't Explain" for the very first time in the room's background atmosphere. After filling up two glasses of red wine for the two of us to toast, she came to sit close to me on the couch. I could sense that the wine's relaxing effect had begun to take its toll on us. But because that was her last night in Miami, and time was of the essence, Suzanna was not about to wait for me to make the first move on her. She got herself up and came to sit her entire bottom on my lap. The next thing she did was to go for my lips. It was just the start of one of the most memorable nights that I had ever spent with a brunette and not a blonde. I would spare you all the usual, erotic, wild details of that nightlong sexual encounter with the Mexican bombshell. But I could tell you, it was bloody and an all-out war all throughout the night, where no one at the end was left standing. I can certainly assure you that she left the Sunshine State the following day with a sparkling aura around her and a large, bright smile on her pretty face. On my end, I lived out the wildest sexual fantasies I had about Salma Hayek through her.

In the class of 1984, all of us had one thing in common: the single horrifying fear of being put on the spot by Dr. Max Rosemberg, whose spooky habit was to call on anyone in the group without any warning to comment on the evening reading assignment. He made it a mission of his that we all came prepared in his class. The accomplished scholar and geopolitologue that he was wanted to make us aware how rigorous a discipline we were embarking on. For my part, I had to give him full credit for his steadfast stewardship by turning me into a lifelong student of geopolitics and International Relations. Dr. Rosemberg had a selection of students he always came back to pick on. Students rightly or wrongly suspected that they were either not keeping pace with their reading assignments, or he was cynically enjoying watching them turning red and embarrassed, especially when they were asked to go in front of the class, using the green board for their graphic exposé. If you were prepared and not shy, you would do fine and survive the onslaught, but if you were not and were shy, you would have your most agonizing moment when called upon by him.

Again, for some odd reasons, Dr. Rosemberg had his top two favorite victims in the class of 1984: Joanne Biondi and Anna. They happened to be the two most attractive looking females in our group. The former had held so many grudges against him that nearly four decades later when she caught up with Dr. Rosemberg, who by then had become FIU's President, and goodness gracious if she let him have it with a vengeance! It all happened days before the fake, false flag COVID-19 pandemic when Dr. Rosemberg sponsored an event, a sort of in memoriam, post-eulogy for Bernard Diederich, the famous writer who passed away recently.

The evening function was held at FIU's Tamiami Campus, and Joanne, for the occasion invited three to four of us from the class of 1984 to attend it. Three of us made it to the event, and when Dr. Rosemberg, who remembered us as his old former students, came to greet us, Joann went for an all-out verbal assault against him within minutes. The fiery red hair never got over the way he embarrassed and humiliated her in front of the whole class, not just one time but repeatedly. I was there when she went into her virulent, vicious attack, blaming him for the FIU's recent bridge collapse, which occurred under his watch, causing the death of six people. She pointed her finger at him, all the while accusing him of being irredeemably corrupt, and thanks to his corruption, he got away with murders while still holding on to his top position at FIU.

Dr. Rosemberg was obviously taken aback by Johanne's tirade of mostly unfounded accusations of murder and corruption by him and his office. He handled her ferocious pit bull-like attack in a surprisingly well-composed manner by ignoring her completely, all the while continuing imperturbably with the conversation, he was having with the rest of us. The fiery red hair Johanne, at last, vented out her decades-old anger against Dr. Rosemberg, whom she perceived as the absolute embodiment of white male's timeless patriarchal oppression. She let out all her anger against what she perceived to be an endless battle for gender equality, freedom and justice against the oppressive white male-oriented world order represented by him.

Anna was the class of 1984's bombshell beauty, and yet that did not spare her from being put in the spotlight by Dr. Rosenberg. In fact, rumors had it that he had the heart for the blue-eyed, blonde-haired ballerina girl who was blessed with a majestic six-foot slim figure. If the rumors were true, he would not have been the only one in the Department's teaching staff to desire her. Everyone was hitting on Anna, including some male students in our own group. The class' Ballerina girl was obviously coming from a well-to-do family judging by the quality of the elegant, fashionable clothing she wore in class and the bourgeois, sophisticated air she displayed in her body demeanor. She was quite reserved and was not the outgoing, friendly type. My very first impression of Anna was that she was a snob. I even joked with one male student in the class that she was so full of it that she might have convinced herself that her poops could pass the test of smell. So, I barely paid any attention to beauty Queen Anna, assuming that she was way beyond my range, even though she was the type of blonde female conquest that would have catapulted my male ego to the stratosphere.

But again, I was not living in isolation in the group, as I was often seen in the equally attractive female companies of Jeanne de Quinne, Joanne Biondi and others. And to paraphrase one last time Alfred de Musset, "Chercher la femme elle vous fuit et quand vous la fuyez elle vous cherche" [Look for the woman she runs away from you, and when you run away from her, she searches for you], might have repeated its magic turn and twist once more between me and the inaccessible Anna.

She began to befriend me by engaging me in a discussion on a topic related to the class's course. I would afterward uncover that her extreme reservation, far from being a snubbing act, was rather a convenient cover mechanism for her extreme shyness, and of course, to also kill two birds with one stone by keeping away many of the unwanted male advances coming at her from left, right and center on the school campus. Our unlikely friendship from the beginning of the semester had now turned into a stunning twist of friendship causing many uproars and jealousy in the group.

A few of my lady acquaintances who never were too crazy about Anna in the first place, did not see with a welcoming eye that sudden rapprochement between me and her. Indeed, it was seen by them as a flagrant, if not a serious territorial encroachment by Anna on their turf, even though I was not involved in any romantic

331

escapade with any of them. The same unsettled atmosphere was also there with some of the white male students in the class who would rather wish to be in my 'poor' Haitian shoes to receive all the attention that I was now getting from Anna in the classroom.

I was barely recovering from Anna's charm offensive toward me, when she invited me to come to her house so we could both study together and help her get better on par for Mark Rosenberg's periodic raid on prepared and unprepared students alike. It was beginning to look like a 'déjà vu' scenario that I lived once before with the beautiful, sassy Cuban princess, Mariana, from Little Havana when I was in Dr. Alex Stepick's class! Apparently, she watched in class how well I seemed to navigate whenever I was put on the spot by the 'bullying' tactic of Dr. Rosemberg. Thus, Anna's targeted friendship could have been not because I was kind of cute to her eyes but simply because of my geopolitical understanding of the complicated Galtung's Center-Periphery model theory she seemed to have serious issues with.

Anna was living with her wealthy secular Jewish parents at an expensive oceanfront property near the Morning Side Park's wealthy neighborhood off Biscayne Blvd. and 54th Street, a mere walking distance from where I once lived when I first arrived here in Miami. I remember that it was not long ago when I often came to the Morning Side Recreational Park on weekends to enjoy its natural charm and its vast ocean view. I was always fascinated and taken by the sumptuous mansions along the seaside with their yachts and well-manicured landscapes. Anna's family mansion was the one nearest the edge of the park. Little did I know back then that there would come a day when I, the nearly broken, destitute Haitian migrant, would be an invited guest at one of those properties.

Though Anna's mother never worked a day in her life, her father was a lifelong careered Federal judge. I met both parents for the first time the Sunday I went to study with her at her family's home. I was able to see clearly why she had the attitude she had. She could not help feeling the way she did, as she came from serious wealth and was raised with not just a silver but also with a golden spoon in her mouth. Added to that, she was the only girl in her family, thus, Daddy's little darling! I also understood why, from day one, upon picking up on her condescending body language and mannerisms, she automatically triggered in me that long, undying existential resentment that I abhorred rightly or wrongly toward the rich. As I had not one iota of doubt in my mind that the rich got rich through a set of gross and unfair advantages, like exploitations, thefts, and cronyism to name just a few.

Subsequently, my relentless attempt at conquering or seducing Anna started on the wrong foot and under the wrong kind of vibrating energy from the start. I wanted to have her not for the sake of genuinely having her, nor for who she really was inside, but for her outside look of what she represented and symbolized in my

333

arrested, militant world vision of white elitism. And despite discovering later that I had more things in common with her than I had previously anticipated. Yes, I came to realize that though Anna was born and raised in wealth and abundance and in a conservative secular Jewish family, she was nevertheless a rebellious soul, an anti-bourgeois, and anti-capitalist individual. And it seemed that her stand was quite genuine. I never ceased to admire her for that and for accepting the very fact that she had no say on being born white and wealthy.

I could not judge her for her bourgeois upbringing in as much as one could not judge me for my own petty-bourgeois upbringing. Sure, I imagined her attending Ivy League institutions like the Miami Shores' Catholic School of St. Rose de Lima or St. Mary of Notre Dame Academy for girls her entire life, but who was I anyway to resent her for that and for being born into a privileged class for that matter! Funny that the same Anna that I once thought was too white and too much of a bourgeois snob for me, would reproach me years later for being whiter than she was from the inside thanks to my Frenchy ways, mannerisms and upbringing. In short, she accused me of being a classic victim of neurosis identity as portrayed by Frantz Fanon in his revealing book on our racial alienation, "Black Skin, White Masks".

Anna was among the rare few white women I was with who never bought into any of that suave French image of mine seen in her eyes as dysfunctional. If she was in any way attracted by me, it was not for my "Frenchy" ways but by something else beyond her own comprehension. Perhaps she was attracted by that good genuine Haitian chemistry that she sensed was deeply hidden in me. But she was quickly deceived and deterred by how entrenched that heart of gold was buried under piles of insurmountable layers of protection. She found all that out with much chagrin the closer she was getting to me. But again, I'm getting way ahead of the story of Anna and me, which was in and of itself another missed opportunity by me, as I came that close to falling in love with her and vice versa.

To start with, Anna was by a country mile the hardest female conquest I had ever encountered since I began my compulsive dating spree with blonde women. It took me almost three months of nonstop courting before we officially went out on what I could call a date. Sex, despite my many pressing demands, was still off the menu with her. She reminded me so much of my typical bourgeois conservative Haitian women who were trained at the art of playing hard-to-get. She was, in so many ways, the reverse phenomenal thing she reproached me for. Yes, she was white on the outside but black on the inside. For as strange as that may sound, I never felt discouraged throughout the long ordeal of romancing Anna. I felt that she was worth the wait. Meanwhile, we had lots of fun hanging out with one another, as we shared many vices in common, like Reggae music, reefer smoking, concerts and eating out. She introduced me to a deeper version of non-commercial roots Reggae by taking me to many related local venues in Broward and Fort Lauderdale. We even went on to my first and only Reggae Sunsplash together in Montego Bay, Jamaica and what a memorable event that was!

We had been seeing each other for quite some time now, and I stopped pressuring her to give in to my sexual want of her, but one evening, while we both were hanging out at my Isidor's bachelor pad as we often did, I got my one and only lucky break with Anna. We were making out as usual with no expectation by me that it would ultimately lead us all the way to her promised land when she, for reasons I would never know to this day, made up her mind not to stop me this time from disrobing her all the way to her nature given birthday suit. And what a sight that was! For the first time in a long time, she allowed my fingers to explore parts of her attractive, lean body that were until now sacred and ferociously defended and protected by her.

My insane, wild desire for Anna had never subsided until that very instant when she allowed me to strip her naked and subsequently offer herself totally to me unconditionally. However, I felt as if I just got hit by some unknown, overpowering force coming out of nowhere. That invisible overwhelming entity seemed to have suddenly taken a strong hold of me, which was utterly beyond my control. My epic sexual desire for Anna instantly metamorphosed itself into a weird, estranged, enveloping, if not a contemptuous, spooky feeling toward her. I felt a strong, emotional resentment in me toward her which could only be translated as, "Now that you want it, bitch, it's my turn to punish you and humiliate you for daring to hold back from me for so long". Subsequently, I skipped all the existing foreplays in the book of lovemaking to stimulate Anna and went straight for the kill. The sex act between me and Anna was anything but love. It was a purely adulterated banging act that had resulted in the quickest, lousiest sexual performance ever by me on record with anyone I ever made love to.!

The scariest aspect of the entire sexual ordeal was that the sooner I crossed Anna's Rubicon, I seemed to purposely not make any effort to resist the overwhelming temptation of an early premature ejaculation. Instead, I made it a point to do just that and did not seem to care about pleasuring her, as I had done countless times with several women before and after her. And to add insult to injury, the sooner I came inside of her, I moved to the other bed in the sleeping quarter, pretending that I was too darn tired and exhausted and that I needed some rest without even a "Wham, bam, thank you ma'am" acknowledgment to her.

She left my place that night completely devastated, disappointed and humiliated. It was only the following day, when I woke up that I really realized the gravity and the magnitude of my despicable sexual act toward Anna last night. "What was so darn sinister about falling in love with Anna that scared the living daylights out of me." I asked myself later in hindsight. She was, in so many ways, the closest I ever allowed myself to be with a woman, emotionally speaking, even though she reminded me so much of my typical bourgeois Haitian woman that I could never get but in my dreams. Did I feel so undeserving of her love that I had to act that nasty toward her, crushing whatever feeling she had for me?

My despicable, nonsensical performance with Anna was an unrepairable mistake, as I crossed an unforgivable redline with her. I spent hours on the phone with her the day after, apologizing and giving all sorts of excuses to her, but to no avail. I begged her for another chance and even told her that the devil made me do it and act the way I did last night, and that the man she had sex with, in that room was not me. But she made up her mind not to give me another chance to right the wrong, as she came close enough to me to sense that I was perhaps beyond redemption when it came to opening myself for love and emotional commitment with a woman regardless of her race, wealth and social status. Did I just blow a once-in-a-lifetime opportunity to forge a steady, meaningful relationship with a person? Could she have been the woman of my life, the woman I had been waiting for all this time? And yet, I inadvertently missed her train. I blew the first and only chance I had with her last night by acting like an epic jerk and lost her!

## Miami, Florida: A Sunshine State's Unauthorized And Unredacted Journey

Anna was a very sensitive person, and she would not allow herself to be hurt any further by me despite any genuine feeling she might have had in her heart for me. She was more than convinced after what I did to her that I had some serious, personal issues with women and that I needed to deal with them on an individual basis, by seeking appropriate help with professional therapy. We managed to at least salvage something by remaining friends, as we had so many things in common, all the while lamenting over what a loving relationship it could have been with Anna if I had the courage to conquer all my inner demons by accepting love and by being emotional and vulnerable.

The ballerina girl, over the years, became an educator and had gone into some fundamental transformation of her own. She turned into a dedicated member of the Rastafarian religious sect which originated in Jamaica. The last time I saw her was in a show at Gusman Hall on Flagler Street. Three years had passed since I last saw her. So, I had a hard time recognizing her at first, as she put on some much weight. She was no longer the lean, skinny ballerina girl that she once was at FIU's Class of 1984. Her lustrous, long blonde hair had turned into a pile of entangling dreadlocks. Anna was no longer wearing her collection of brands of fashionable western clothing like Louis Vuitton and Cartier. Instead, I saw her wearing the typical multicolored Rastafari dress reminiscent of traditional African clothing. I lost contact with her again, but teacher Carline,

339

an endearing friend of mine, who worked with her in the same school, told me that her secular Jewish parents disowned her when she converted into the religious 'cult' and became a Rasta woman. She moved out of her family's bourgeois mansion to shack up with her black Jamaican Rastafarian lover.

# The Inspiring Parties at Mike and Peter's Chicken Coop Pad

My old friend Mike Jarvis, a.k.a. Jack, whom I met at Harvey's Printing shop and who had introduced me to Coconut Grove's outdoor Art festivals, cafes and restaurants, had moved out from his Grove's house to roommate with his friend Peter at an old chicken coop place which used to house poultry in the past. It was remodeled into a chic, charming home that stood in the middle of two to three acres of land, right under a panoply of lustrous South Miami vegetation and tall pine trees. It was always a delight to take my date for a visit there. Both handsome buggers had the right, perfect chemistry with each other to turn their old chicken coop apartment into an oasis of fun and entertainment. A welcoming hangout headquarters for several of their respective friends.

Peter and Mike were incorrigible bachelors and knew lots of cool folks in the Grove and South Miami areas. Hence those two were instrumental in staging a series of mindboggling gatherings known as the 'famous' Mike and Peter's Chicken Coop parties. I never missed on any of their get-togethers, as it was not a reasonable option for anyone to miss out on such a unique and rare energy filled ambiance attended by an eclectic mix of beautiful people.

When I first saw, amid all the dashing couples and singles at my very first party there, the handsome Italian-looking couple, Bob

341

Pelligrini and his late beautiful wife Chris, I thought they had just torn themselves up from a Hollywood celebrity magazine to come grace with their starlike presence Mike and Peter's party. It was so packed that the small, limited space of the low-ceiling chicken coop could not possibly accommodate that many people. So, a large overflow of the invited guests hung out through the immense outdoor yard amid the surrounding trees and vegetation. But my favorite spot was the Chicken Coop's inside atmosphere. Something about its over crowdedness, the nonstop talking of people conversing and breathing on top of one another, made for a compelling, marvelous tribal ambiance that made us all humans. With, of course, the added pleasant vibe coming from a fully packed space garnished with beautiful, invited guests. Though meeting with people was not an outlier; in general, the entire Chicken Coop party experience could be felt by just being there and letting oneself seemingly float around and enjoy the magic of the evening.

By attending Mike and Peter's landmark parties, I learned many important pointers and clues on how to throw together one fabulous party and the important elements needed to make it a memorable, successful one.

I had been wanting to throw a party at my bachelor pad for the longest time, but I was a little self-conscious about the limited available room. But after witnessing the success of Mike and Peter's parties in their small, confined space, I grew more confident that I could pull such a similar stunt at my even smaller bachelor pad, but with a limited number of guests, while having in mind to use the reception lobby space and the outside front yard of Isidor's apartment as backup plans for a potential overflow if more people showed up to the party.

So, with such a contingent plan, I made up my mind to plan my first-ever major house party. I went to work diligently by mobilizing all the possible players, contacts and connections I knew.

First and foremost, obtained Isidor's okay to have the party and use the building's entrance lobby to house some of my guests. The next thing I needed to work on was to carefully select the list of 25 invited guests, and if each would bring a date, that would take the number up to fifty. Peter/Mike South Miami connection would bring up to eight guests. My old Coconut Grove Village Inn's connection would take care of at least ten, and my FIU class of 1984 would cover the rest.

Aside from my various mixed international music collections, I needed to add some surprising shock and awe elements to the party. First, my old girlfriend Melodee agreed to entertain all my guests with a belly dancing performance. Second, on my list of surprise was to introduce to the mostly white and foreign audience a Haitian folkloric female dancer in an exotic Yanvalou dance. The final presentation would be a Haitian male dancer performing in three different dangerous magical voodoo exhibitions. Most invited guests were timely contacted for the scheduled Saturday party. All the entertainers were booked. People were asked to bring covered dishes, bottles of wine, liquors and drinks to supplement what I already purchased and stored for the anticipated number of guests. I had to remove the two medium-sized beds from the sleeping quarters and the kitchen table to my brother Willy's pad next-door to create more moving space for the standing partiers.

Finally, on the day of the event, I could not help being nervous. I started feeling better when the first guests began to arrive around the 7 pm scheduled time. My Village Inn's connection buddies were the first to arrive. Patrick Duperval, the reputed suave, sweet talker, was unsurprisingly accompanied by two hot-looking white chicks, immediately followed by his other partner in crimes, Ti Harold Estimé, the grandchild of the most progressive Haitian President in Haiti's history, Durmasais Estimé. He showed up with a date. Next was the FIU's class of 1984 contingent with the party animal in chief Kervin, his brother, his friend Andrew and the girls who accompanied them. The South Miami crowd, headed by Mike and Peter, was the last group of guests to arrive. By 10 pm, the party was in full-blown momentum where it had taken on a life of its own. I was pleasantly surprised when Bob Pelligrini and his wife Chris graced my party with their glamorous Hollywoodian presence.

By 11 pm, the number of guests was in the estimated range

of over 50, which triggered an immediate overflow of the guests to the front yard outside the building. Some guests were seen walking down the half-block stretch leading to the sea walls for a night view of the ocean. At 12 midnight, it was showtime when as scheduled Melodee opened the evening's entertainment hour with her tantalizing belly dancing piece revealing her killer curvaceous body moves to a crowd in awe. Immediately following Melodee's performance came Diane, a foxy looking, Haitian female dancer with her dazzling, tantalizing 'Yanvalou' dance performance, which left the entire audience asking for an encore.

However, the coup de grace came when Jean, an all-lean, muscular black Haitian dancer, started with his mystical, hypnotic fire folk dance show, invoking the allure of a real voodoo ritual ceremony. Following his folk dance was his barefoot jumping on hundreds of sharply pointed knells purposely placed on a large piece of wood with no blood spilling from his feet, at the audience's amazement. finally, Jean closed the show by chewing nonchalantly on several pieces of glass while asking the audience for water to help him take some of the stubborn pieces down, which was, of course, an intended act to send chill down the audience spine.

In all, the party was an even greater success than I expected. It lasted until the wee morning hours, a sign that the guests were having a marvelous time and did not want to go home. What I felt that I achieved in the success of my first party was the realization that we all could really get along regardless of race, language, culture, social status and wealth. The gathering crowd at my party was a mix of all the above. I had white Europeans, Americans, Jews, Hispanics, Jamaicans, Haitians and others among the fifty-some guests attending the party that night at my small, humble bachelor pad. I was amazed to observe how fifty-some guests at the party managed to get along so well and enjoy themselves immensely in such packed confined space. And all that regardless of their differences.

That in and of itself spoke volumes that we can all coexist on that green, fragile planet of ours against our worst instincts and beyond many of our apparent differences if only we have the will to take down our fear of the other. If only we began the process of deprogramming ourselves from the 'Us Versus Them', from that unproductive warlike mindset to welcome and accept one another for what we are, meaning TRANSIENT HUMANS!

I was so darn poised by the positive outcome and feedback received from many of my guests upon leaving my first ever bachelor pad's party that I promised to continue that pacifying path in the future by throwing this type of life-celebration gathering parties aiming at consolidating and reinforcing that fundamental existential link in us. I committed myself to do all that I could to promote and awaken the best we had in us and that we all shared, i.e., our common basic humanity.

# Francis Fukuyama Ought to Rewrite His End of History Book

Looking at today's unprecedented World events like the current ongoing proxy war between NATO/ Ukraine and Russia, the current powder keg in the Middle East, with a no less dangerous looming war between US and China over Taiwan, would lead anyone to conclude how close we are to the mid-night's doom clock hour from global extinction and self-annihilation.

In 1992, if we were to believe Francis Fukuyama, the renowned political scientist and philosopher, in his "End of History" book, humankind had arrived at a pivotal end game from its longest ideological and historical struggle between the Capitalist, neo-colonialist and imperialist North led by the US against the impoverished, super-exploited Communist/Socialist South championed by the Soviet Union and China. He argued that with the dismantling of the Warsaw Pact, along with the communist/socialist ideology, came the uncontested ascendency of liberal democracy and the hegemonic unipolar reign of the Collective West.

The former Soviet Union, which had historically held the mantle of the leading opposite pole of worldwide resistance against the rampaging Globalist exploitation, defaulted from its longtime historical role under the surrendering naive regimes of both Mikhail Gorbachev and Boris Yeltsin. The so-called civilized Western

Capitalistic/Neoliberal vision and its win-lose economic dicta appeared to have won one decisive battle against the Socialist/Communist alternative economic model following the vassalization of Russia under the Yelsin regime by Wall Street and the City of London vultures.

How did the instrumental dismantling of the Warsaw Pact alliance, the last vestige of check and balance against an ever-expansionist Capitalist/Imperialist West, come to such an abrupt end? Most students of History knew about Russia's massive resource-rich territorial holding and its never-ending war to protect and defend itself from repeated outside invading forces, all aiming at the balkanization of Russia to loot and plunder its vast oil and rare earth mineral resources. From Russia's pre-Napoleonic War to the First and Second World Wars, the hidden agenda behind all those wars had always been about subjugating Russia in the same way the rest of the Global South was. However, history had shown what those past Capitalist wars against the old Soviet Union failed to achieve, a handful of mujahideen in rags, sandals, and shoulder-fired antiaircraft missiles supplied by the CIA and MI6 had done the unthinkable by giving the former Soviet Union its own Vietnam and its subsequent demise.

Once the political, social and economic unraveling of the Soviet Union started, there was no way to stop its inevitable historical collapse. As a student of History and Geopolitics fresh out of FIU's International Studies, I went on an expansive trip behind the Cold War's Iron Curtain just weeks before the fall of the wall separating East and West Germany. First, I visited many Western European cities like Berlin, then went through Bonn in East Germany, Warsaw, Kyiv, Belarus' Minsk, Moscow, and Saint Petersburg. In Moscow, I experienced firsthand the epic collapse of Russia's economy. It was on free fall, and Wall Street and City of London vultures were on a rampage frenzy, buying off all of Russia's orchestrated devalued assets.

The Global Money Empire, through its Central Banking cabal, was back then in a rare historical position to substitute strategically their tiring win-lose neoliberal economic model for a much gentler win-win model but they failed. Instead, they doubled down on the old way of doing business. The immediate windfall had the winning Collective West embarked on such an innovative economic strategy worldwide would have been into trillions of dollars. As there won't be no urgency for the trillion dollar a year spent on the North's global defense budget to protect and defend their win-lose economic paradigm.

A genuine Kennedy Pax Americana, or something like the current China's Belt and Road initiative approach would have been a welcoming change to the centuries-old genocidal, colonial project of exploitation and subjugation of the mostly nonwhite Global South. The wicked Global Money Empire instead felt for the easy "hammer nail analogy", whereby the only tool they ever had in their hand dealing with the Global South was always a hammer; thus, every issue was seen as a nail. And, of course, the Deep State, unelected, faceless culprit behind the Collective West, felt that their ideological/economic victory had given them 'carte blanche' to do as they pleased with the wretched losers, including Yugoslavia, Russia, and China to name just a few.

The triumph of the 'winners take all' approach, like France buying Niger's uranium at a disgraceful price of e0.80 per kg to resale it for e200 on the international market, became the norm in the aftermath of the neoliberal 'End of History' win championed by Fukuyama. Not even nuclear Russia was spared by the reckless, ferocious economic exploitation of Wall Street and City of London's economic foes and hitmen. The triumph of the Neo-fascist Global elite, which could only strive on the systematic thefts of other nations' oils, rare earth and mineral resources, had nothing beneficial to offer to the nonwhite Global South but under-development, chaos, destruction, famine, poverty and genocidal wars in return for their stolen riches.

The Northern neo-liberal democracies of Europe and North America were never in the business of helping to develop the Global South, to begin with, but to extract as many resources as possible along with the super-exploitation of their cheap labor. As the ongoing proverbial joke rightly argued, If their economic assistance were truly genuine, the entire African continent, along with several of the South Asian countries, would have been fully industrialized by now, considering their decades-old fake developmental aids and plans that had been pledged and financed over and over by the IMF and the World Bank.

In the aftermath of the Globalists' so-called ultimate victory in their ideological bipolar world rivalry with the old Soviet Union, they appeared to have overplayed their hands in the newly created unipolar world completely dominated by them, as the potential multipolar world is yet to be delivered by a midwife. Meanwhile, Global governance by the lonesome American Empire was a fait accompli, as there was no real opposing military hegemon that could possibly challenge US full power spectrum then. Russia under Yeltsin was simply licking its wounds in sorrow and regret over its glorious dying Empire. However, the white Western's hubris and arrogance vis-à-vis Russia and the rest of the nonwhite Global South had done more in the way of reviving and resuscitating the dying, beaten and bankrupted old empire by provoking the coming of Vladimir Putin onto the seat of power in Russia. The diehard nationalist in Putin suffered silently the vexing excesses of the Capitalist West's pillages and systematic looting of Russia's oil and mineral resources through the sold-out Russian oligarchs until he discretely maneuvered skillfully around his supposedly installed 'puppet' regime to consolidate his power and began to turn things

351

around in his beloved Russia. He, quietly under the nose of the five eyes intelligence networks, rebuilt Russia's deteriorating military-industrial complex into that formidable deterrent force to be reckoned with in less than two decades. He then slowly started to take care of the Russian oligarchs trojan horses who conspired with the Global Money Empire's agents in the orchestrated economic destruction and general looting of Russia.

History has shown over and over that colonialist, neo-colonialist and imperialist powers alike could not have kept their centuries-old plundering of the Global South for this long without their unmatched formidable military machines and weapon technology. Both maritime empires of Great Britain and the US were subsequently able to project anywhere in the world their overwhelming naval superiority and dominance to reinforce and maintain their win-lose economic exploitation model. But with the latest development of hypersonic weapons, the Collective West, for the first time in their ageless militarism, seemed to be lagging considerably behind Russia, China and even North Korea and Iran. This gap represented an undeniable game changer in the global rapport of forces.

The fast-moving hypersonic missiles had overnight rendered obsolete the once mighty Aircraft carrier fleets of the American Maritime Empire, including its vassal allies France and England. For the first time in the Collective West's millennium-old history, they realized that their once conventional military dominance over the Global South was no longer able to protect and reinforce their "Rules-Based International Order" on any position of strength.

China, of course, had not forgotten its century of humiliation, intervention and subjugation from the First Opium War by the West, was now biding time for its cold-blooded revenge. Russia, on the other hand, had not forgiven itself for being played like a violin by its sworn, lifelong enemies in the West where it was utterly humiliated under Gorbachev and Yeltsin. Nor had Russia forgotten how it miserably failed to stop the Globalist balkanization of its sister Slavic nation of Yugoslavia or the nonstop encirclement of NATO's encroachment of its territory seeking nuclear primacy over Russia through Ukraine. Subsequently, following the Maidan massacre in Kyiv, and the overthrow of Yanukovych by yet another orchestrated color revolution in Ukraine, Russia swiftly moved its forces to annex Crimea, where it had the only warm water naval port for its Black Sea Navy Fleet and could not afford to be cut off from it. And in 2015, Putin also moved decisively into Syria to save the strategic Russian naval facility in Tartus when the Syrian regime of Bashar al-Assad was about to be defeated by the Western proxy forces armed, trained and financed by CIA and MI6. Without that strategic military intervention by Russia, a potential ISIS takeover of Syria would have taken Moscow out of the Middle East.

With the current ongoing NATO/Ukraine-Russian war, it's

being shown that the US, absent of its nuclear triad arsenal, was unable to keep pace with Russia's artillery dominance, and overwhelming missiles dominance on the Ukrainian battlefield. NATO miserably failed to establish a no-fly zone over Ukraine or prevented the Russians from establishing a near total dominance of Ukraine's airspace by Russia's effective use of its conventional triad system consisting of a combination of land-based, submarine-launched and strategic bombers with their latest unstoppable hypersonic conventional missiles. The Western alliance's quickly depleted stocks of supply and military hardware, on the other hand, spoke volumes on how the once mighty Military Industrial Complex in the US had become a shadowy institution of its old self in less than a three-decade time. Some political analysts in the West would put the blame solely on the neo-fascist ideology which had recently taken complete hold of the American Empire's major economic, military, public and private institutions such as the Arms Industry, Wall Street, the banking institution, Big Pharma, our food production, schools, water, electricity, and a whole host of things that should never have been privatized for profit, as they were simply too vital for America's national security.

Neo-fascism's absolute control of the US' Four Estates of Power, the Executive, the Legislative, the Judicial and the Mainstream Media, followed by a total lack of oversights and accountability, had led the Empire that dared not speak its name to the direst situation it found itself today. A completely bankrupt American Empire with more than 35 trillion dollars in deficit, a weapon industry entrenched in astronomical price gouging of the US taxpayers and the systematic looting of the US treasury for so-called state of the art weaponry that constantly malfunctioned or failed to work. And finally, a Wall Street and its Banking Cartel's acolytes preying on millions of American retirees' Social Security, Pension Funds, manufactured pandemics, unnecessary wars, created inflation and stock market manipulations, just to name a few!

Systemic corruption had gotten so rampant and, like an out-of-control cancer, kept spreading everywhere with no hope for the once striving nation on the shining Hills to recover from it.

The nation's political elite that had long been in the pockets of a shadowy, unelected, comprador Deep State elite with a hidden agenda for America's ultimate destruction, kept pushing for more afflicting, suicidal wars with near-peer nations like Russia, China, North Korea and Iran. American exceptionalism had never been so tested ever since its epic debacle in Vietnam and recent failures in the Balkans, the Middle East, Africa and Southeast Asia, notably in Afghanistan! America's boastful exceptionalism started to run its course thanks to its many unwise, unnecessary wars on too many fronts. The US had been at war with the rest of humanity for most of its historical lifespan, and it began to show signs of fatigue toward an eventual general collapse sooner rather than later.

Traditional use of military muscles to reinforce US Imperial might had lately been challenged, with the revolutionary development of drone technology and hypersonic weapons. The US has been forced to keep its Aircraft Carrier fleets beyond the range of Iran's hypersonic missiles and their long-flying drones. Furthermore, US bases throughout the Middle East are highly vulnerable and have come under repeated attacks by Iran-backed Iraqi and Syrian militias since the start of the Israel-Hamas war.

Being the world's lonesome bully could come with a hefty price, for at some point in time in the international bullying schoolyard, every boy nation there wished for the day when someone would muster enough courage to punch back at the hated big bully. One of the notable incidents of punching back the bully straight in the face was when the Iranian integrated system of Air Defense Forces took down a US Global Hawk surveillance drone over the Strait of Hormuz. We also witnessed one brazen manifestation of hitting back at the schoolyard bully when in the aftermath of the US drone assassination of the Iranian commander of the Quds Force, General Qasem Soleimani. It happened on 8 January 2020, when Americans were stunned once more upon learning that two of their airbases in Iraq were destroyed by 12 ballistic hypersonic missiles from Iran. Rumors had it that the so-called state-of-the-art defense system protecting the two US Military bases there went stone-deaf and blind minutes before they were hit, by Iranian unstoppable hypersonic missiles. The only plausible explanation for such successful attack by the Iranians was the use of their superior electronic jamming system, viewed as one of the best in the world. The Iranians purportedly deprived the bases' defensive electronic radars with their eyes and ears to see and hear any of the incoming missiles. At first, the US Department of Defense denied that none of its soldiers were injured or killed to later admit that 110 of their servicemen were being treated for traumatic brain injuries, which was, of course, a euphemism for being brain dead or in other words, clinically dead.

As if the proxy war in Ukraine was not costly enough for the Collective West's treasury, now came the latest exploding war in the Middle East opposing Israel and Hamas. Since the October 7th border breach attack by Hamas, Israel went on a bombardment rampage against the 2.5 million Palestinians living in Gaza. Several International observers called the enclave an open-air prison where over half of the civilian population are children and women dying under the genocidal, indiscriminate carpet bombing of the City by the IDF, while Hamas militants were known to be safely hiding in their deep underground system of tunnels.

Several independent observers feared that due to the unprecedented military mobilization in the region by US Aircraft Carriers, added to Russia and China's own warships near the trouble region, something even bigger than the actual Israel-Hamas conflict seems to be in the making. The Middle East's volatile powder keg, more than the Ukrainian one might become the war theater to lead us to the real end of History as we know it.

We are living in an unprecedented time in history where the millennium-old hegemony of the morally bankrupt, deindustrialized, neo-colonialist, neo-fascist and racist Collective West, which had been long manipulated by the Global Money Empire, had found themselves with their back to the wall of history and on the wrong side of it. Living under a Himalayan pile of debts that could never be repaid and outmaneuvered by its enemies' electronic and hypersonic weapon development, the lonesome US Empire had now begun to panic when realizing that their old master-slave Imperialist role to dictate to the rest of the non-white world when and how they ought to live and die will soon be a thing of the past. One does not have to be a rocket scientist or a Nostradamus to see the writing on the wall. The dizzying speed through which the decolonization process of Africa and the rest of the super-exploited South had been occurring could not have been any more mindboggling to the long impatient students of history and geopolitics exhausted and fatigued by the eternal white Western hegemonic knees over the Global South's sore broken neck.

Even the seventy-five-year-old neo-colonial project of Israel's creation in 1948 by the City of London and Wall Street, in cahoots with one another and under the strict directive of the Global

Money Empire, as an advanced post to control the Middle East's vast oil resources, began to falter. Subsequently, the only unthinkable suicidal option left to salvage the neo-colonial, neo-fascist Globalist vision of a unipolar world built and made for them could be a reckless use of a first, all-out nuclear strike on the axis of resistance nations as a last, absolute final solution. If this end-of-time potential scenario is where we are all heading, it would reveal how prematurely unwise Francis Fukuyama was when he wrote and declared his 'End of History' in his 1992 book following the dissolution of the Warsaw Pact Bloc headed by the old Soviet Union. Though he never anticipated that as soon as the white Collective West had found themselves as the World's lone imperial hegemon without the check and balance of a strong opposite force, the winners would have become in less than a three-decades-time frame, losers by becoming their own worst enemy.

This real potential end of history that all living things on earth are now facing makes Francis Fukuyama's 1992 book a big nothing burger in comparison to the unprecedented worldwide nuclear carnage that could ensue if and when the white Western hegemonic powers chose their suicidal, nuclear path and not go softly into the crepuscle of the descending night. And guess what, there won't be any Francis Fukuyama left standing to write about that absolute end of history, as we will all be turned into a wide array of nuclear dust piles.

The latest unprecedented historical event at the end of 2023 when the State of Israel was attacked by Hamas and the former began the systematic obliteration of the Gaza strip which is still ongoing to this day, the so-called enlightened Western Civilized World stood into a deafening silence. They looked the other way while Israel snuffed its nose at the democratic, humanitarian North by continuing with its genocidal, final solution, a rampaged killing of the defenseless Palestinian population. Such indiscriminate carpet bombing of Gaza has passed a biblical high of over 35,000 dead Palestinians. Subsequently, Israel's denial, arrogance and hubris at the Hague when facing the ultimate crime of genocide filed by South Africa, was nothing less than a display of the Collective West's lies, falsehood, hypocrisy, and extreme moral depravity. I was programmed to believe that the West stood for decency, human rights, freedom and, above all else, the sanctity of life. But their spineless responses to Israel's actions exposed them for what they are in their biased double standard approach.

It also revealed that America along with its European vassals are mere despicable minions of the tiny, little state of Israel and the Global Money Empire cabal standing behind it. One must take a look at the multiple, unsuccessful trips of US Secretary of States, Anthony Blinken and Lloyd Austin, US Secretary of Defense to reign on Israel to conclude that America is not a sovereign State entity, as it has no real control of its foreign policy. Therefore, US's vital, national interests had always taken a back seat behind Israel, as demanded by the Global Money Empire's last ultimate project of settler colonialism in the Middle East.

Will America save itself by asserting its national priorities from Israel's genocidal and suicidal war agendas against the Axis of Resistance? Or will it come down to the intervention of the Global South nations, hence saving the Collective West from their own hedonistic corruptions, and depravities.

Lyonel Gerdes

# **Epilogue**

This third memoir book, "Miami, Florida: A Sunshine State's Unauthorized and Unredacted Journey…" is a follow-up to the last two preceding memoirs, "Joie de Vivre and Decadence: Growing up in the Golden Age of Les Cayes, Haiti", and "Port-au-Prince, Haiti: Duvaliers' Pax Haitiana Dynasty and my Coming of Age in the Time of Compas Direct and Mini Jazz".

Tome I of this third trilogy started with a petrified yet seemingly composed twenty-year-old flying on a one-way ticket from Port-au-Prince to Miami. I only had twenty US dollars in my wallet, and between paying for the taxicab ride from Miami International Airport to Fougères' home, where it was arranged for me to get room and board, and buying ice creams for his kids, and finally posting the $10 left from the twenty back to Haiti, I was penniless the day after my arrival here in Miami which so happened to be my 21st birthday!

The start of my Miami journey was not, by any stretch of the imagination, a leisurely, casual walk in the park. My sudden wake-up call came on the very first evening of my arrival when I was told that the room they had earlier scheduled for me was taken by someone else; then, I would be staying at an alternative home, which I later found out was one of Fougères' mistress houses, located just five blocks away from his marital family home. One quick observation in passing, was the proximity of the two houses confirmed that some old Haitian marital habits and practices continued 'belle lurette' to strive here in Miami despite the different, foreign environment. I found myself overnight living in a small, doorless space with no window and privacy, sleeping in a stranger's home. The confined area was such that there were no possible side paths to get in bed other than to jump at the foot of it. The only sense of privacy I had was a thick side fabric hanging by the ceiling entrance that I pulled sideways as a privacy substitute each night before going to bed. My first night was sleepless. Noting that it was just the night prior that I went to bed feeling safe and totally secure in my house's bed on Titus Street in Port-au-Prince. And now, what a difference a day made in little less than twenty-four hours!

That was just the commencement of a host of hurdles thrown at me from my tempestuous Miami journey from day one. I went through a series of unpleasant experiences. My inability to speak a word of English did not help me find or keep a job for long. From a somewhat spoiled petty bourgeois lifestyle in Haiti, as an independent journalist at 'Le Petit Samedi Soir', a popular weekly magazine in Port-au-Prince, I ended up within days at a North Miami Beach restaurant, washing dishes. I desperately needed that job, any job, to begin earning money not only to pay for my weekly room and board but also to begin to send money home on a regular monthly basis. For it was understood that the reason I was chosen to migrate here was for me to take over the monthly remittance check that my adopted father would no longer be able to honor. It was an essential part of their informal divorce agreement.

A washing dishes job that I was lucky to get lasted no more than three days, as I was fired for my dismal inability to communicate in English. It was my first unflattering series of low-status jobs that no black Americans, let alone whites, wanted. My next window cleaning job at a North Miami Beach Resort Hotel, was followed by two factory jobs. Then came Harvey Mordoff's Printing shop, which was status-wise a marked improvement right before my first white collar job, as an HRS social worker. I was able to get this job thanks to my resiliency in furthering my education despite many hardships. I first attended English classes at Lindsay Hopkins in downtown Miami; then, I diligently earned an AA Degree at Miami Dade College North, and finally, a BA degree in Sociology at FIU's South Tamiami Campus.

However, before I managed to stay afloat and keep my head above the waves, there was a time in my struggling journey I needed to be rescued by the Gelin's brothers, Georges and Jerry, when I could not pay for my room and board at Fougères' mistress home. Georges was like a brother to me, if not altogether an angel sent to me when I needed help the most. I remember all the hard, trying days when we were all three living in that one narrow space apartment room on 53rd Street between Northwest 2nd and First

Avenue. Some days, things were so dire that my dear, beloved friend Georges had to split his own dinner in half to share the other half with me. All throughout such an epic ordeal, I never once lost hope as I was confident that I was simply going through a violent but temporary storm and that all I had to do was to stay put and weather the whole thing. I stoically endured the worst part of it and never once gave in to facile but dangerous offers and temptations, nor did I ever blame my adopted father for dropping me off like a sack of potatoes in Miami with a non-relative to fend for myself.

In a sink or swim situation, I decided to swim. In hindsight, I remember to have managed well beyond my own expectations. I did not know I had that much resiliency in me until I was faced with unrelented challenging situations. The passing of my regretted journalist friend Gasner Raymond when he was martyred in Haiti was a hard, depressing news that stayed with me for a long time. Still, despite the grimy aspect of those early first years in Miami, I was able to somewhat turn many of the unfortunate early experiences into something of a life lesson to learn from. Ergo, many of my most memorable moments, believe it or not, came from amid those trying days when I was hanging out with the Pepe group. But you would not have known or noticed that I was living under tremendous stress from behind my stoic, calm and collected outer demeanor. I hung out for as long as I could with the Gelins in solidarity for their invaluable support by continuing to share rent and other miscellaneous things and activities with them until we went our separate ways.

My first efficiency room experience was quite a milestone move, as it marked the start of a completely new chapter in my Miami life journey. At the historic apartment building where I moved in, I met with Jean Anduze and Pierre Mendes Alcindor, a.k.a. Dada, who, like me, rented a room on the second floor. We developed a longtime friendship. Jean was the culprit who introduced me to the use of the Cannabis herb that had amply contributed to a significant fundamental change from the way of I used to look at life or at the everydayness in general.

I met with two interesting fellows, Limoné Joseph, a known playwright, and his poet friend Inavy Joseph. Both were Miami's early pioneers in the nascent Little Haiti community, as volunteers working at HACAD, a Haitian American organization that was providing social services to the just-arrived Haitian refugees in Miami. Through them, I began to frequent the HACAD's office and help on my off days. They were also involved in many cultural activities, and that was how I was introduced one evening to Madame X, a very attractive Haitian lady who was a staunch supporter of the art. She was also the wife of a successful Haitian leader in the Haitian community and was about twice my age. Rumors had it that their marriage was a sham and that he, as well as she, had affairs outside of it. Reportedly, she had a compulsive physical attraction to much younger man.

The first thing in her that caught my attention was the physical resemblance she had to a certain Tante Paulette, a one-of-a-kind Haitian lady that I had an epic crush on two years before I migrated to Miami. And like Aunt Paulette, she was one voluptuous looking grimelle herself with an equally pleasant face and an imposing physical build. We immediately clicked, and before I could even blink, she ended up in my first efficiency room to be the first woman to grace it with her presence. With her in my bed, I lived out all the sexual fantasies I had for Aunt Paulette. Our affair lasted until I could no longer live with myself in the aftermath of a social function with the nameless socialite and her husband.

The absolute game changer came when I moved to the Isidor apartment on 25$^{th}$ Street off Biscayne Boulevard and subsequently started a new job at Harvey's Printing Shop, thanks to Pierre Mendes' connection. There I met with lots of interesting characters, the likes of George Fishman, Mike Jarvis a.k.a. Jacques and several 'premis' belonging to a religious sect called Guru Maharaj Ji. I could not help being intrigued and fascinated by the group's contagious energy and the way that seemed to rub off on me or on anyone else just by being around them. George, who was a member of the group, took me to an evening Satsang. When I got there, I was so overwhelmed and taken by what would later be understood as a gentle, pacifying version of the notion of general mass psychosis.

I came close to being converted that evening to the group. I cultivated an interesting friendship with Maggie whom I met at my first evening Satsang. She was an attractive, notorious member of the group. We met often for dinners and drinks to such an extent that some people in the group thought that we were lovers. She never gave me any sex, but what I believed she had given me was that thing the cult members called 'knowledge'. Consciously or subconsciously, she might have given it to me, as she was trained to do. In possession of such a powerful, charming tool, considered by me as a far more beneficial thing than any sex I could have had with her, I came out swinging. I became an overnight walking magnet, especially with the white ladies.

Adrien Besson, the friend who sold me my first car, a black Cadillac, was in the habit of taking me and my friend Georges clubbing whenever his wife Michelle was in New York. It was at one of those all-white clubs on Biscayne Blvd. and 114th Street that I realized how much of a romantic pull I seemed to have on white ladies. I remember well what a disaster I was at getting a normal Haitian date back home in Port-au-Prince or even here in Miami. One thing was evident from the dazzling romantic interest displayed by white women toward me got me thinking about where my sexual, romantic interest should lie from now on!

Soon, I began to develop the incorrigible bachelor image when I moved from my first efficiency room to my new Isidor's bachelor's pad, which had become a favorite hanging out spot for many of my male and female friends alike. It was non-stop traffic on weekends and holidays where the best Ganja was being smoked and where the latest Pink Floyd, Supertramp and Pet Shop Boys' music were being played. In those days, it was not unusual to see an interesting gathering of friends like Gregory Carré, Claude Wells, Philippe Carrie, George Gelin, or Abner Perodin make their usual weekend stops at my place to chill out. Jean Willy, the oldest of my three younger brothers, moved to Miami and was living right across in his own bachelor's pad. It was the best of times!

I had one of the busiest daily schedules ever, between my work at Harvey's Printing shop, my undergraduate Sociology classes at FIU's Tamiami Campus, and hanging out late at party events in the Coconut Grove area. The Village Inn's matinee Reggae with the unforgettable Roots Uprisings band was by far my all-time favorite ambiance, for the whole magical atmosphere there opened me up to a sort of ongoing existential peak experience.

From a shy, provincial nerdy look, I began to change my outer physical appearance, by wearing a cool collection of pants and shirts and elegant black long coats. I had my hair braided à la Milli Vanilly, giving me a stunning, if not an exotic, look. A picture of me in a cross like pose with my wild braided long hair lying in bed will be gracing the Tome One's front cover of this third volume of my Miami memoir as a testament to a crazy, wild bygone era in my unauthorized and unredacted life journey here. I started to develop a certain animal magnetism of my own thanks to the therapeutic recreational use cannabis, the projection onto others of that feel-good contagious energy that Marggie had passed on to me, and my latest newfound discovery of the magical essence of Reggae music's transformational power.

I became very popular with the ladies overnight, as I was ravishing blonde babes everywhere I went, at work, on school campus and at many of the bar scene venues in Coconut Grove. I solemnly declined the unflattering label of the heartless womanizer for the much softer, romantic appellation of the 'man who loves women', for I was like that overly excited little black kid who suddenly found himself in a room full of delicious white chocolate and was told by an empowering magical voice inside my head to help myself with as much as I could possibly taste. And, oh boy, had I gone on an epic blonde frenzy!

My sweet avenging rampage of seducing and dating white women was seen by me as a small but annoying way of getting back at the white supremacy ideology. It started innocently with my risqué affair with the screamy fountain lady, dirty blonde bombshell Cindy, whose emotional and heartfelt physical attraction for me was startling at first but had convinced me later that if I could have someone like Cindy, I could have any white woman given the right and perfect circumstances.

Miami, Florida: A Sunshine State's Unauthorized And Unredacted Journey

I came out more engaging and more assertive with the ladies by projecting and releasing that feel-good energy of sensuality and animal magnetism that I never thought I had in me before. Put in other words, I was able to sort of projecting my own sexual excitement and desire into the ladies who were the objects of my romantic attention. My Village Inn's partners in crimes bluntly put it this way: "Mwen fè anvi raze kenbe fanm blanch yo" [ I gave those white ladies an unbelievable sexual turn on].

Despite my unsettled bachelor's lifestyle, I managed quite successfully to remain childless, as I refused to put a child of my own into such unpredictable, complex, unjust world of ours. In my old ancestors' days on the slave plantations, many of the enslaved mothers chose all sorts of indigenous, leaf-based medicines to abort their fetuses, preventing themselves from giving birth to children born in slavery, but in my case, the simple continuing use of rubber condoms had done the trick!

There were, of course, ample other reasons behind my fierce, incorrigible bachelor stand. First, I wanted to build a solid foundation for a comfortable life in the future. Next, more importantly, I wanted to live a little, travel, and explore life, as I could barely afford to do any of that while growing up in Haiti. The bulk of my poetry and writing essays as a French poet and journalist at LPSS weekly magazine were partly coming from my fecund imagination, research, and observation than they were from personal

371

experiences. I remember the very first time I met the famed journalist and radio personality, Marcus Garcia, in his Radio studio in Port-au-Prince; he told me jokingly that I had him fooled into thinking that my poetry and essays were coming from "Un homme qui a vécu" [A man who had lived] while I was a teenager with not an extensive real-life experience.

It was no accident that I went out of my way to avoid dating any of my countrywomen, as all they worried about back then was getting married to beat their biological clock of reproduction. I would not have been on the same page with any of them, as I just wanted to have fun, further my education and travel the world. I could not have accomplished any of that interesting life journey I had lived so far had I allowed myself to get married and 'getting' pregnant that early in the game.

The danger of not being trapped in a relationship by a girl was not totally guaranteed, even though I was dating the more liberal, free-spirited white ladies. In fact, I ran into a few close encounters, starting with dirty blonde Cindy, Gil and others.

My deliberate, frugal lifestyle living at my Isidor bachelor's pad had a certain logic to its thriftiness. First, I refused to buy into the established systemic debt trap by living beyond my means like most people do. I was only working for starvation wages until I started working as a social worker for HRS. Second, sending money to my family left stranded in Port-au-Prince, was a non-negotiable priority for me. Shacking up with a girl in a suburban house and buying brand-new cars would mean guaranteed starvation for my relatives back home, whose only reliable source of income came from me. So, I did not really give a rat's ass attention to people criticizing me for living my frugal lifestyle, though I was kind of taken aback when the criticism came from my ungrateful little brother Carlos who was himself the prime recipient of the beneficial saving deriving from my modest, frugal lifestyle.

As we reached the end of my third trilogy Tome I memoir "Miami, Florida: A Sunshine State's Unauthorized and Unredacted Journey..." I trusted that I did not bore or offend you in anyway with many of my erotically detailed content of adult themes, as a significant part of my Sunshine State's Unauthorized and Unredacted journey toward the ultimate search for myself!

I can promise you that there will be even juicier stories from my continuing Miami journey that will soon be gracing the pages of Tome II, as I had gone international by traveling all over Western and Eastern Europe, Asia, India North America, South America, Australia, New Zealand, North Africa, and many parts of the Caribbean, while keeping Miami as my base.

Let us all keep our fingers crossed and our spirits up high that we will all be alive and well to meet up once again next time.

Humankind had never been in such direst predicament than it had found itself today, as a genocidal, suicidal Globalist elite is determined to fight to a bloody finish to maintain their neo-colonialist, neo-fascist, and imperialist old habits of economic plundering and looting of the world.

To quote Antonio Gramsci, amid the current insanity and depravity of the Global Money Empire's latest debacles in Ukraine and the Middle East, there seemed to be so far no sane, real responses against such pure evil and madness, for "The old world is dying, and the new world struggles to be born". let's all hope that life on earth will be spared from a looming sixth extinction of all living things. Let's all hope that the power that be will ultimately regain its long-lost sanity at the eleventh hour and choose to go gently and kindly into that last good night!

# About the Author

Lyonel Gerdes had already published two books of his memoir Trilogy about his life growing up in Haiti. His first trilogy book, "Joie de Vivre and Decadence: Growing up in the Golden Age of les Cayes, Haiti," recounts a simultaneously joyous and difficult childhood while living in a loveless family environment as a child adoptee. His second book memoir, Port-au-Prince, Haiti: Duvaliers' Pax Haitiana Dynasty and my Coming of Age in the Time of Compas Direct and Mini Jazz" continued with Gerdes' harrowing tale of his near destitute family, who was forced to seek refuge in Haiti's Capital, Port-au-Prince, to avoid political persecution by abandoning their well-to-do bourgeois lifestyle in Les Cayes.

Gerdes' family's financial situation worsened to the point that that his adopted father was forced to migrate to the State as the only last alternative left to save his family from reaching financial rock bottom in Haiti. In this third book trilogy memoir Tome I, we found the twenty years old Gerdes on a one-way ticket flight to Miami, where he had been sent by his adopted father living in Waukegan, Illinois to a non-relative home to fend for himself with only $20 US in his wallet. The author of "Miami, Florida: A Sunshine State's Unauthorized and Unredacted Journey…" recounted another horrifying tale of his early struggling years, to survive and make it in Miami, the so-called land of plenty. Gerdes had known days where he lived on half a meal a day and was about to be kicked out from his room and board for lack of payments, as he could not find work because he could not speak a word of English. He was that close to be homeless had it not been for the rescuing help of the Gelin brothers.

"Miami, Florida: A Sunshine State's Unauthorized and Unredacted Journey...Tome I" is a breathtakingly written memoir with an impressive tale of resiliency, redemption and self-searching identity. Those readers who had been following Gerdes' trilogy memoir about his life journey going back to Les Cayes and Port-au-Prince, will undoubtedly be served once more by another no less fascinating and unpredictable tale of a journey!

Made in USA - North Chelmsford, MA
11798_9798884264489
04.09.2024 1452